AF567078

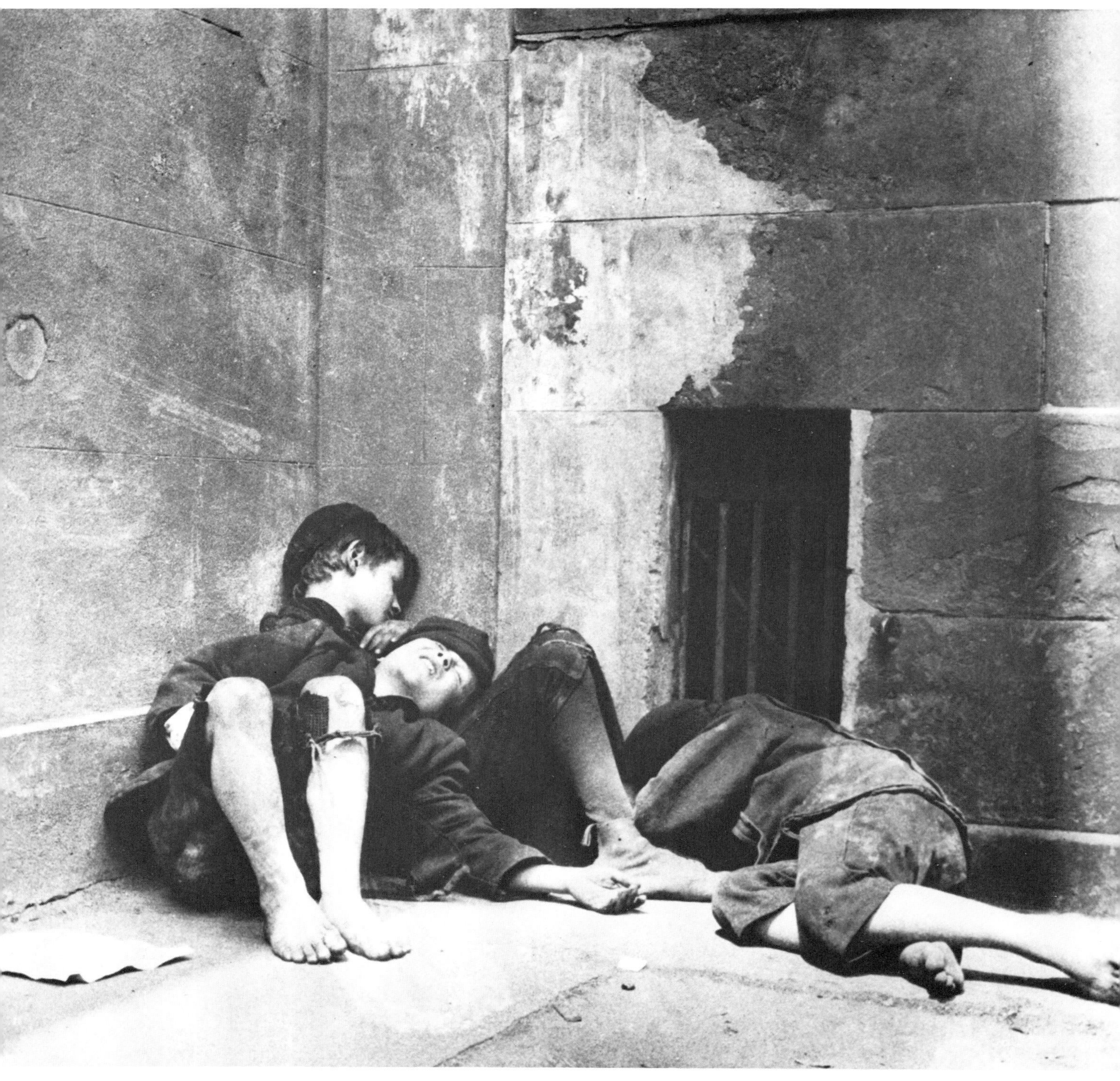

NEW YORK STREET KIDS

136 Photographs

Selected by
THE CHILDREN'S AID SOCIETY

with captions by
JOHN VON HARTZ

DOVER PUBLICATIONS, INC.
New York

ACKNOWLEDGEMENTS

The Children's Aid Society gratefully acknowledges the assistance of Marina Sevastopoulo, Special Projects Coordinator for The Children's Aid Society, whose original idea sparked this book; Linda Voorsanger, her assistant; Mary Black, Curator of Painting and Sculpture at The New-York Historical Society; and Jane Sugden, photo researcher.

Note: Photographs credited *c.a.s.* were supplied from the archives of the Children's Aid Society.

Frontispiece: **Homeless Children Sleeping in an Alley.** Homeless slum kids found little to cheer about in the "Gay 90s." Without a warm, safe place to sleep, they huddled under stairways, curled up in empty delivery carts, clung together in rat-infested cellars and dozed in blind alleys, as seen here in a famous photograph by Jacob Riis. On winter nights their favorite sleeping niches were the heated lobbies of office buildings. To discourage this practice, building superintendents doused the kids with cold water and drove them into the freezing night. The prevailing attitude toward the street kid paralleled that expressed about the poor man—he could improve himself if he really wanted to. *(The Jacob A. Riis Collection, Museum of the City of New York)*

Published in Canada by General Publishing Company, Ltd., 30 Lesmill Road, Don Mills, Toronto, Ontario.
Published in the United Kingdom by Constable and Company, Ltd., 10 Orange Street, London WC2H 7EG.

New York Street Kids is a new work, first published by Dover Publications, Inc., in 1978.

International Standard Book Number: 0-486-23692-7
Library of Congress Catalog Card Number: 78-57823

Manufactured in the United States of America
Dover Publications, Inc.
180 Varick Street
New York, N.Y. 10014

NEW YORK STREET KIDS

136 Photographs

Selected by
THE CHILDREN'S AID SOCIETY

with captions by
JOHN VON HARTZ

DOVER PUBLICATIONS, INC.
New York

ACKNOWLEDGEMENTS

The Children's Aid Society gratefully acknowledges the assistance of Marina Sevastopoulo, Special Projects Coordinator for The Children's Aid Society, whose original idea sparked this book; Linda Voorsanger, her assistant; Mary Black, Curator of Painting and Sculpture at The New-York Historical Society; and Jane Sugden, photo researcher.

Note: Photographs credited *c.a.s.* were supplied from the archives of the Children's Aid Society.

Frontispiece: **Homeless Children Sleeping in an Alley.** Homeless slum kids found little to cheer about in the "Gay 90s." Without a warm, safe place to sleep, they huddled under stairways, curled up in empty delivery carts, clung together in rat-infested cellars and dozed in blind alleys, as seen here in a famous photograph by Jacob Riis. On winter nights their favorite sleeping niches were the heated lobbies of office buildings. To discourage this practice, building superintendents doused the kids with cold water and drove them into the freezing night. The prevailing attitude toward the street kid paralleled that expressed about the poor man—he could improve himself if he really wanted to. *(The Jacob A. Riis Collection, Museum of the City of New York)*

Published in Canada by General Publishing Company, Ltd., 30 Lesmill Road, Don Mills, Toronto, Ontario.
Published in the United Kingdom by Constable and Company, Ltd., 10 Orange Street, London WC2H 7EG.

New York Street Kids is a new work, first published by Dover Publications, Inc., in 1978.

International Standard Book Number: 0-486-23692-7
Library of Congress Catalog Card Number: 78-57823

Manufactured in the United States of America
Dover Publications, Inc.
180 Varick Street
New York, N.Y. 10014

INTRODUCTION

This book depicts the many moods and faces of the children of New York's poor from the 1890s to the present. It is a fascinating study, a tribute to the courage, creativity and resiliency of children who can rise above the problems and constraints of poverty to find adventure, beauty, fun and humor in squalor and adversity. In one sense it is a history of the great city itself—the gateway and barometer of a mighty nation. In another, it tells the story of a caring, pioneering agency, the Children's Aid Society, which has worked on behalf of children in distress as advocate and service provider for 125 years. It is a distinguished history of assistance to more than three million children since its founding by Charles Loring Brace as one of the first organized efforts in this direction. Brace saw the means of salvaging slum children with a clarity of vision rare in any age. Yet this prophetic reformer was neither widely known nor celebrated during his time. A minister by training, Mr. Brace devoted his professional life to slum children after a frustrating year of work among the hardened, cynical adult poor at Five Points in Lower Manhattan. An idealistic 26-year-old in 1853, he joined with a handful of eager reformers to establish the Society.

Mr. Brace's desire to help needy children sprang from his devout Christianity, but his methods were sheer pragmatism. His answers for the salvation of these children from misery and degradation were simple—education, gainful work, wholesome family atmosphere and economic self-reliance. His book, *The Dangerous Classes of New York, and Twenty Years' Work Among Them,* spells out his fervent beliefs and practical applications. Indeed, it reads like a modern primer for approaching today's social problems.

For 37½ years Mr. Brace quietly put his sensible theories to work at the Society. At the turn of the century, he stepped aside for his son, also named Charles Loring Brace, who ran the CAS for another 37½ years. Thus, for the first 75 years of its life, the Society was guided by a father and son who left their mark on the city by saving countless numbers of poverty-stricken children. The Society has responded to the needs and problems of children ever since without regard to race, creed or place of origin.

The Society's primary concerns have always been children who are needy, homeless, neglected, exploited, abused, sick, handicapped and troubled. Its goals have always been to provide secure, loving homes, to help each child realize his full potential, to assure his physical and mental health, to keep families together where possible, to improve the quality of life in the communities in which children live and to address the critical problems which adversely affect the lives of children. The Society's priority of service has always been on prevention where possible, remediation where necessary. Its fundamental emphasis is on self-help.

Its record of developing new and innovative services in response to children's needs is truly unique. In December 1853, the first industrial school for poor children was established. By 1893, 21 were in operation. In March 1854, in the midst of the era of the almshouse and of the asylum, the first working-boys' home and lodging house in America was established in the loft of the Sun Building. A few years later, six were in operation. Also in 1854, the first organized movement to place orphaned and abandoned children with families in the country was undertaken—the "free home" movement which ultimately placed thousands of children throughout the nation. Our predecessors, no chauvinists, established a home and training school for working girls on 12th Street in 1861.

In 1862, an agent for the Children's Aid Society was appointed visitor to the Tombs Prison "to investigate the causes of arrest of boys and to receive in his care, first offenders and the more hopeful cases." The importance of this prototype of the probation officer was recognized and endorsed in 1900 when the Society's Probation Committee, acting with the Court of Special Sessions, employed the first official probation officer in New York.

A public health program, precedent for the Visiting Nurses Service model, began operations in 1873 when the Society organized physicians' and nurses' visits to tenement houses in its Sick Children's Mission. In 1876, the first free kindergarten was established in the Society's 18th Street Industrial School. In 1881, a group of trustees, in concert with other leaders, built a model tenement midtown on the East Side. The Health Home, the first seaside sanatorium for mothers with sick infants, was established by CAS in 1884 at Coney Island, to be followed in 1887 by the first Fresh Air Cottage for children disabled by tuberculosis and other diseases, a forerunner for CAS convalescent homes established after the turn of the century. A farm school for homeless boys was developed in 1894 and three years later the first upgraded classes for "restless, wayward boys" and chronic truants were set up in the West Side Industrial School. That same year, a "model flat" to teach girls housework was set up in connection with the Avenue B Industrial School. The following year, New York's first day school for crippled children was initiated in the Henrietta School and in February, 1900, a class for crippled children was developed at the Avenue B School. A horse-drawn omnibus brought the children to 16th Street from the area from Stanton to 59th Streets and from 3rd Avenue to the East River. The Auxiliary Board which oversaw this program decided to separate from the Society in 1907 and incorporated as the Association for the Aid of Crippled Children. In 1902, the first free class in New York for mentally retarded children was started in the Rhinelander School, which also ran classes for handicapped children, and a year later the first home for homeless mothers and infants was opened on 12th Street. The first free school dental clinic was established in 1907.

Because the Society has operated from its inception on the theory that what it does today, it need not do tomorrow, it has continued to develop innovative programs, discarding or passing on pilot models as the need has diminished or as other have assumed the functions and the responsibility. As an example, when the public education system adopted their vocational school program, the Society converted its industrial schools into community recreational and guidance centers. But as life grew more complex and difficult, recreational programs were retained as a minor theme in a broadened spectrum of protective, preventive and supportive social services.

Parallel with services was the constant effort to effect legislation in the best interest of children. Successful efforts included the compulsory school attendance laws and child-labor restrictions, as well as laws enabling the development of public services for children and funding partnerships of the public and private sectors. Mr. Brace did not restrict his work to this country. In 1873, as a consequence of his efforts, the Italian Chamber of Deputies framed a bill for the suppression of the padrone system (the criminal exploitation of children), crediting the CAS for its crusading role. This pattern of study directed towards legislation continues in high gear today.

Through its long-established centers in seven neighborhoods, the Society now offers a wide spectrum of major services to children and their families. These range from direct service to referral to other appropriate public and private agencies supplying the assistance required.

The Foster Care Services Department deals with adoption, work with unmarried parents, family counseling, foster boarding-home and group care (a substitute for the costly and often dehumanizing public shelters), tutorial and psychiatric services for children in placement, and homemaker services.

The programs extended through the City and Country Branches Department include those devoted to group work, recreational and informal education, community-based health and dental services, mental health clinics, Head Start, drug prevention, a preschool program for retarded children, alternate education, pre-trial diversion, a special tutorial and preparation for the world of work (LIVE) sponsored in conjunction with five major corporations and the public education system, an agency-operated boarding home and a group residence for diagnostic and treatment purposes linked directly with the Foster Care Services. There is also a specialized residence camp for handicapped children, as well as year-round weekend camping and summer day and home camping.

The program of the Health Services Department includes health screenings for both foster and center children, follow-ups, information and referral, community health education, special services for overweight children and dental services (including prosthodontia and orthodontia).

The pictures in this book reflect some of the changes that have taken place since 1853. Horse-drawn wagons, knickers and children in factories are relics of the past, but some of our children, unwanted and unloved, still wear old faces and nurse hidden hurts. Amid the most affluent society that has ever existed, malnourished and poorly clad children still live in dwellings unfit for human habitation, without dignity, privacy or hope. In a nation whose technology has put men on the moon and resolved problems that could not even be formulated ten years ago, there are still children who are unlettered, unskilled and untrained, ill-equipped to cope with a complex urban society. They hold low priority in a nation that professes its love for children but spends more for liquor than on its young.

What has not changed or wavered since 1853 is the Society's commitment and mission on behalf of children in need. Almost 100,000 children will turn to it yearly for the foreseeable future. Children imperiled by deprivation of the body and spirit, children in crowded tenements, without sound values or love, scarred by beatings at the hands of parents who were similarly abused. Children whose families have failed them and whose hope for productive lives lies in foster homes or a group residence. Children without parents who are doomed to dependency and despair unless adoptive families are found. Children of low self-esteem who seek escape in the false security of alcoholism or drugs—or by withdrawal into a world of their own creations. Children who are physically handicapped or retarded, whose hopes for independence and self-fulfillment, though limited, rest with a skilled and helping hand.

While we seek through conscience and through law to assure the protection, the rights and the opportunities that should be afforded to every child, these needy children, who speak with muted voices and who are so eloquently portrayed in this book, are our responsibility and the object of our concern. Their growth to adulthood—to productive, independent and contributing citizenship and to loving parenthood—is our mission and our reward.

Victor Remer
Executive Director
The Children's Aid Society

Hester Street [opposite]. Always a city of extremes, New York in the 90s housed most of America's more than 4000 millionaires and also held stretches of the most crowded slums on the face of the earth. To escape these squalid tenement rooms, kids flocked onto the teeming streets. Here Hester Street on the Lower East Side is seen, looking west from Clinton Street tward The Bowery. Kids rolled up their trousers to wade in the water gushing from fire hydrants or dodged among shoppers in "Pig Market," named for the pork products sold there. The population density on Hester Street—and the entire surrounding Tenth Ward— averaged 522 people per acre, a figure unmatched even by the seething masses of humanity herded into the slums of London or Calcutta. Incredibly, scores of talented, hard-working people emerged from these slums. A list of the alumni of this tough street school reads like that of many established universities. ***(Museum of the City of New York)***

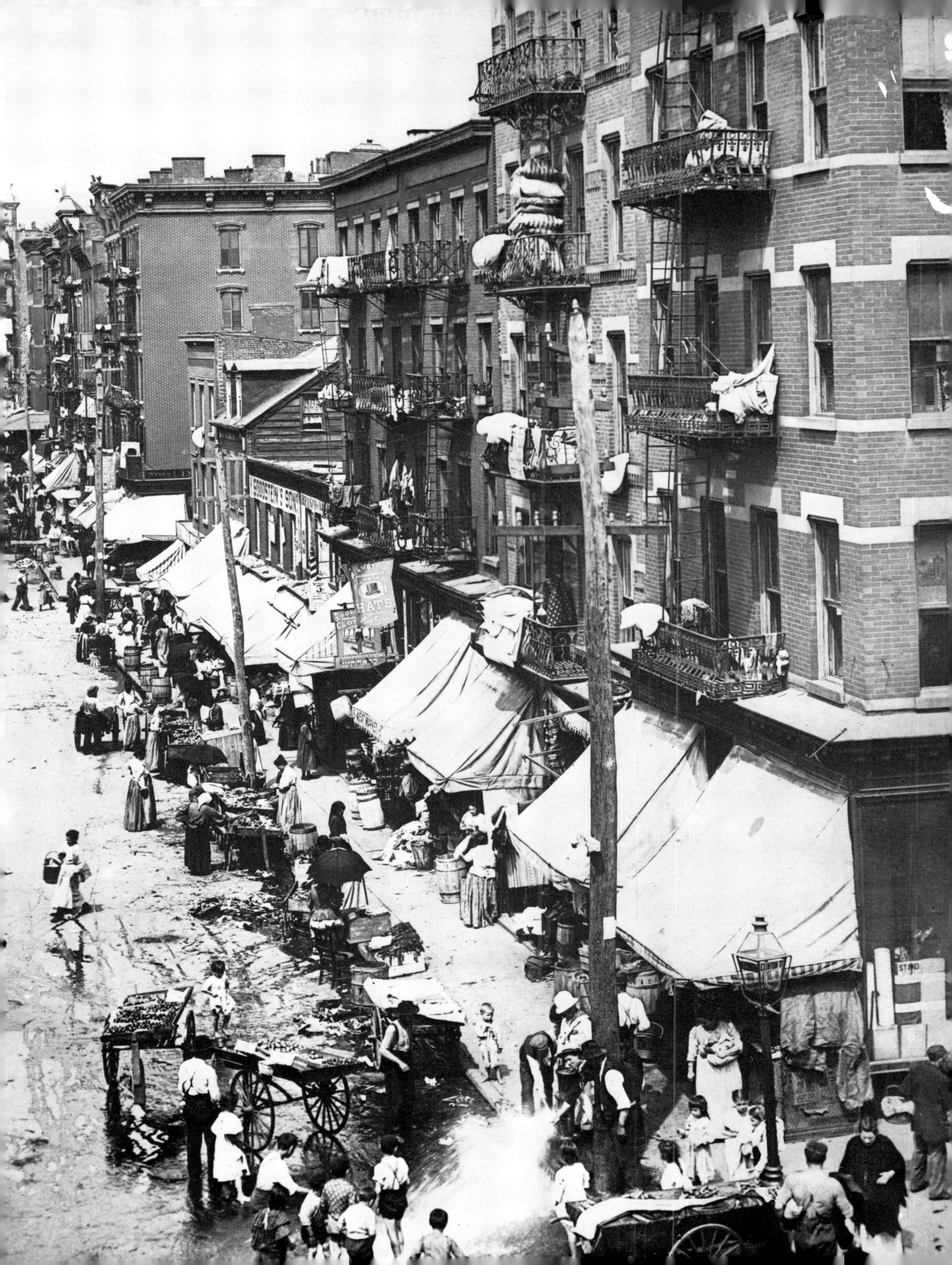
GOODSTEIN'S SONS
HATS

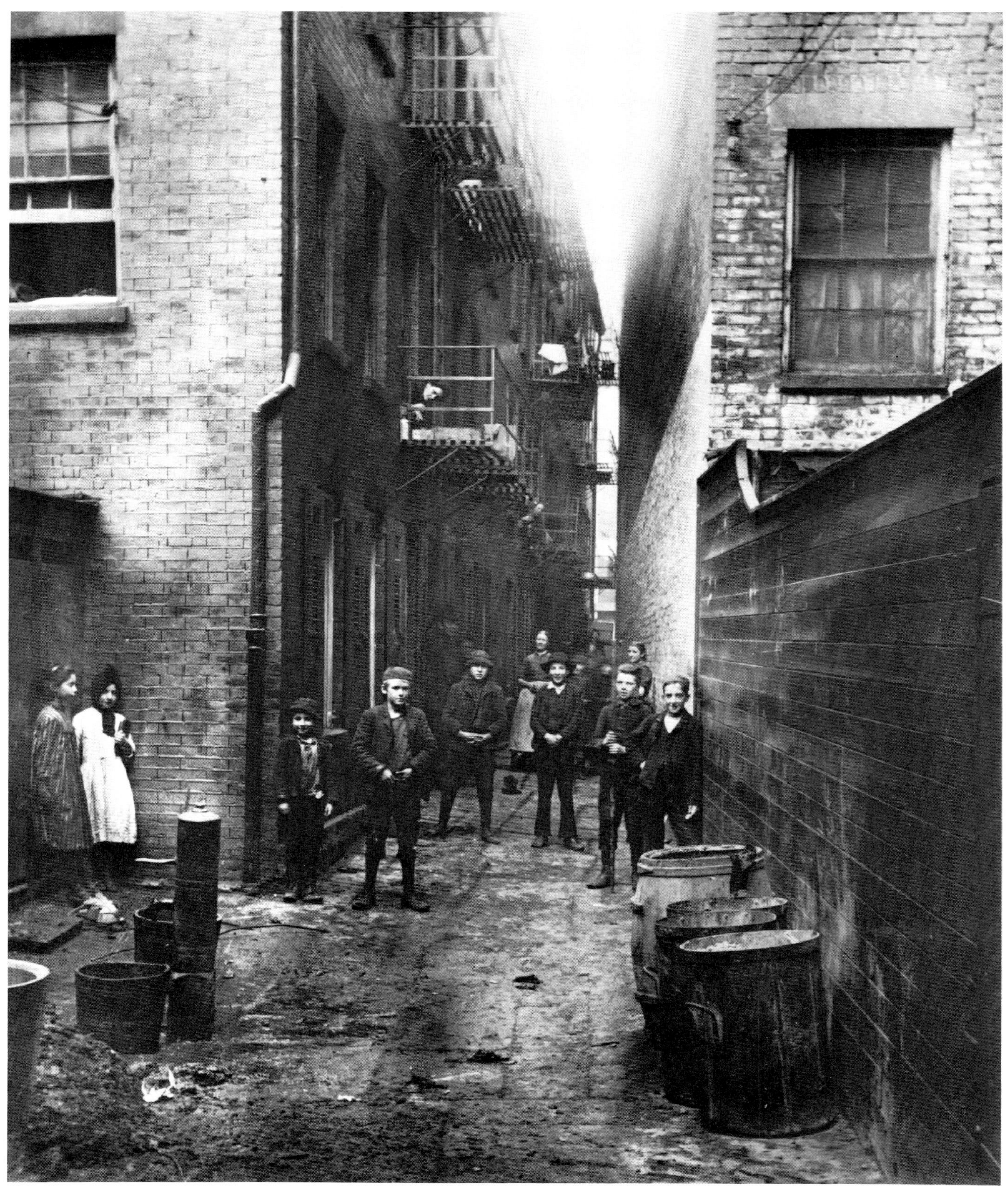

Denizens of Mullen's Alley. Since parks and playgrounds in the slums were rare, children and mothers turned to back alleys for breathing room. As this photograph indicates, these alleys were not without an ominous air. Some were notorious, so clogged with packs of feral kids and gangs of older cutthroats that the police were afraid to enter them even at high noon. *(The Jacob A. Riis Collection, Museum of the City of New York)*

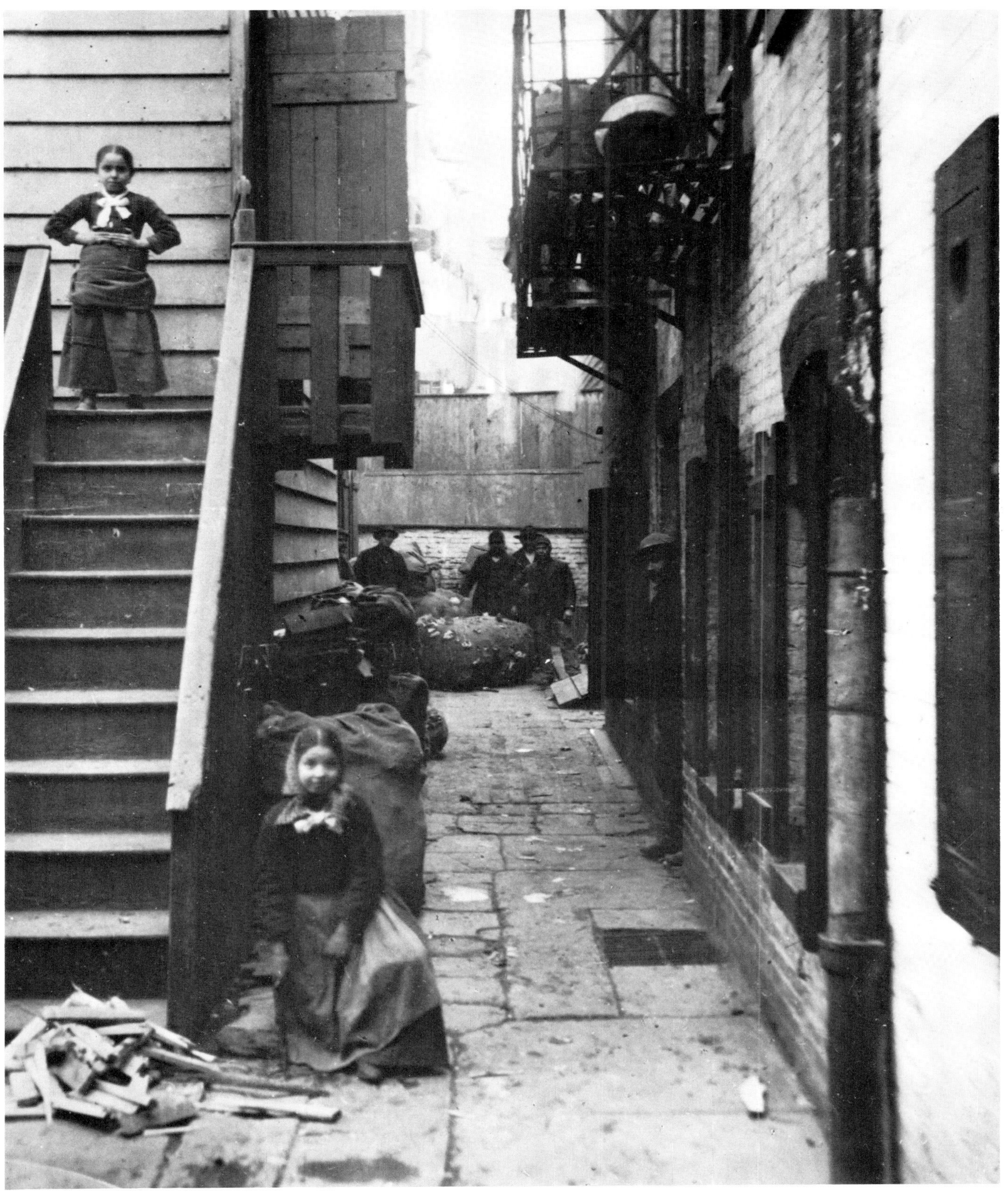

Baxter Street Alley. While the grownups lurk in the shadows, the two girls seen here reflect the maturity that slum kids assumed early in life. The stance of the girl on the porch shows that she is accustomed to adult work. But for her small stature she could be a young mother calling her children for supper. The other girl kneels at the foot of the stairs next to the pile of firewood she has gathered. *(The Jacob A. Riis Collection, Museum of the City of New York)*

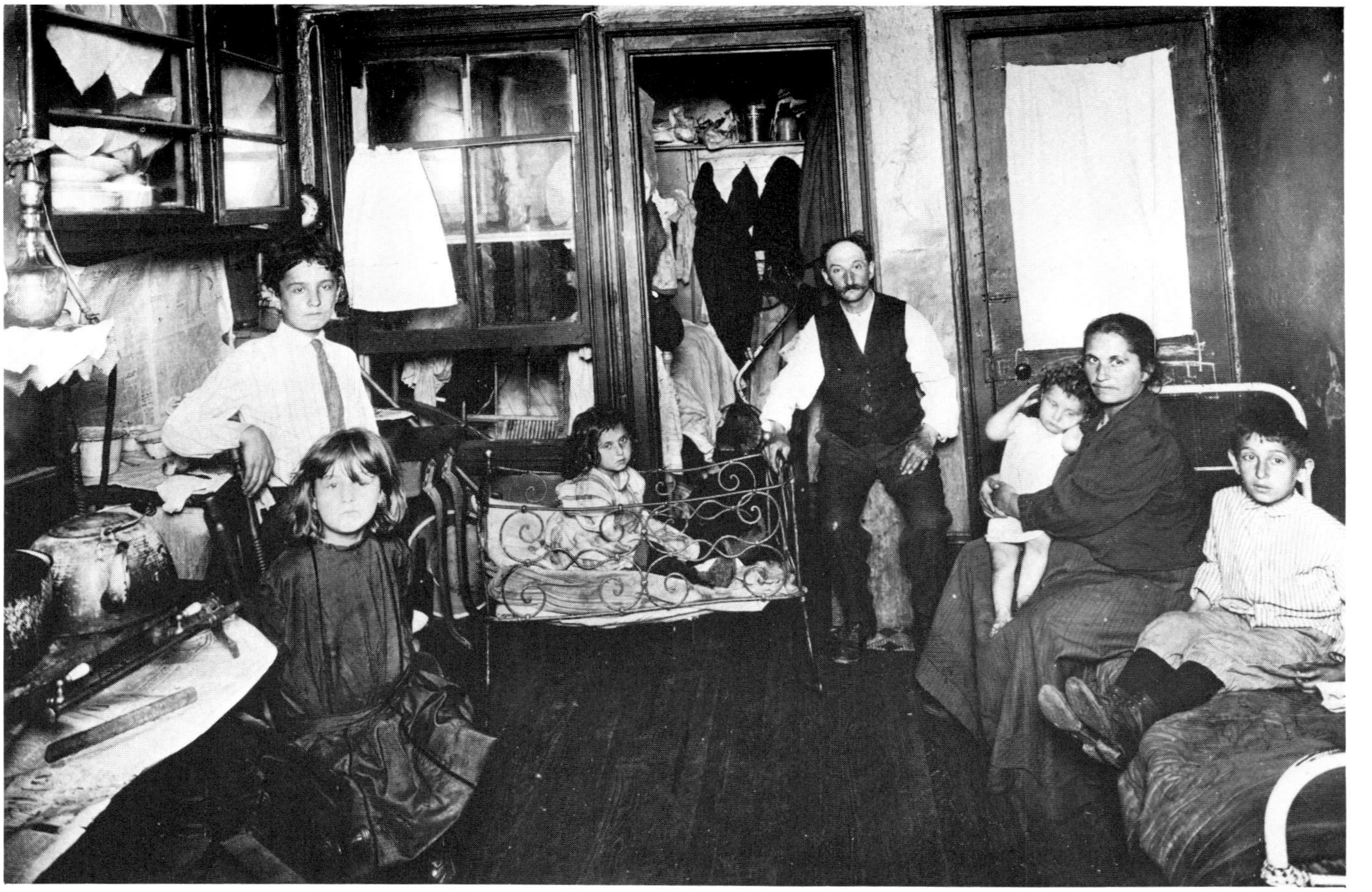

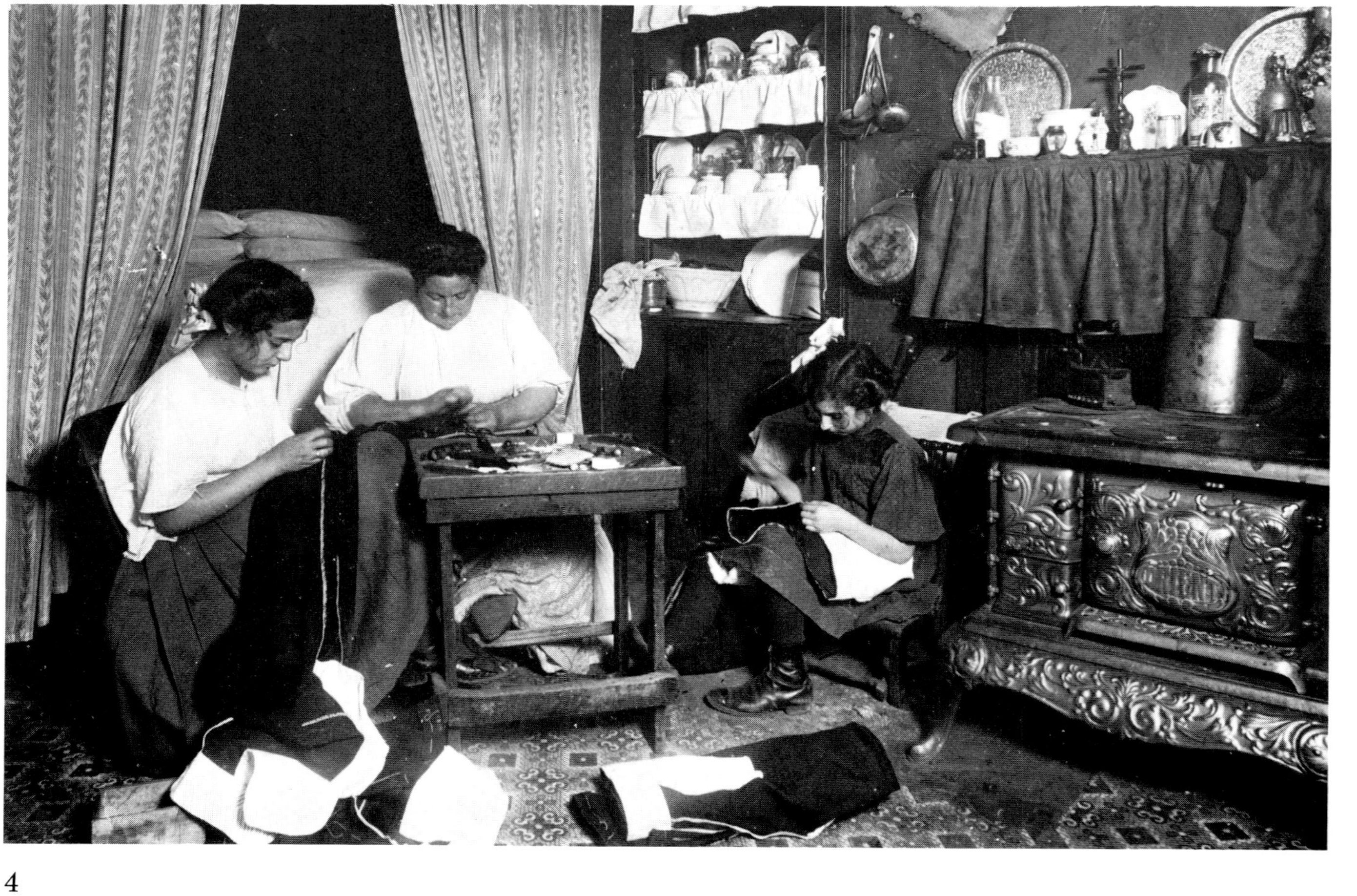

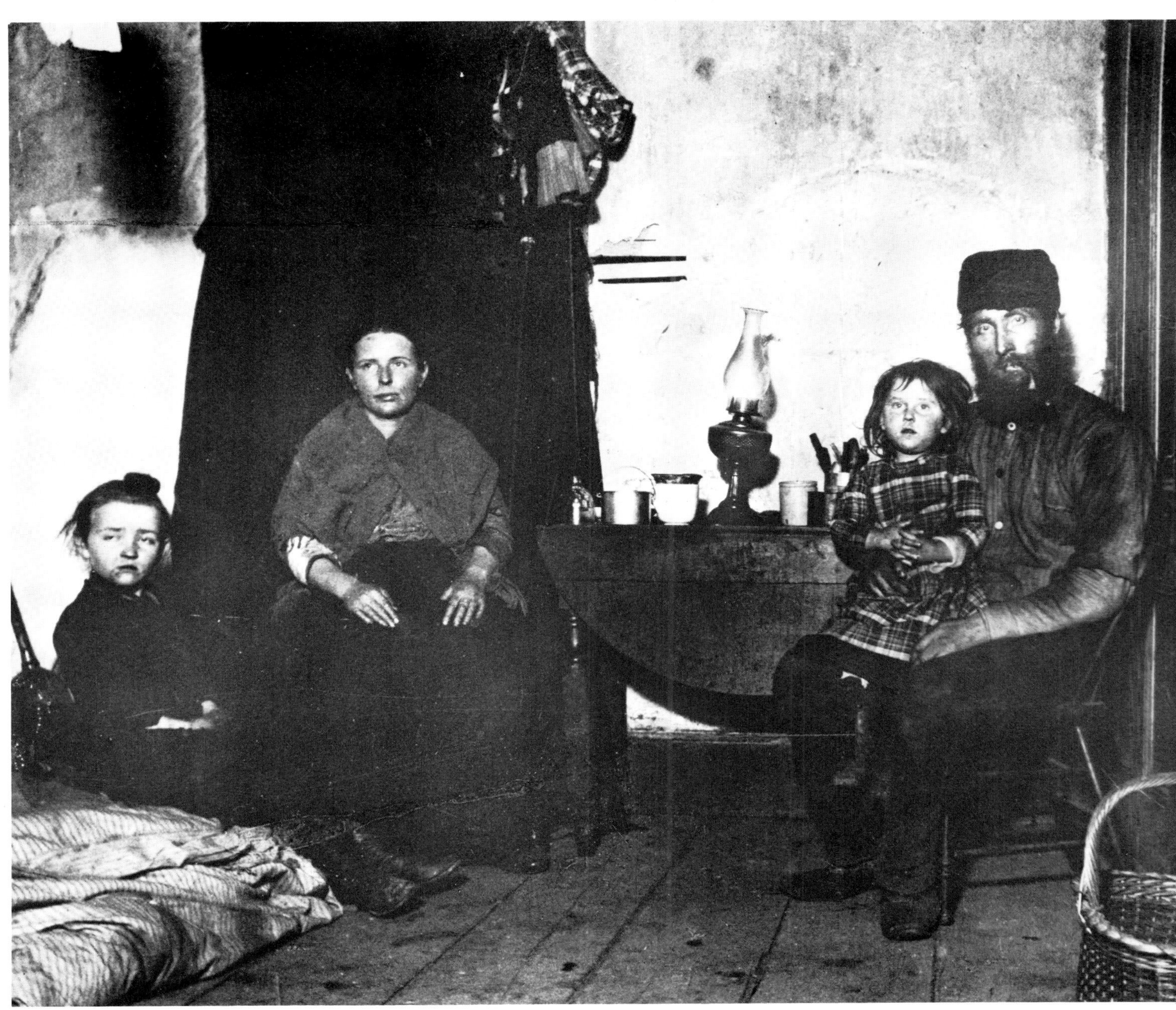

A Ragpicker's Family [opposite, top]. The wretched living conditions of a slum tenement are painfully evident in this candid photograph of an immigrant ragpicker, his wife and five children. In 1890 there were more than 160,000 children five years old or younger packed into the city's tenements. Some suffered in conditions even more miserable than this. An infamous barracks in lower Manhattan held as many as 1500 people in its fetid rooms and foul "sleeping cellar," while on the back lot was a companion barracks just as filthy and crowded. Ground down by such conditions, many children faced a future that was, at best, bleak but for the intervention of the Children's Aid Society (CAS), with schools and programs that offered a chance for survival. The children seen here, for example, were students at the CAS Italian School on the Lower East Side. *(Museum of the City of New York)* **Finishing Pants** [opposite, bottom]. Jobs were never plentiful in the slums, but in the 90s they were particularly scarce. In 1894 a severe economic depression wiped out many sources of employment, which led to street demonstrations and riots by disgruntled workers. To make whatever money they could, children joined their mothers to compete with the men at the finishing tables of the garment industry. Lacking steady employment, they would take home piecework. Still in her child's chair, a daughter proved that she was the match for the older women in the family with a needle. *(The Jacob A. Riis Collection, Museum of the City of New York)* **A Tenement Interior at Poverty Gap** [above]. Like carbon copies of their parents, these little girls wear the dirt and resignation of life in an infamous slum. With characteristic eloquence, the writer-reformer Jacob A. Riis, who took this picture, wrote, "The slum tenement bears to it the same relation as the effect of rags on an old tramp have upon a young idler. He has only to wear them to lose all ambition and become himself a tramp." *(The Jacob A. Riis Collection, Museum of the City of New York)*

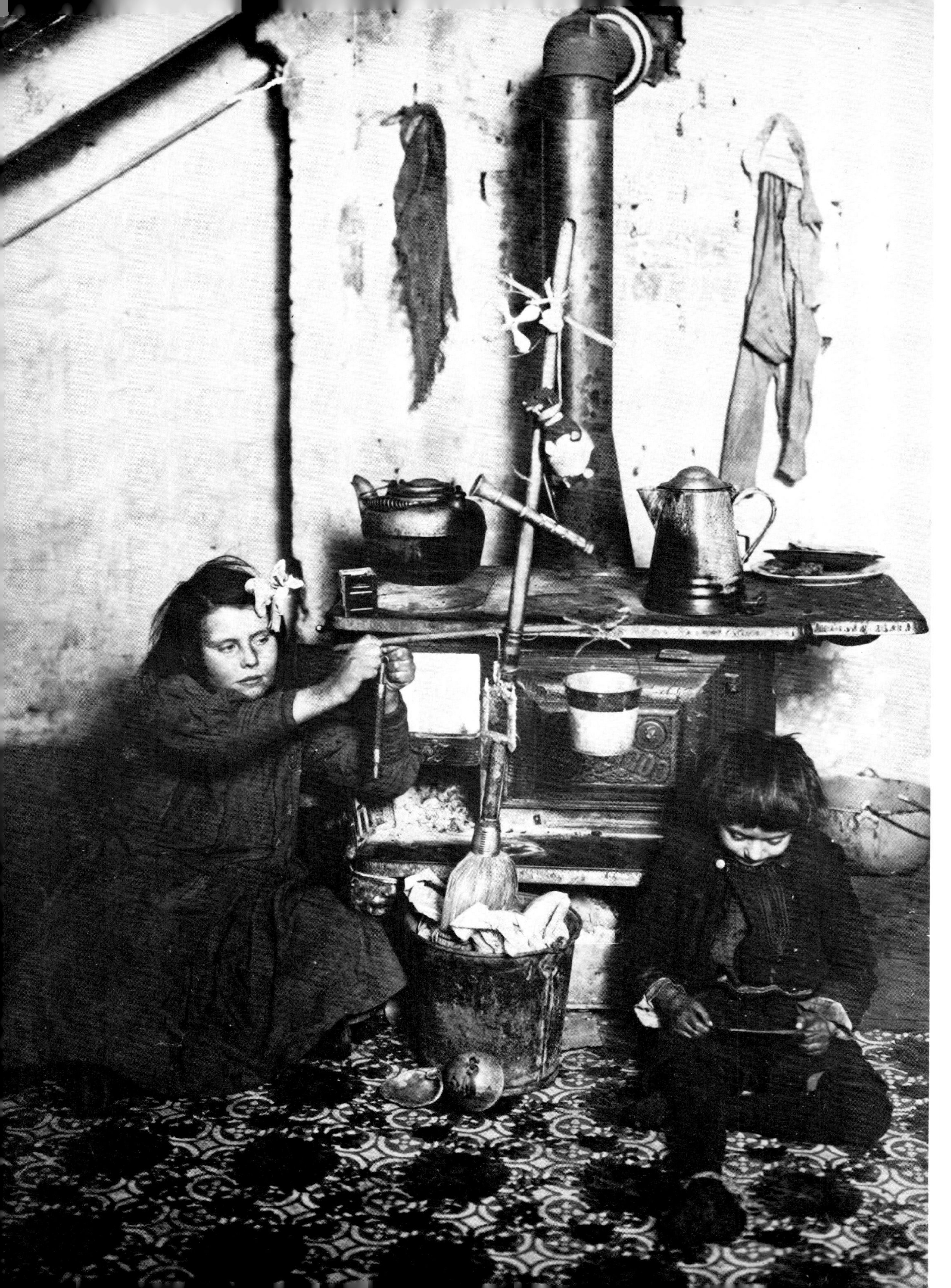

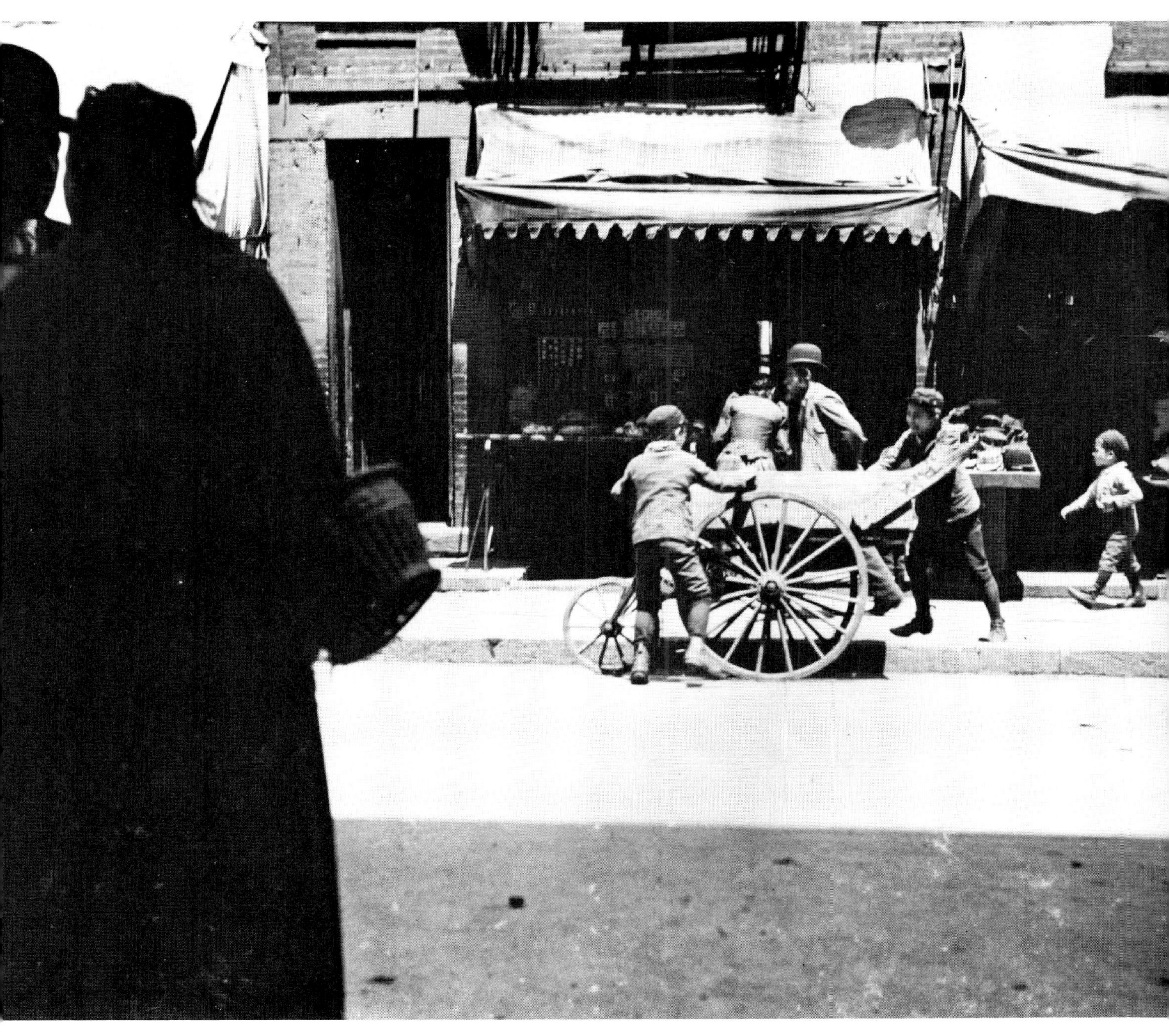

Children Making a Christmas Tree [opposite]. The spirit of city children is unquenchable, even under the most depressing conditions. These two kids use an old broom wedged into a bucket and a few old toys to fashion an impromptu Christmas tree that costs nothing. Ingenious as the broom-tree is, it does have an historical precedent. A decorated broom often served as a substitute or second tree in the homes of working-class Europe. *(c.a.s.).* **What the Boys Learn There** [above]. Stealing fruit and vegetables from a pushcart peddler was part of the education of any poor urban youth during this period. In part, the thefts were acts of defiance that are the standard rites of a growing boy. But the thefts were also for the food to soothe the gnawing pangs of hunger. *(The Jacob A. Riis Collection, Museum of the City of New York)*

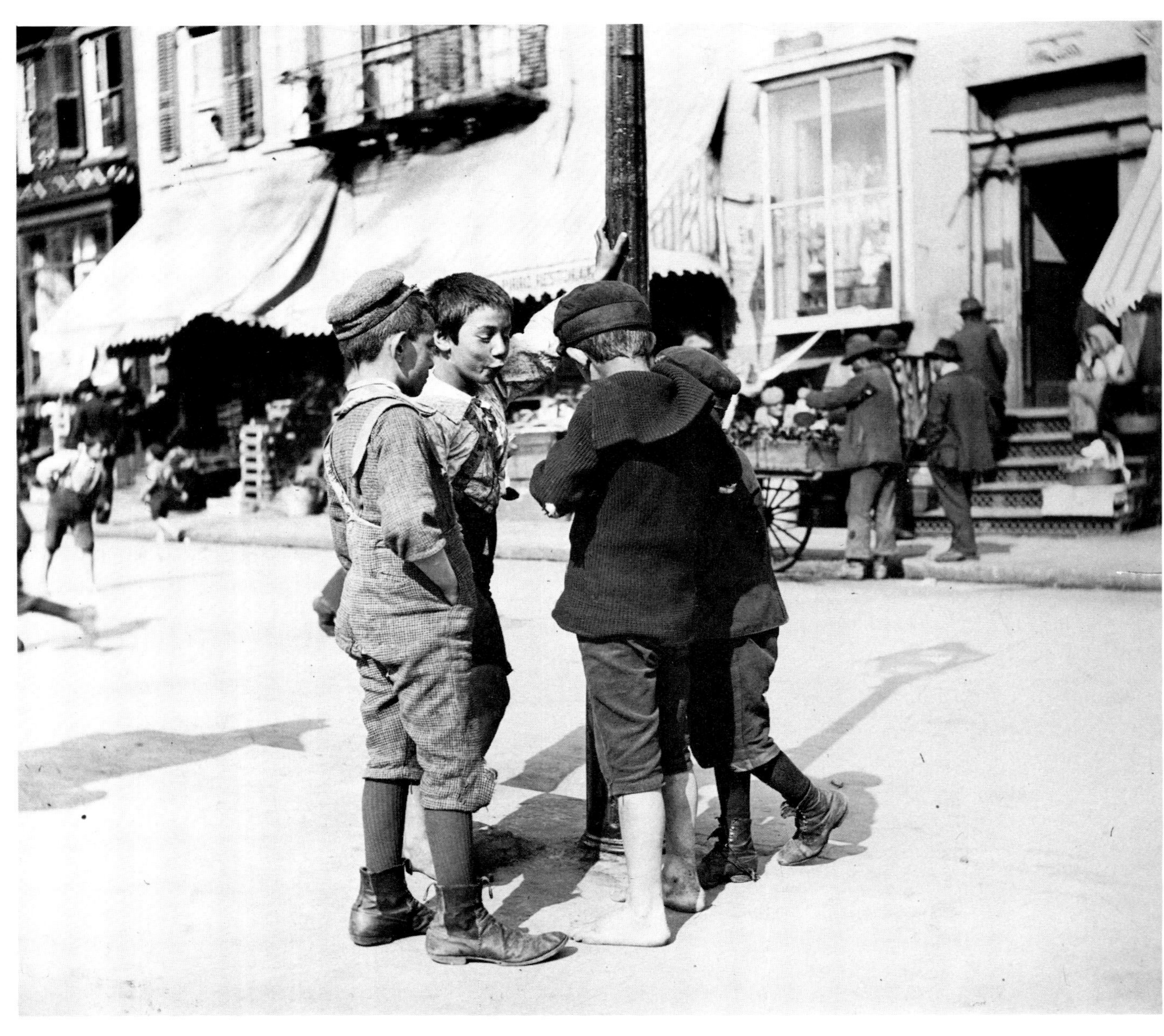

Four Young Boys of Mulberry Street. Clustered around lampposts, boys chat, reveal secrets and display prized possessions. Oblivious to the games being played by their friends, these boys partake in the ritual of lamppost reunions. *(The Bettmann Archive)*

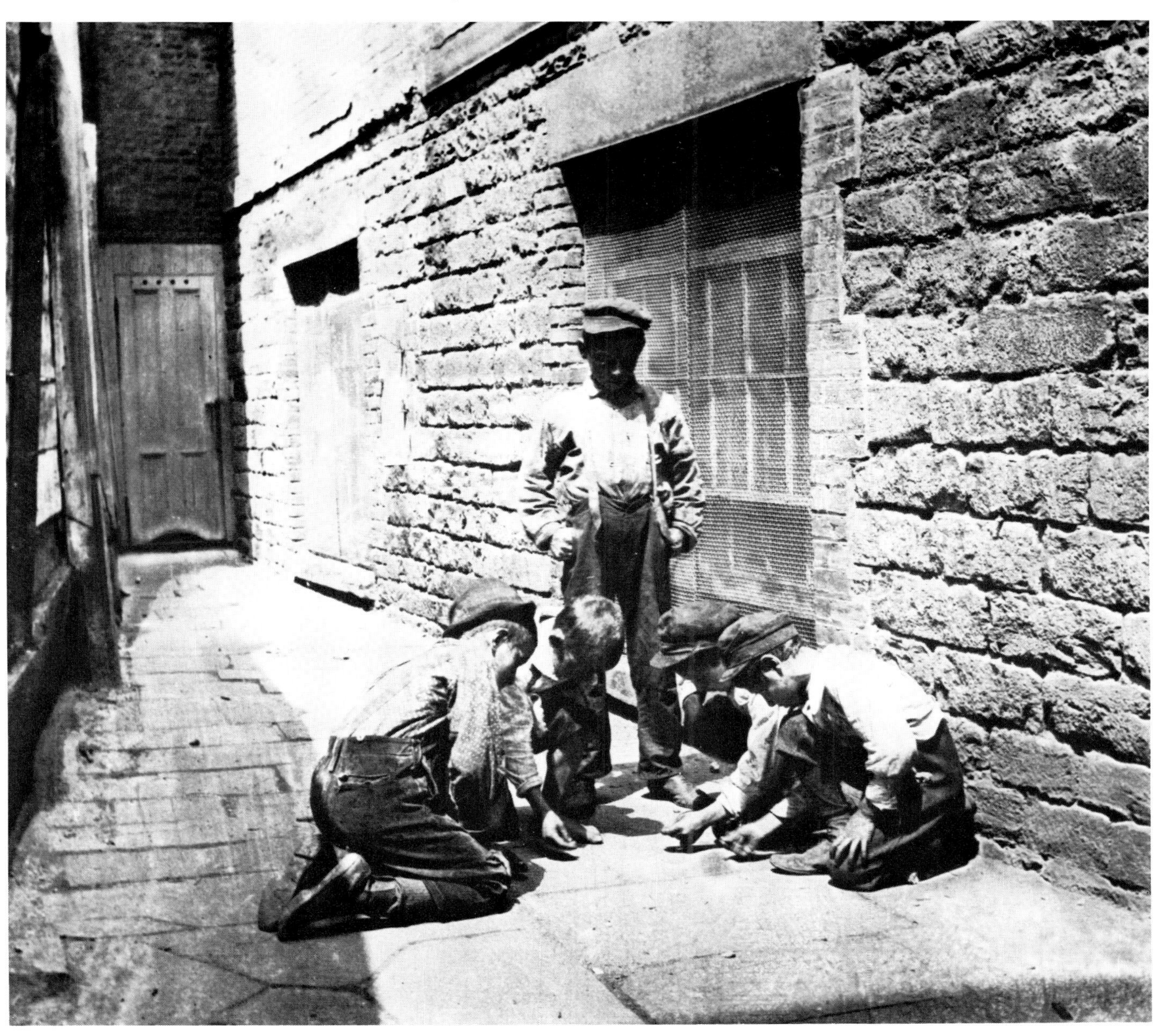

Shooting Craps. Hunkered down in an alley to roll dice, a knot of boys becomes engrossed in a game of chance as old as the streets themselves. The lack of coins suggests that the gambling is all for fun. But the players' intensity implies that before long these youngsters will be dropping coins on the pavement along with the dice. *(The Jacob A. Riis Collection, Museum of the City of New York)*

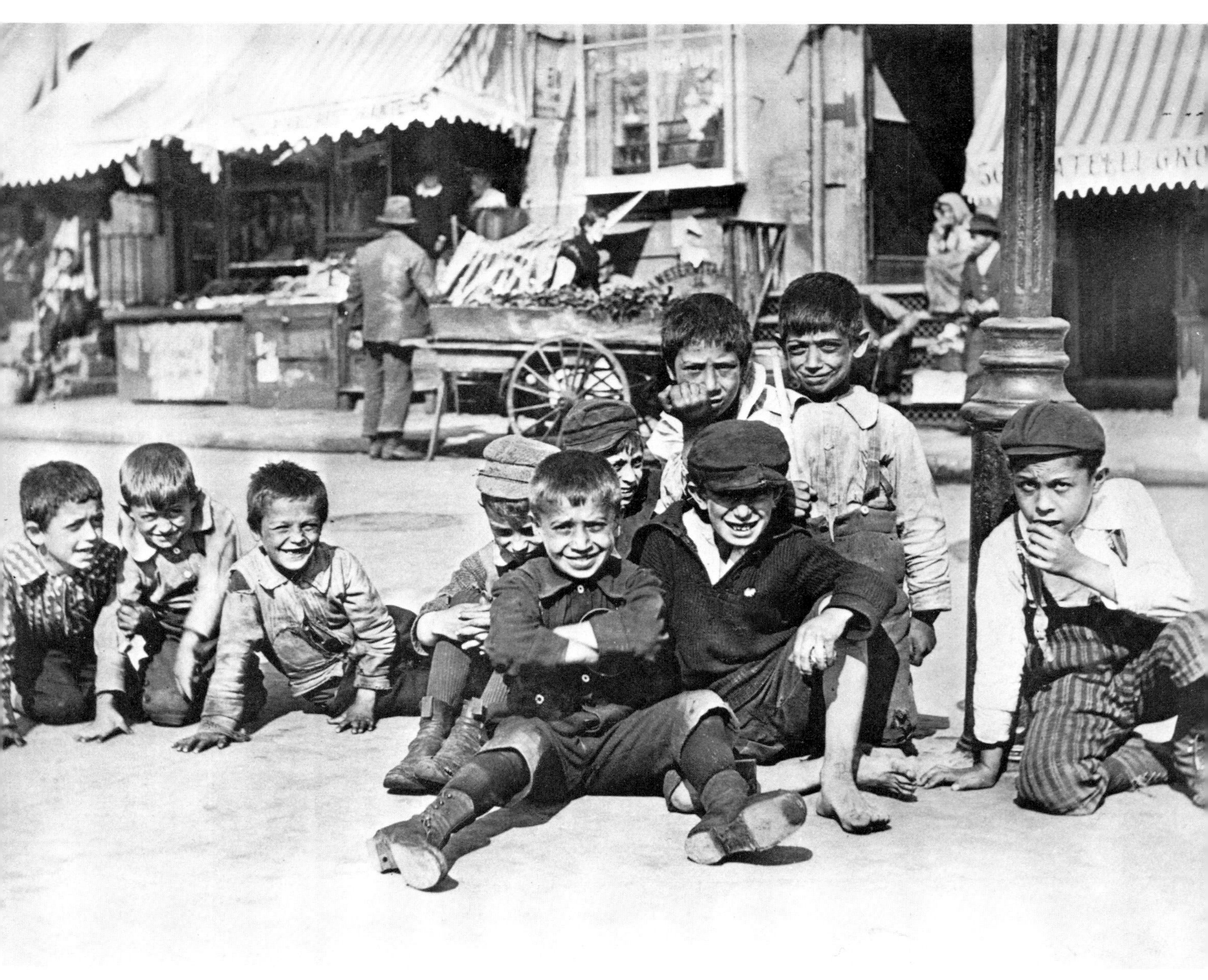

The Boys of Mulberry Bend [above]. Sprawled on an infamous slum street, these ragamuffins flash their gap-toothed smiles to the outside world. Among themselves their shabby clothes attracted little comment or notice. But to their parents, the clothes bore a social stigma. Many were so ashamed of their children's outfits they kept them home from school rather than run the risk of exposing them to ridicule in the classroom. *(The Bettmann Archive)* **Their Playground—a Truck** [opposite, top]. In the slums, where there are neither playgrounds nor parks, the back of a truck is used by two little fellows looking for a place to rest or play. It offers relative quiet and the kind of small enclosure that children enjoy. *(The Jacob A. Riis Collection, Museum of the City of New York)* **A Game of Catstick** [opposite, bottom]. No area was too remote or desolate for street boys to indulge in a game of cat-stick (also known as tipcat). Even though the participants seem to be allowing the summer heat to wilt their enthusiasm, the game helps pass the languid afternoon. In the game, a small piece of wood is laid down. A larger stick (which the boy is holding) is brought down on top of the edge of the small block, which goes spinning into the air. While it is still in the air it is again hit in an effort to drive it as far as possible. *(The Byron Collection, Museum of the City of New York)*

The Fulton Fish Market [over]. For restless kids the piers and docks of the Fulton Fish Market on the Lower East Side were a cool and off-beat place to escape the heat of the city streets. Nude swimmers were so common they hardly caused a ripple of interest among the dockworkers and buyers. So casual was the swim that the pile of clothes on the dock marks the spot the boys chose as their dressing room. *(The New-York Historical Society)*

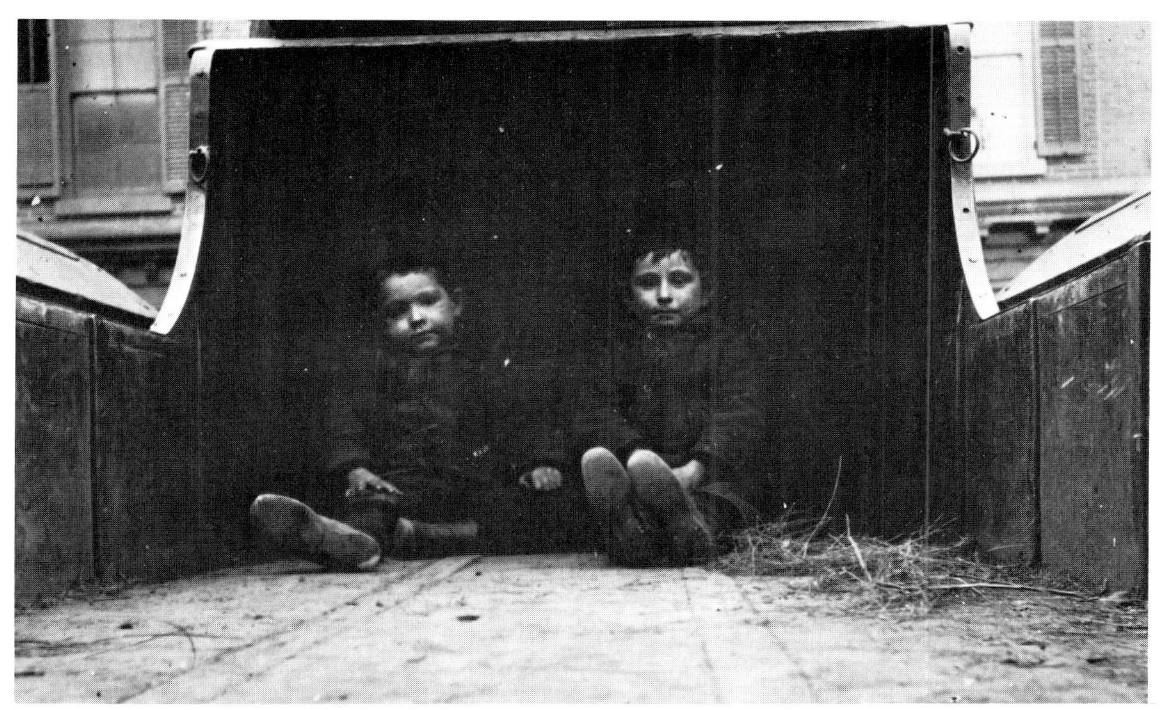

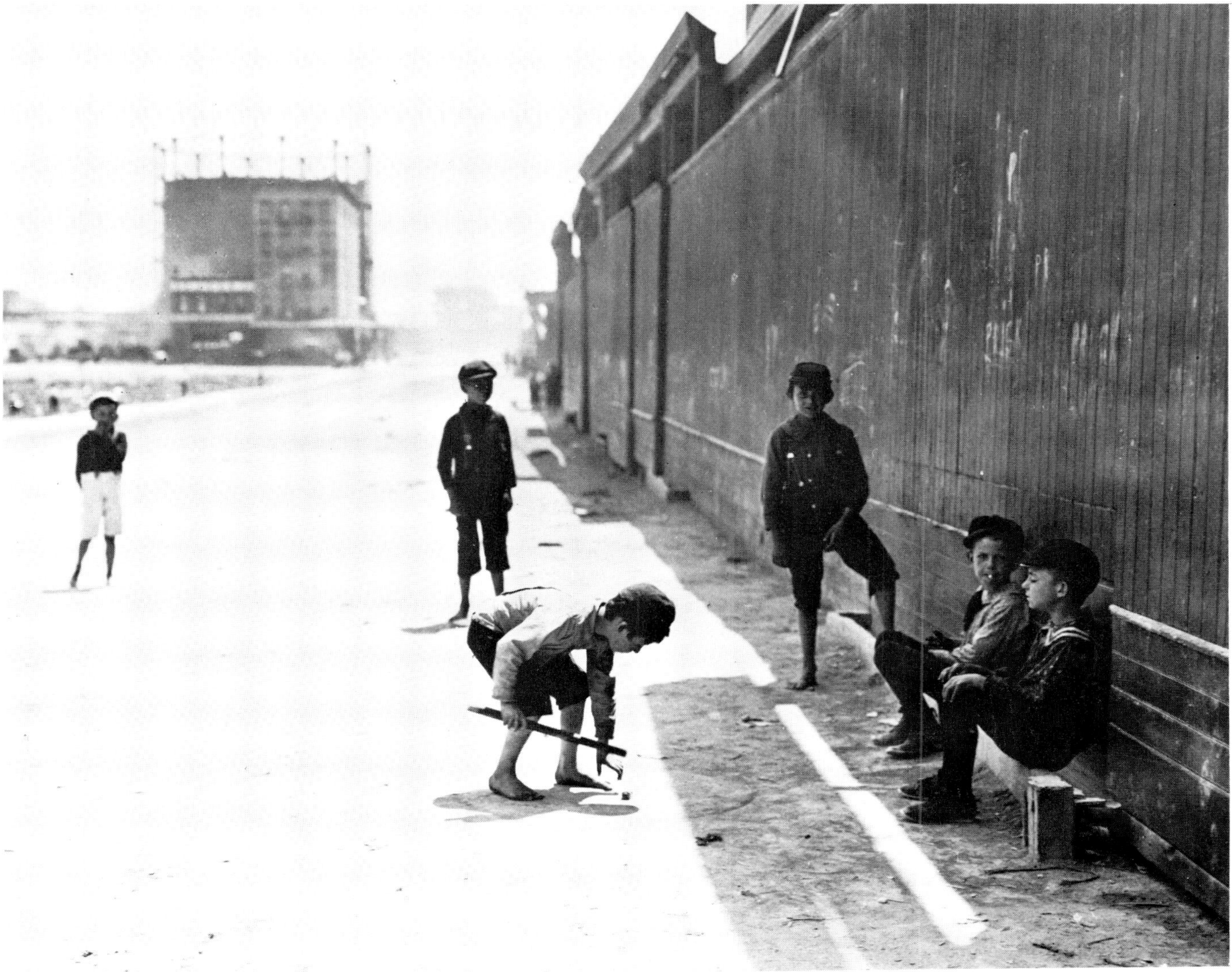

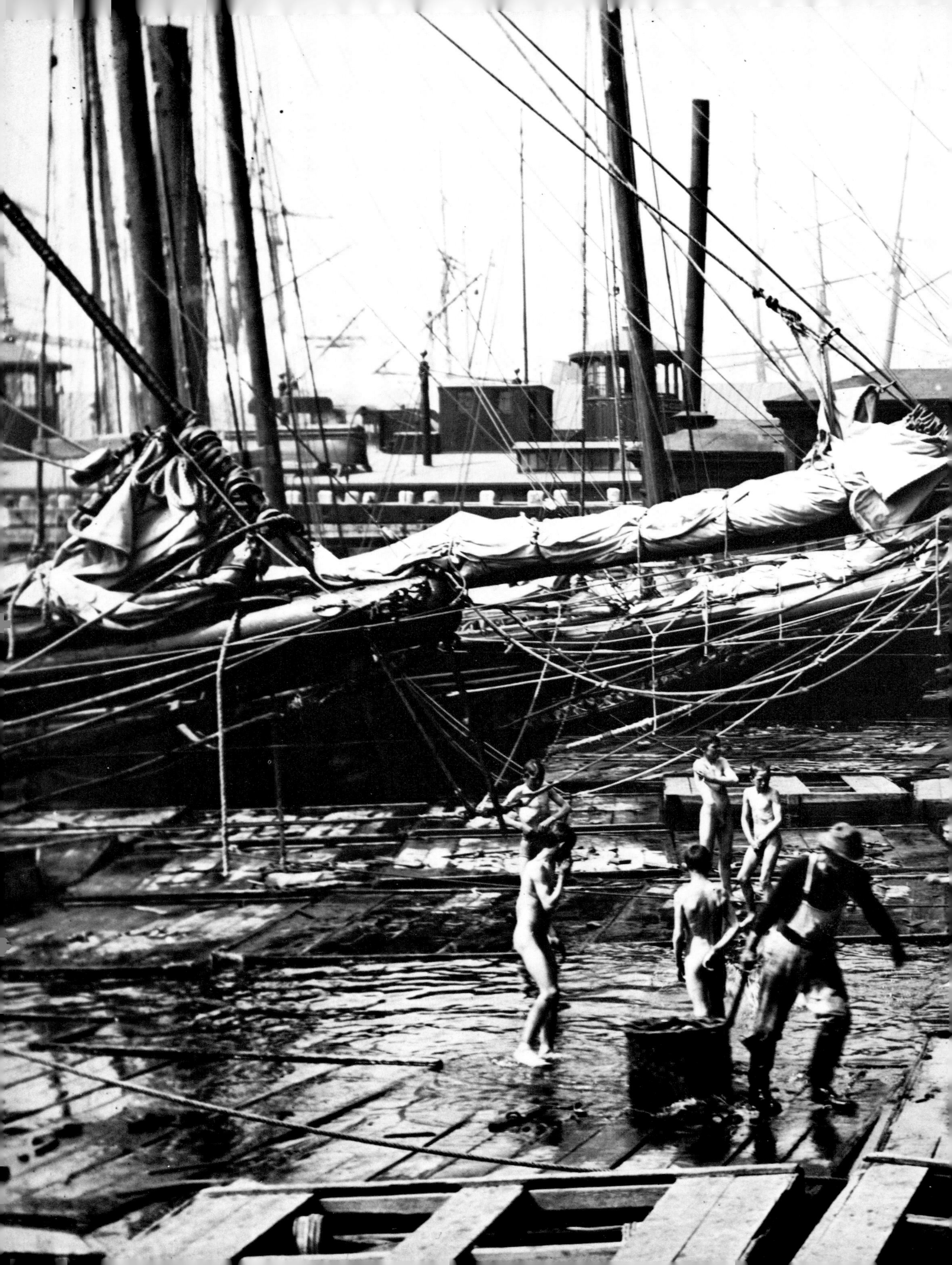

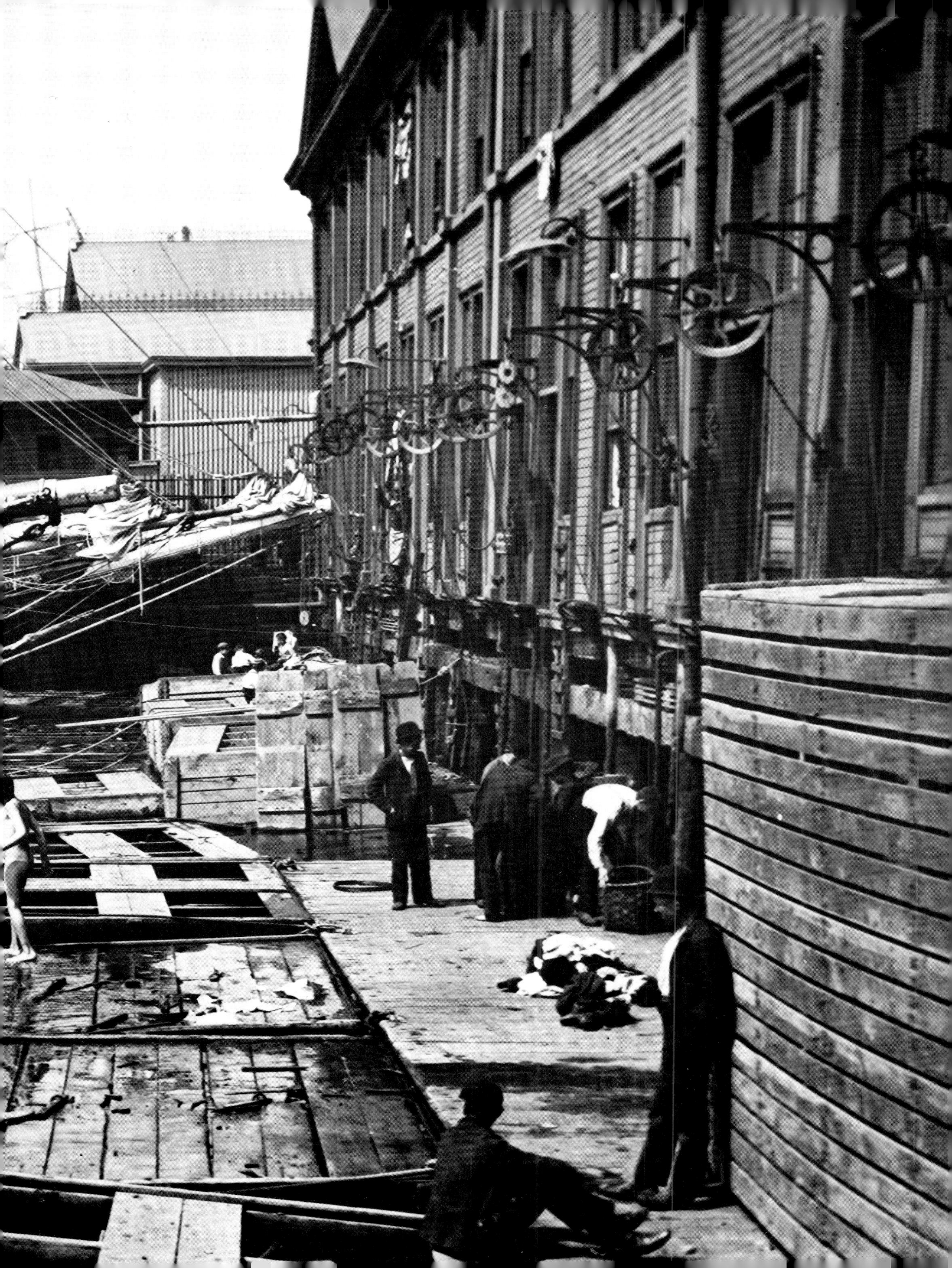

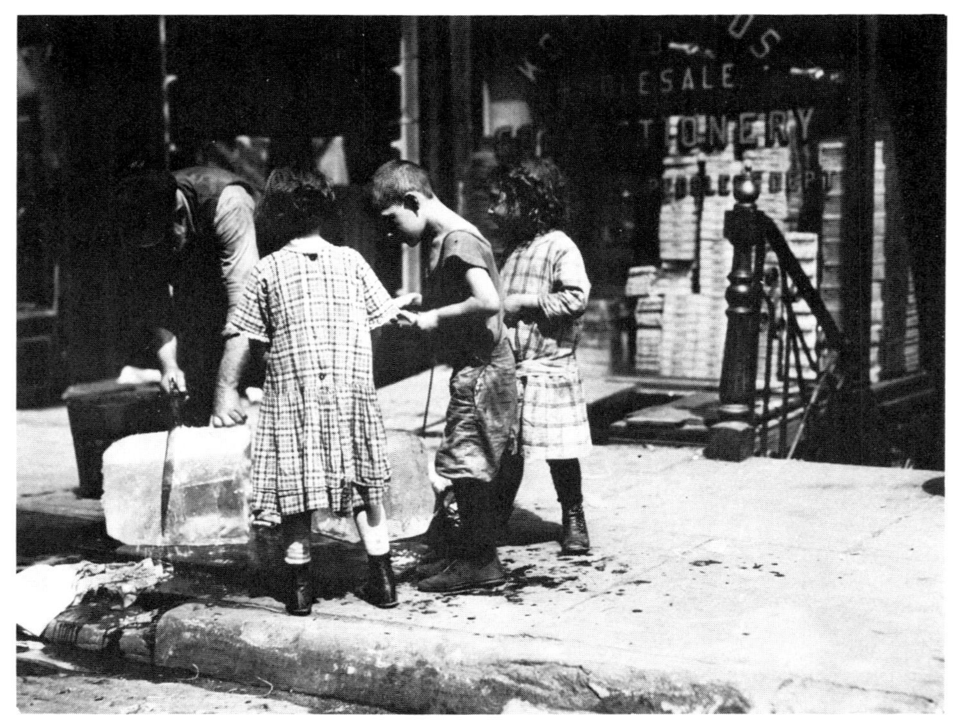

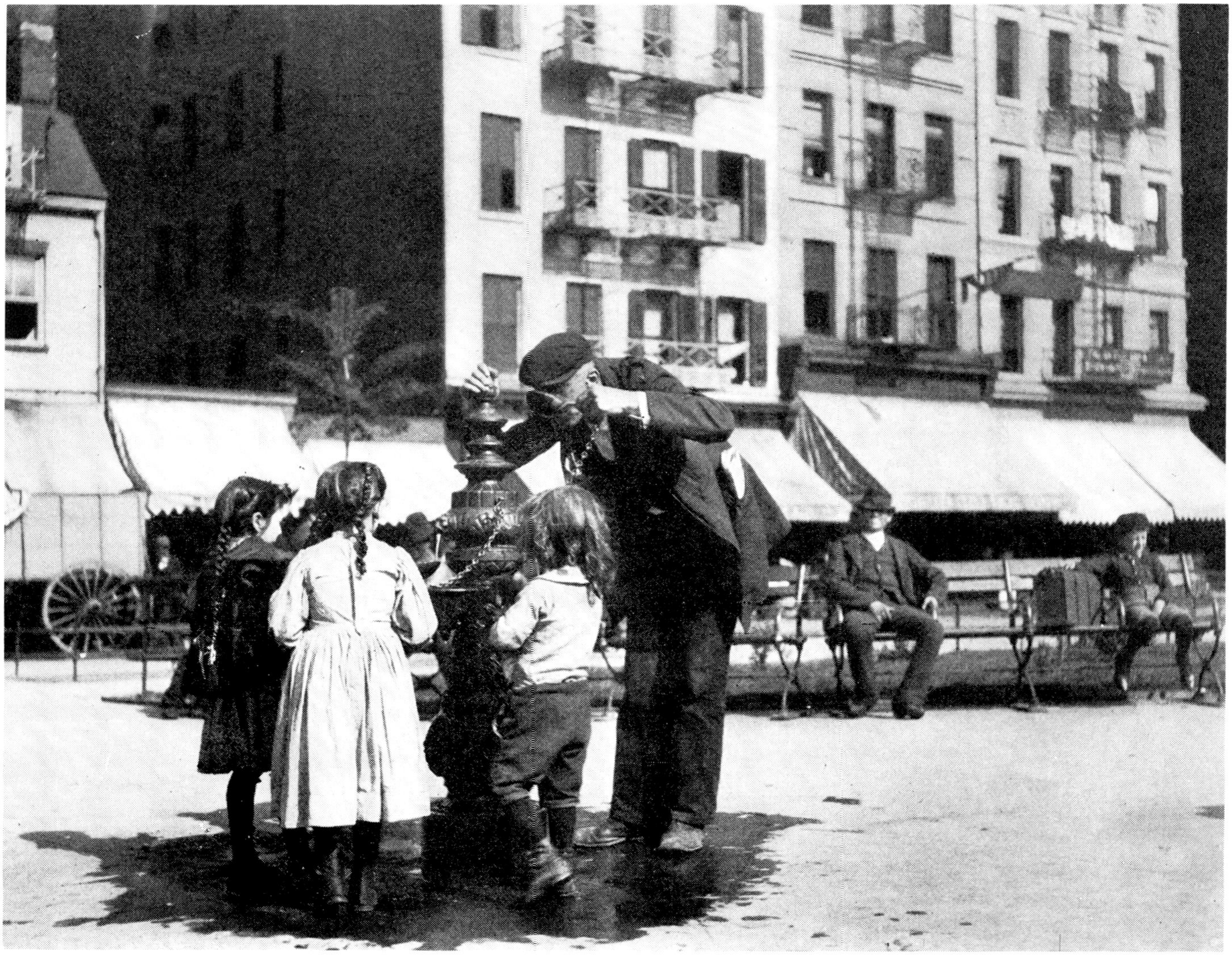

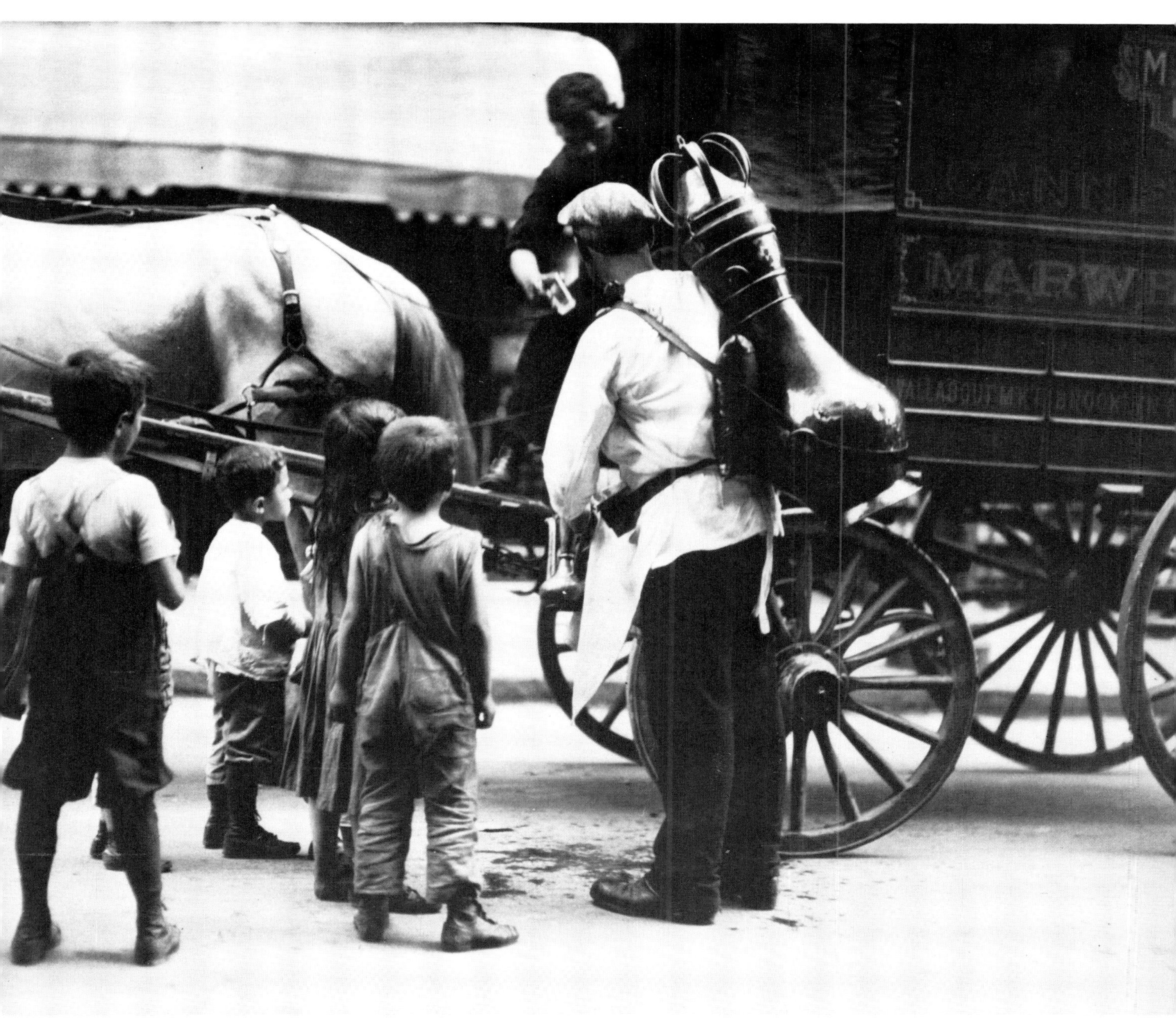

Iceman [opposite, top]. In the days before powered refrigeration, ice was dear. Chunks were bought from the iceman and placed in the tin-insulated compartment of the icebox. The chief purchasers of ice were the kids sent to the streets by their mothers. They clustered next to the cold blocks while the iceman cut manageable portions with swift strokes of his sharp handsaw. Even though the slabs were often heavy and difficult to wrestle up the tenement stairs, they bestowed on the young haulers a blessed cooling dampness. *(Lewis Hine. International Museum of Photography, Rochester, New York)* **At the Drinking Fountain in Mulberry Bend Park** [opposite, bottom]. The outdoor drinking fountains were a natural gathering place for kids and adults. An oasis in a desert of concrete and asphalt, the cool waters never failed to quench the thirsts induced by the sunbaked pavement. **Soda Vendor** [above]. Packing an elegantly shaped container on his strong back, the soda vendor left trails of smiling customers—and crowds of envious children. The vendor sold his sweet cooling refreshment by the glass, mostly to adult working people. However simple the event on the street, kids were always attracted. *(Lewis Hine. International Museum of Photography, Rochester, New York)*

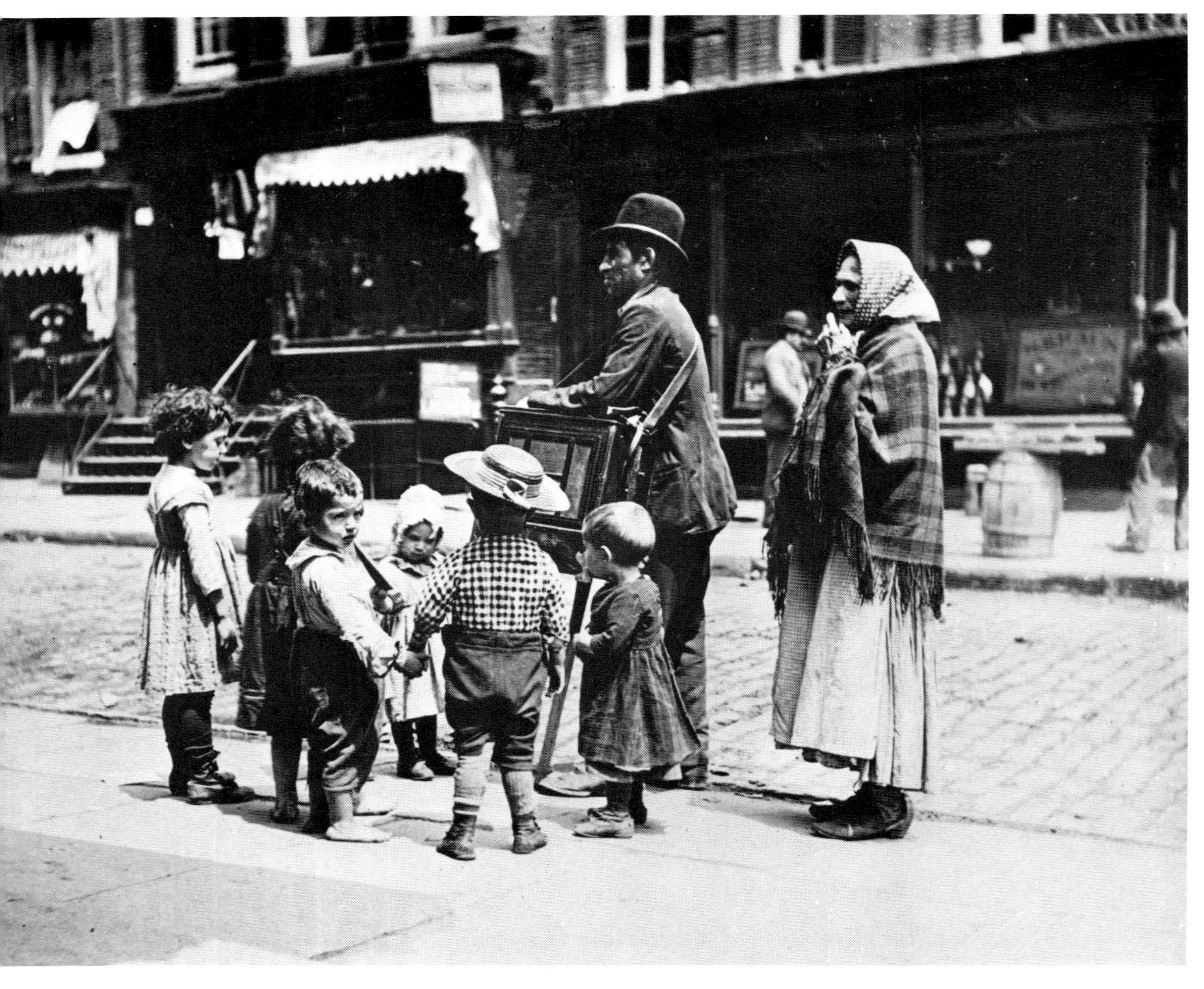

Hurdy-gurdy. The hand organ, or hurdy-gurdy, always provided one of the day's highlights for street kids. Sometimes they formed a circle on the sidewalk next to the street musician, as shown here. More often, they jumped or danced informally to the strains of the strings that played European folk songs. In the 90s the hurdy-gurdy was the domain of the Italian immigrant who arrived in the city with no other means of making a living. To collect the coins for his music and entrance the gangs of kids, the street musician often kept a monkey on a long leash. The monkey wore an embroidered coat and tipped a tiny bellcap's hat in thanks for the pennies offered by the delighted audience. *(Museum of the City of New York)*

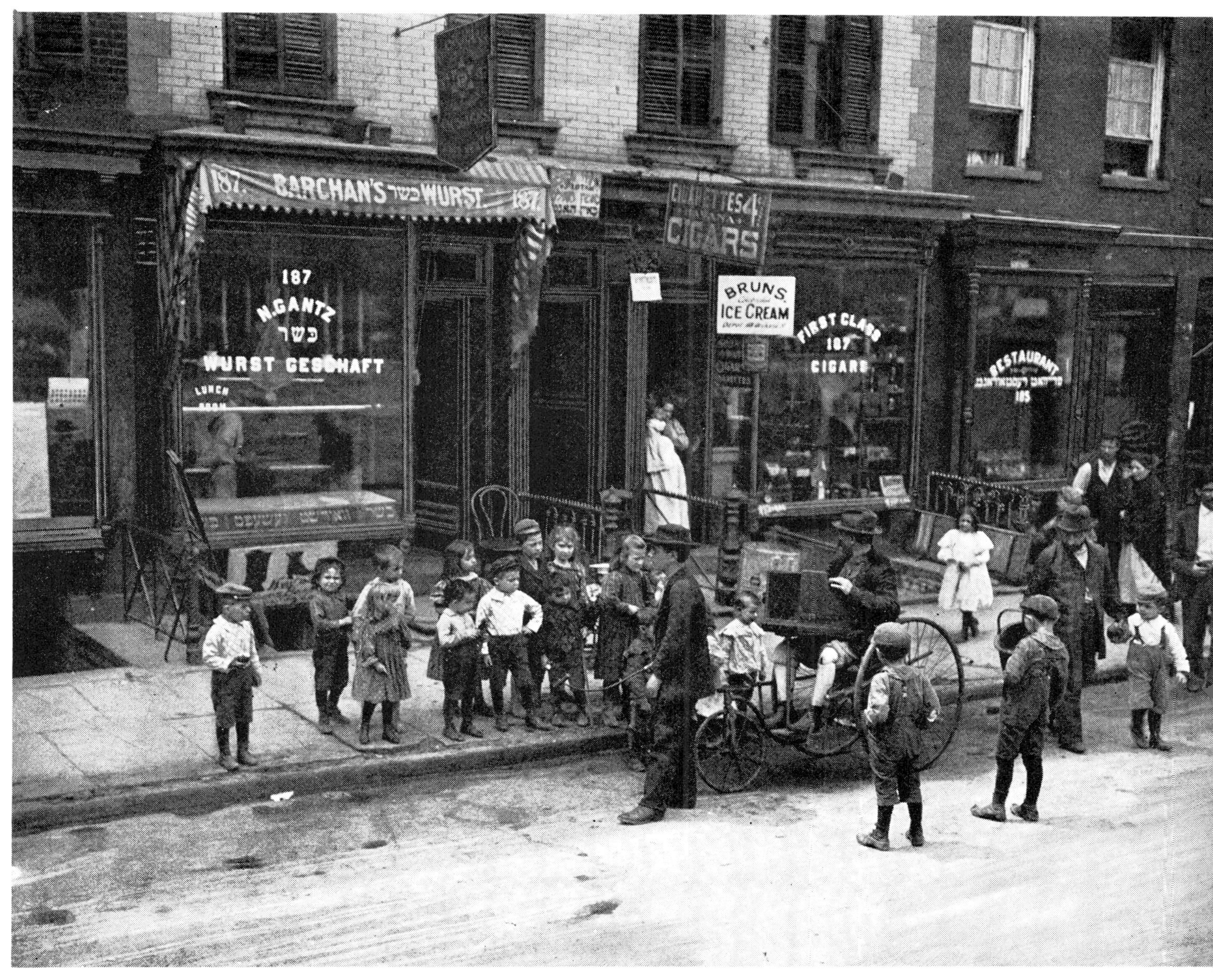

Music Attracts the Children of the Tenements. Sometimes, when the street musician was handicapped, the hand organ was mounted on a veritable chariot hauled by an assistant, as shown here. Immigrant Italian kids were often dragooned as assistants to street musicians through the insidious padrone system. Padrones were organizers in the Italian slums who contracted to bring workers from the Old World to America. When the workers arrived, the padrones were paid a commission by the bosses. Padrones also found lodgings for the workers—at exorbitant rates—and generally extracted portions of every wage their fellow immigrants earned. Naturally, defenseless children also fell under the heavy hand of the padrones; generations of kids were virtually sold into a form of slavery. The Children's Aid Society led the fight against the padrone system so effectively that it forced an end to the system through legislation passed both here and in Italy.

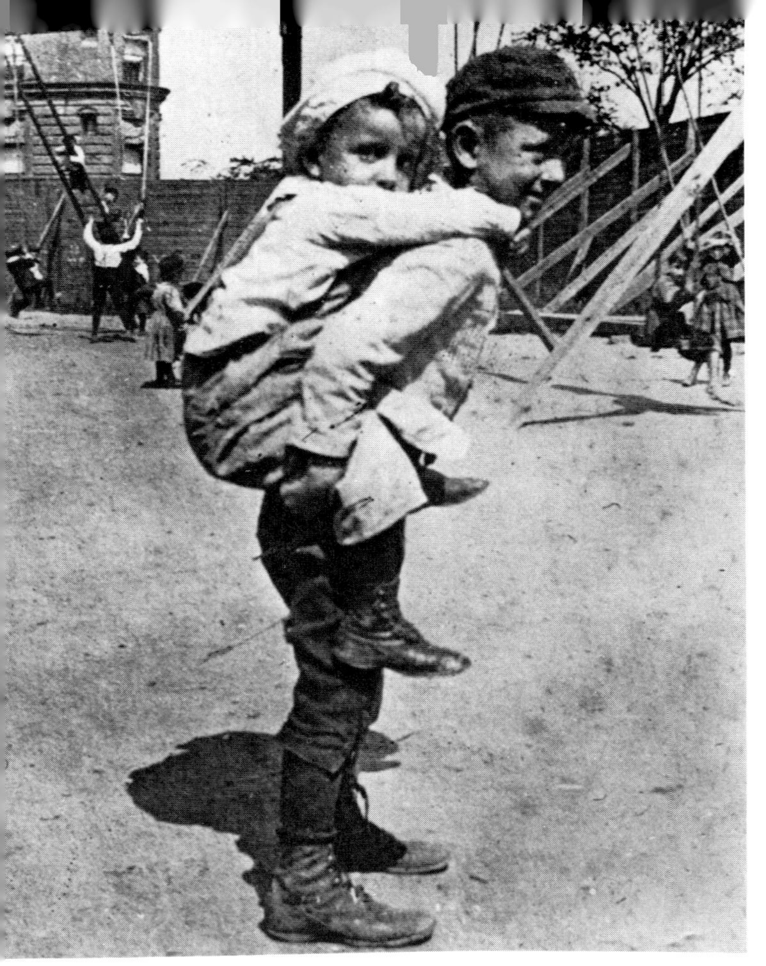

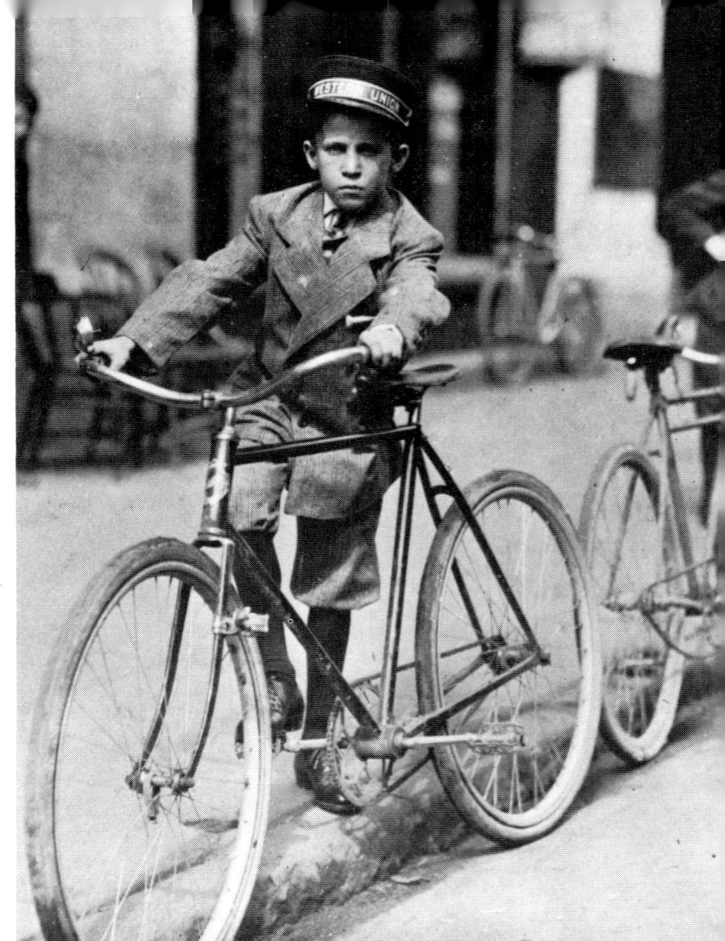

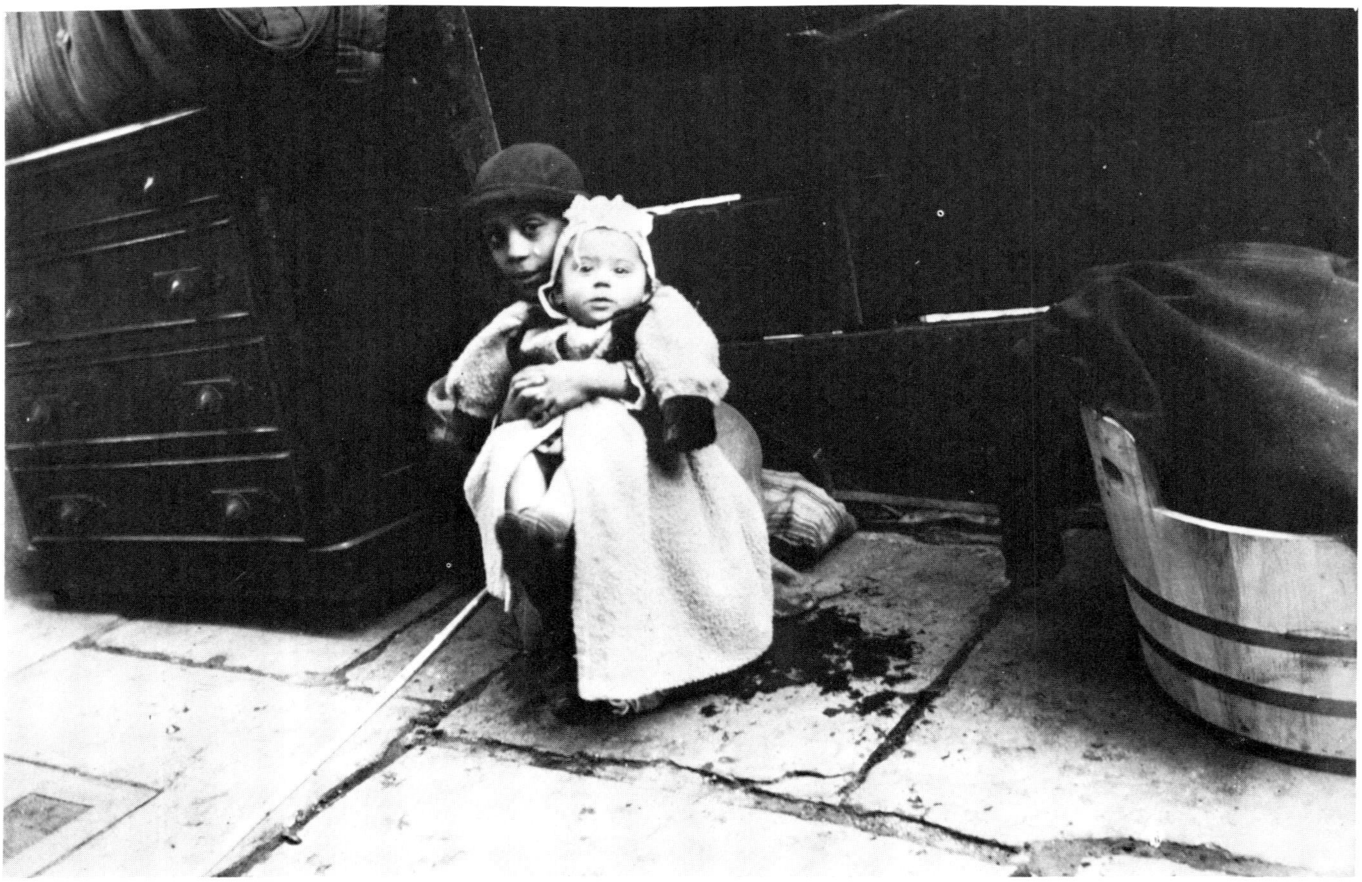

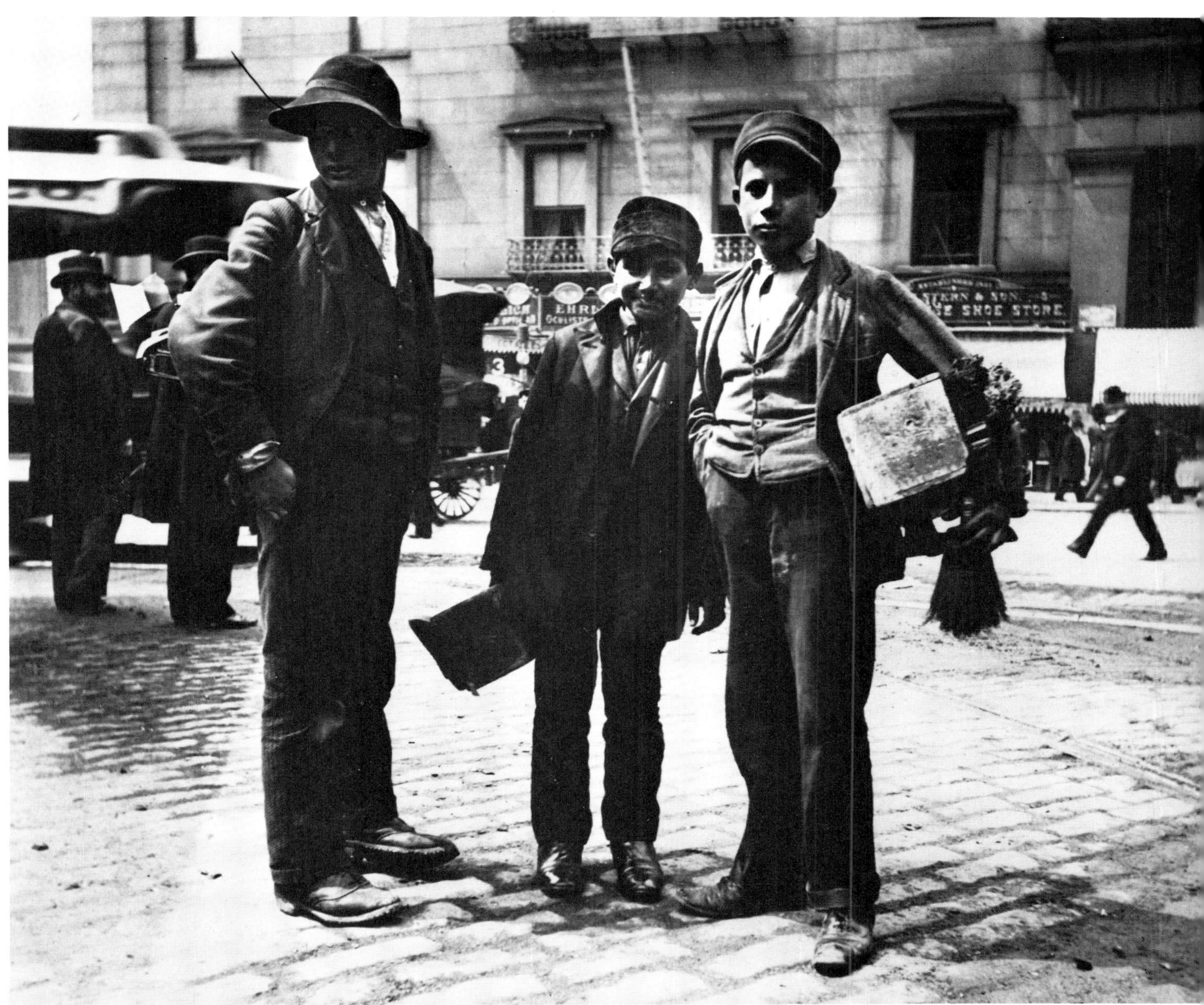

Riding Brother on His Back [opposite, top left]. The dutiful older brother seen here is enjoying his baby-sitting. But to many older children the job was a grim full-time occupation. While the parents were at jobs, the older children became surrogate parents for their younger brothers and sisters, sacrificing their childhood for the sake of their family. *(The Jacob A. Riis Collection, Museum of the City of New York)* **Night Messenger Service** [opposite, top right]. Western Union messengers were sometimes barely able to reach the pedals of their bicycles. Some even lacked the spanking uniform with its shiny buttons. But there was always pride in the work of delivering messages at any hour of the day or night, a pride reflected in the well-pressed and starched appearance of the boy shown here. *(The Jacob A. Riis Collection, Museum of the City of New York)* **Minding the Baby** [opposite, bottom]. A young babysitter—hardly more than a child himself—holds the newest-born on his lap while around him are the family possessions, apparently assembled for a move. To relieve kids from this job and to provide a healthier atmosphere for the babies, the CAS inaugurated nurseries, the 19th-century forerunner of the day-care center. *(The Jacob A. Riis Collection, Museum of the City of New York)* **Bootblacks** [above]. Shining shoes usually falls to those kids from the lowest economic stratum and in the 90s these were the Italians who had just begun large migrations to the New World. *(Alice Austen. Staten Island Historical Society)*

Western Union Delivery Boys [over]. Young faces on a sea of uniforms and brass buttons, these messenger boys from the American District Telegraph Company pose for a group portrait on the steps of the Sub-Treasury Building on Nassau Street. The messenger service, which was part of Western Union, was a welcome source of employment to city kids. Although the pay was meager, the jobs vaulted the recipients into affluence and prestige over their brothers and sisters left behind on the city streets.

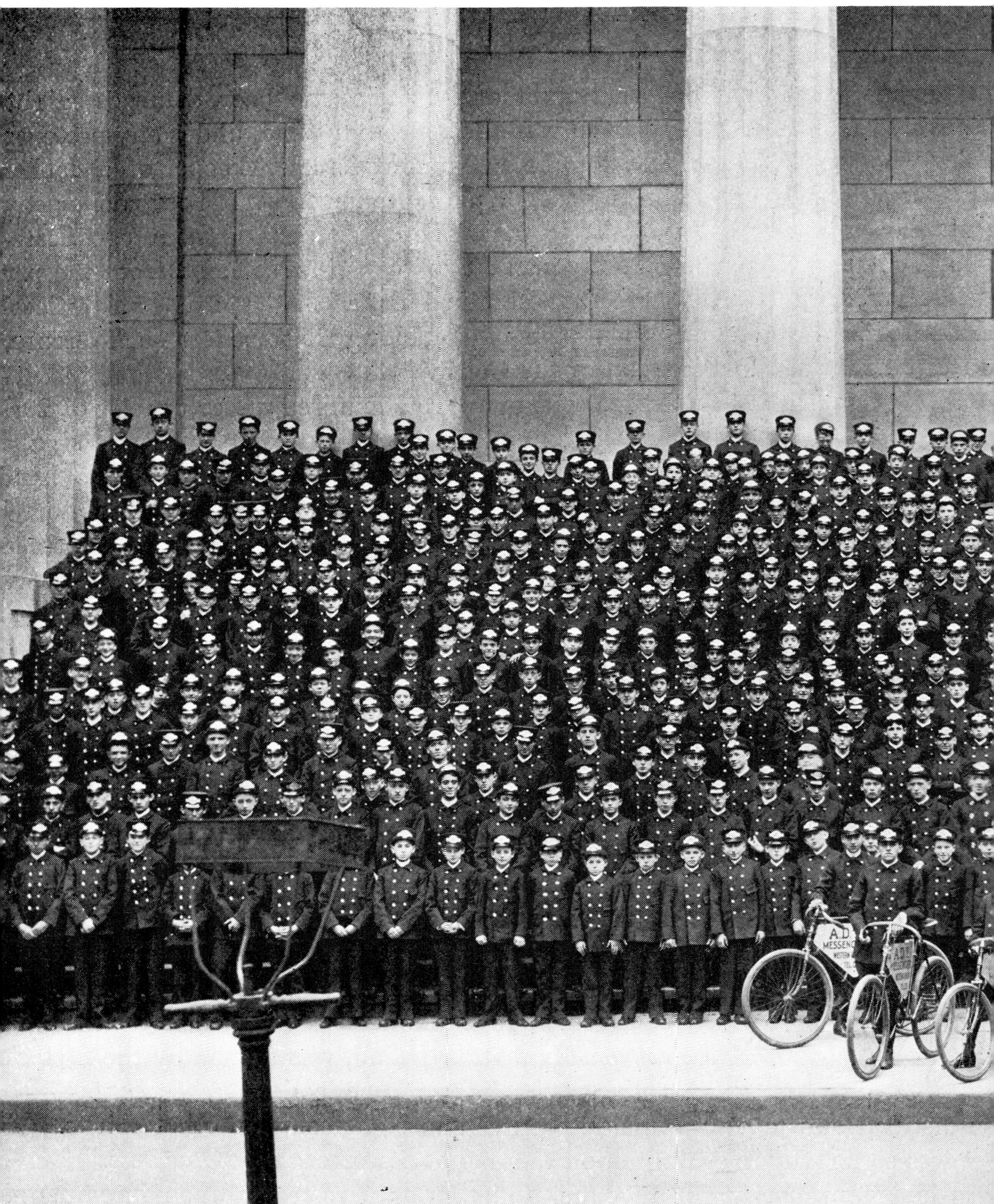
A.D.

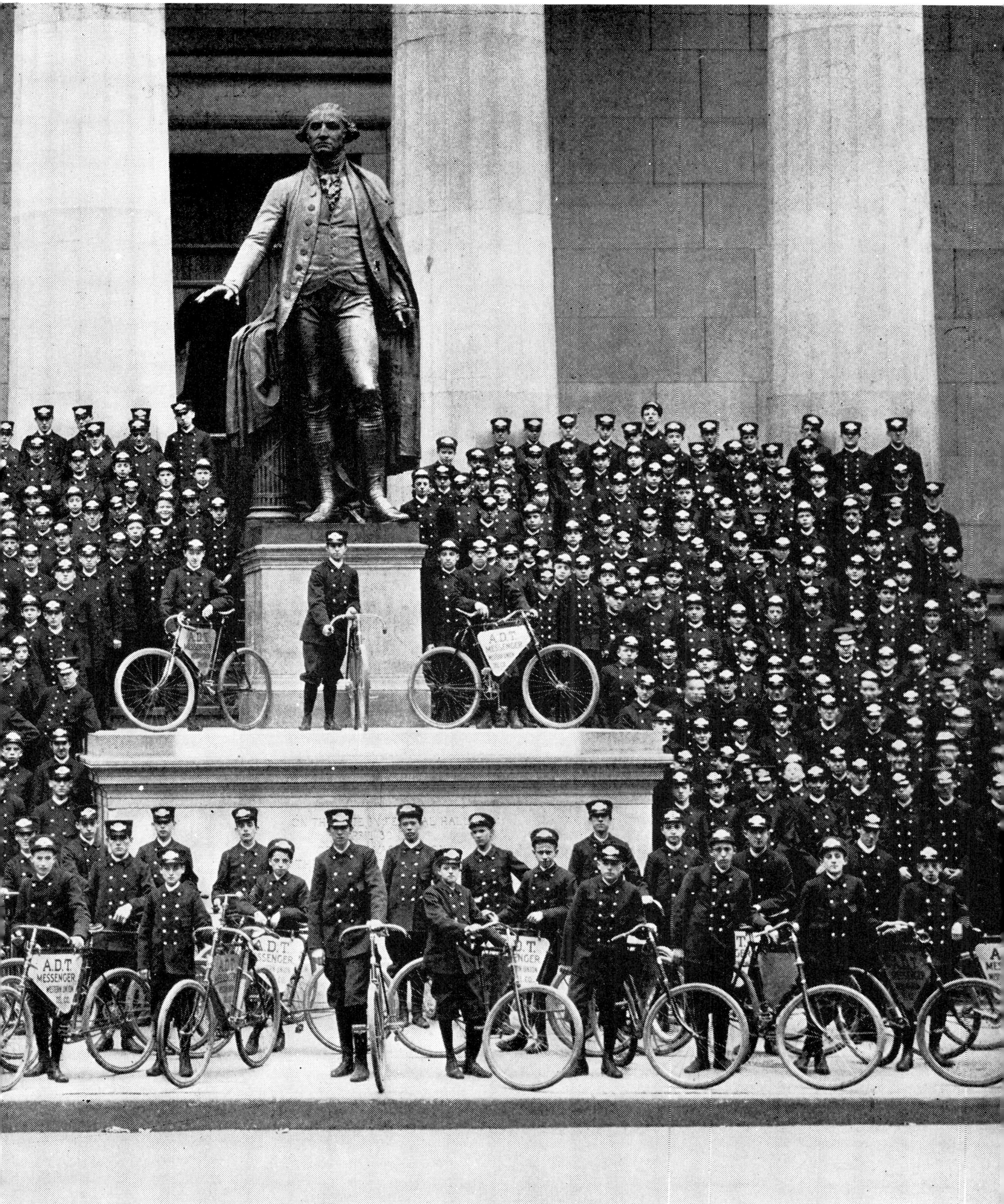
A.D.T.
MESSENGER
WESTERN UNION
TEL. CO.

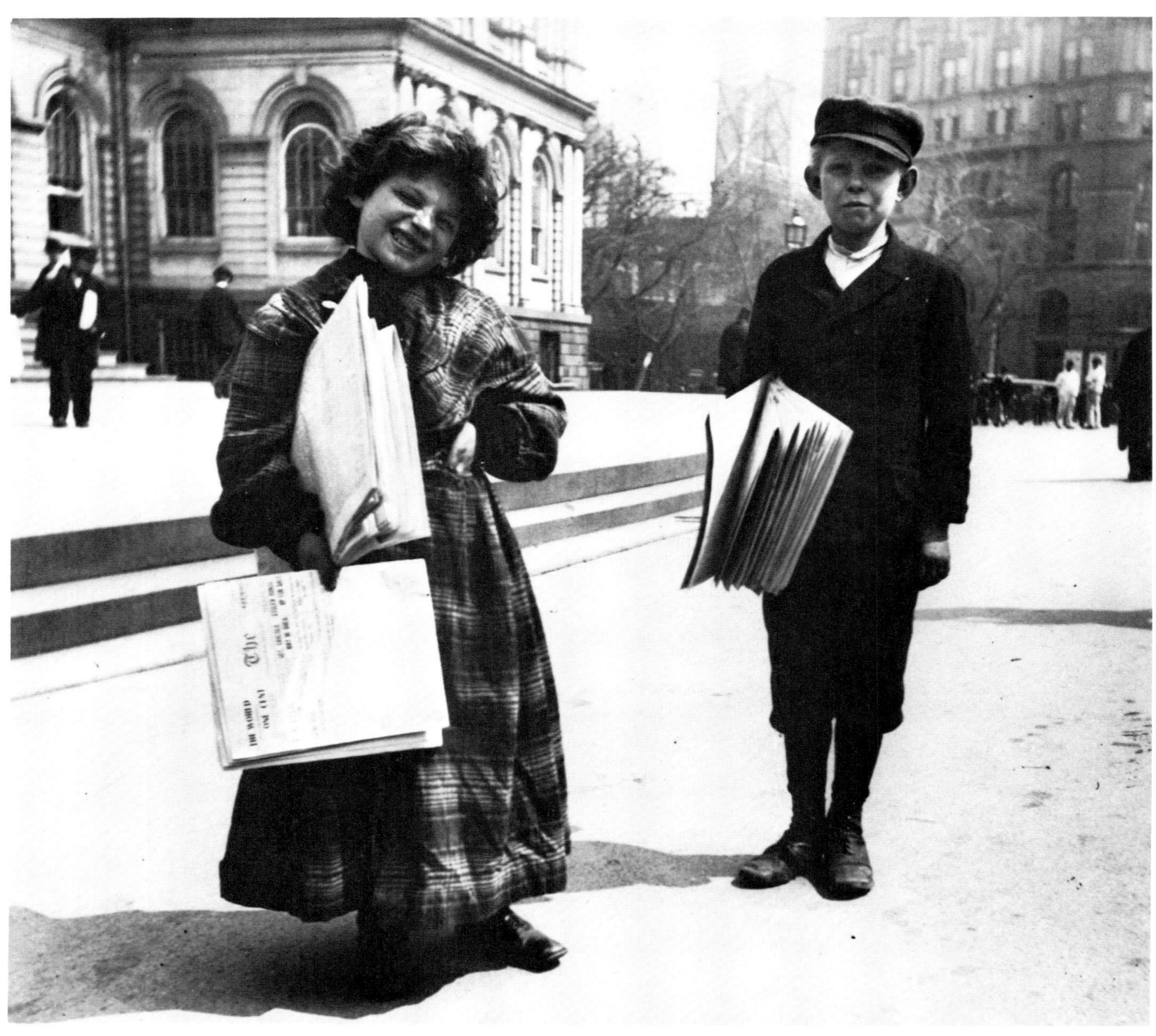

Newsboy and Newsgirl [above]. The sellers of newspapers were as common on the city streets as the horse and carriage in New York of the 90s. Although the term was "newsboy," girls also hawked papers from curbs and corners. The invention of the rotary press in 1847 sped up the process of printing, which led to the launching of the mass-circulation "penny presses." With newspapers now within the reach of the working class, children were recruited to sell them on the streets, hurrying dissemination of the news. As usual, terms for child labor were harsh—"newsies" had to assume the losses for all the papers they didn't sell. This led to unbridled competition, but the newsies' tough private code helped insure their survival as a species. Each staked out a territory that was forbidden to others. Newsies also gained a hard-earned reputation for paying their debts, playing fair and helping each other out in emergencies. Of all the city's street Arabs, the newsboys were considered among the brightest, strongest and most honorable—as well as the best businessman. *(Alice Austen. Staten Island Historical Society)* **Boy with Sticks** [opposite, top]. Lugging, toting, hauling, carrying, the city kid seemed on perpetual missions. This boy carries a bundle of lathing that is longer than he is tall—probably firewood for the family kitchen stove. Once again the remarkable resiliency of the slum child emerges as the boy halts in his work to strike a jaunty pose. *(Lewis Hine. International Museum of Photography, Rochester, New York)* **Children with Bread and Pan** [opposite, bottom]. In their own way, the sturdy little legs of the children carried the tenement family. The errands were numerous and each one meant negotiating the long steep flights of stairs. There was also the trek through the neighborhood to find the best buys and the quick return with the bargain for the mother in the kitchen. *(Lewis Hine. International Museum of Photography, Rochester, New York)*

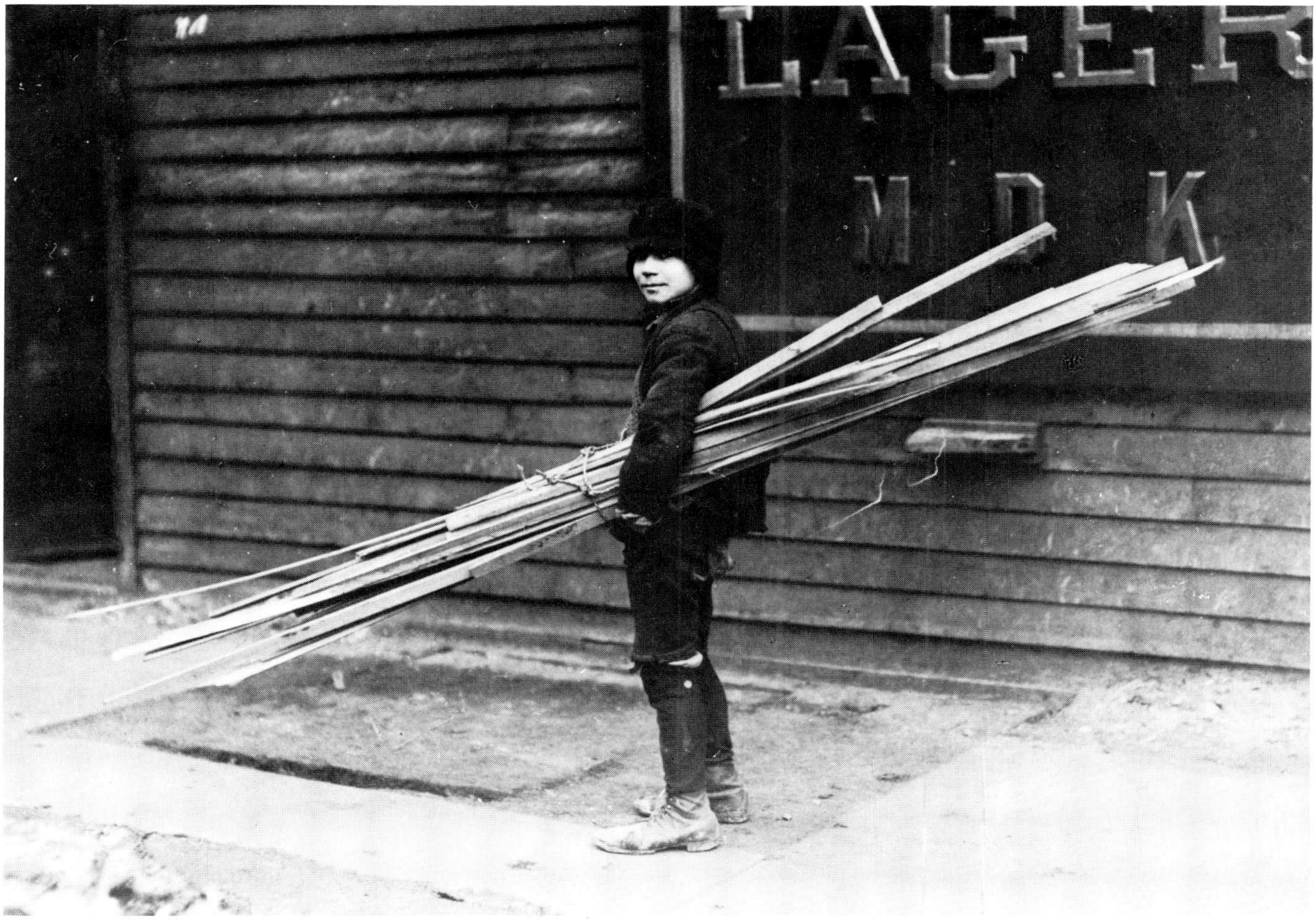

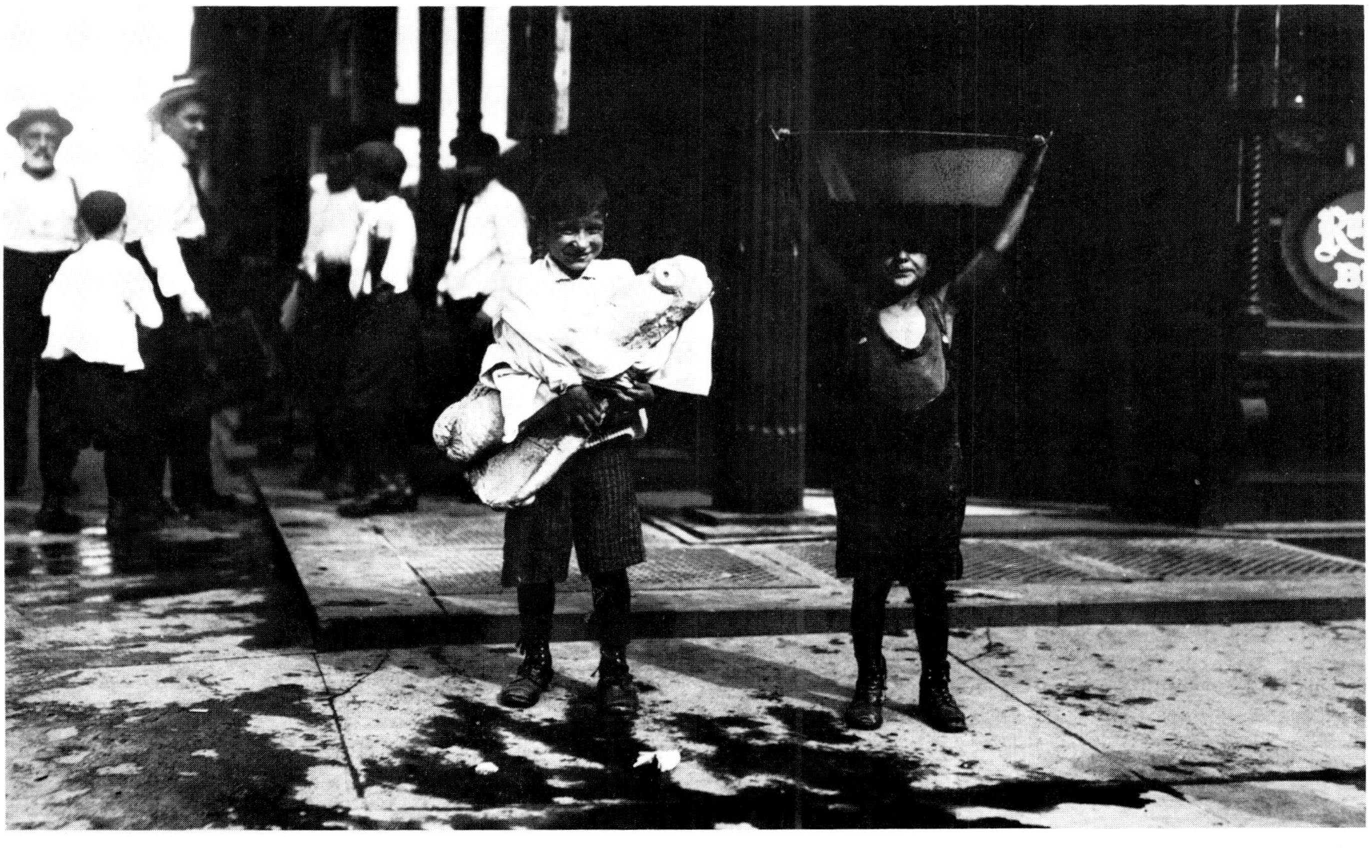

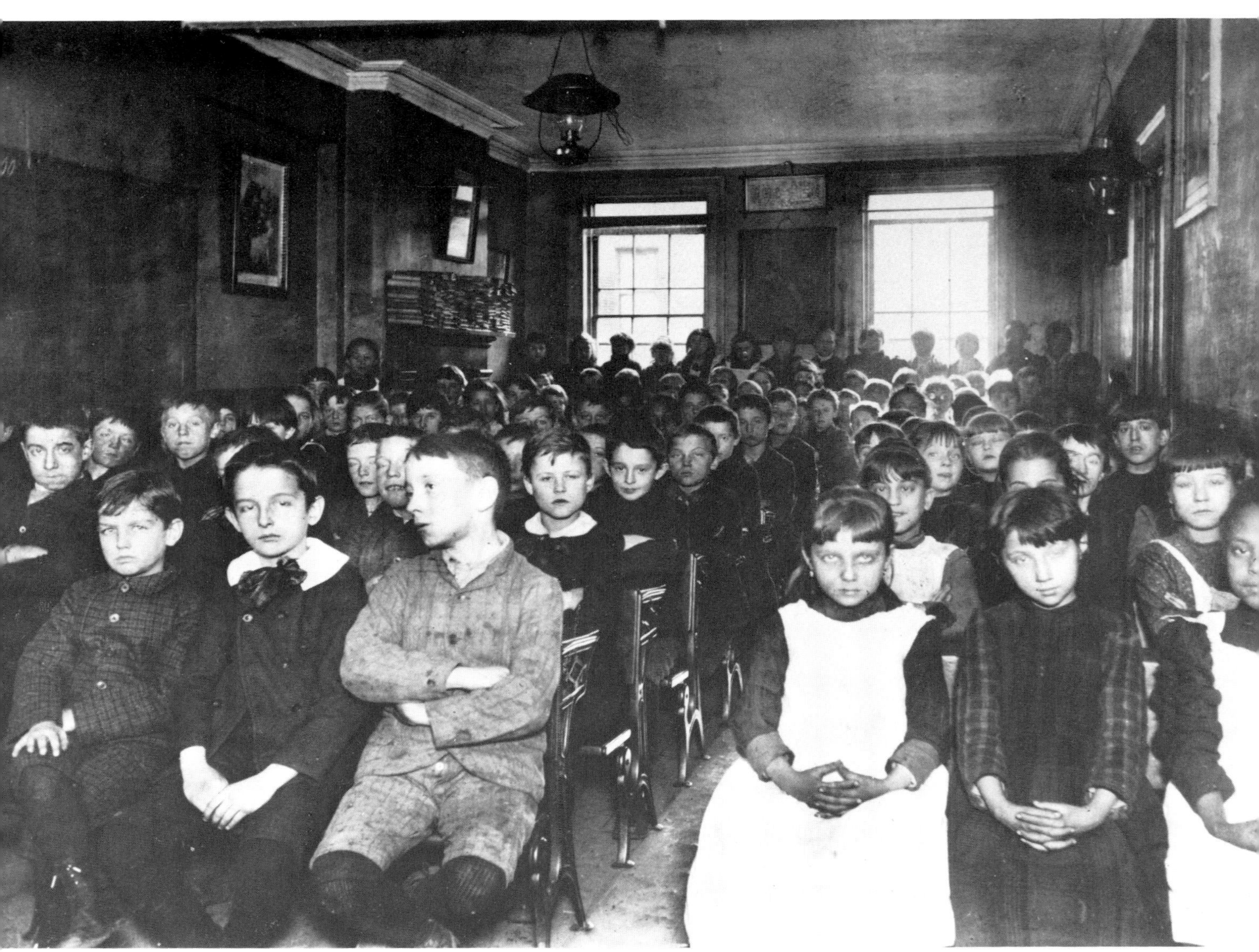

CAS Industrial School, West 52nd Street [above]. If ever there was an institution perfectly matched to a social need it was the Children's Aid Society to the slum children. In 1853, under the leadership of founder Charles Loring Brace, a minister who found his calling among the street kids, the CAS began organizing schools and social centers in some of the city's most oppressive slums. The first school was a trade school for girls—a buffer against the lures of the streets and the gin mills. The CAS schools were subsequently open to teach trades to boys in industrial classes. By 1890 the CAS ran 21 industrial schools with more than 5000 pupils, the precursors of the vocational schools opened by the city public school system in the 1930s. The schools also initiated students into such niceties of life as the proper use of knives and forks at the table. Indeed, the CAS annual report for 1893 stated that the 50 girls in evening classes at the West 52nd Street Industrial school were proficient enough at English to read "intelligent stories." *(The Jacob A. Riis Collection, Museum of the City of New York)* **Circle Game, Nursery of the Italian School** [opposite, top]. Quaint photographs like this one should not impart a false note of romanticism to the work of the CAS. At the insistence of Charles Loring Brace, each CAS program was predicated on tough-minded practical application. Thanks to the visionary genius of Brace, the CAS pioneered so many programs for street kids that its achievements read like a history of the modern urban social movement. The CAS was first to place children in foster homes—in the city and in farms out West. It also established the first trade schools, free lunch programs, nurseries and kindergartens, visiting nurse and school nurse programs, schools for crippled children, free medical and dental clinics, homemaker services and the first schools for Blacks after the Civil War. Politically, the CAS stood up for kids by drafting and backing laws for compulsory education and against child labor. *(c.a.s.).* **Prayer Time at Five Points Nursery** [opposite, bottom]. These tots in fresh nightshirts had every reason to give thanks in prayer at a CAS nursery in one of the city's toughest areas, Five Points in Lower Manhattan. In 1841 Charles Dickens visited the area and registered his shock: "Debauchery has made the very houses prematurely old . . . all that is loathsome, drooping and decayed is here." The area had improved somewhat by the 90s but not enough to staunch the flow of ink from the pens of reformers and social activists. The CAS nursery was an attempt to help working mothers and to give the children a fresh start. *(The Jacob A. Riis Collection, Museum of the City of New York)*

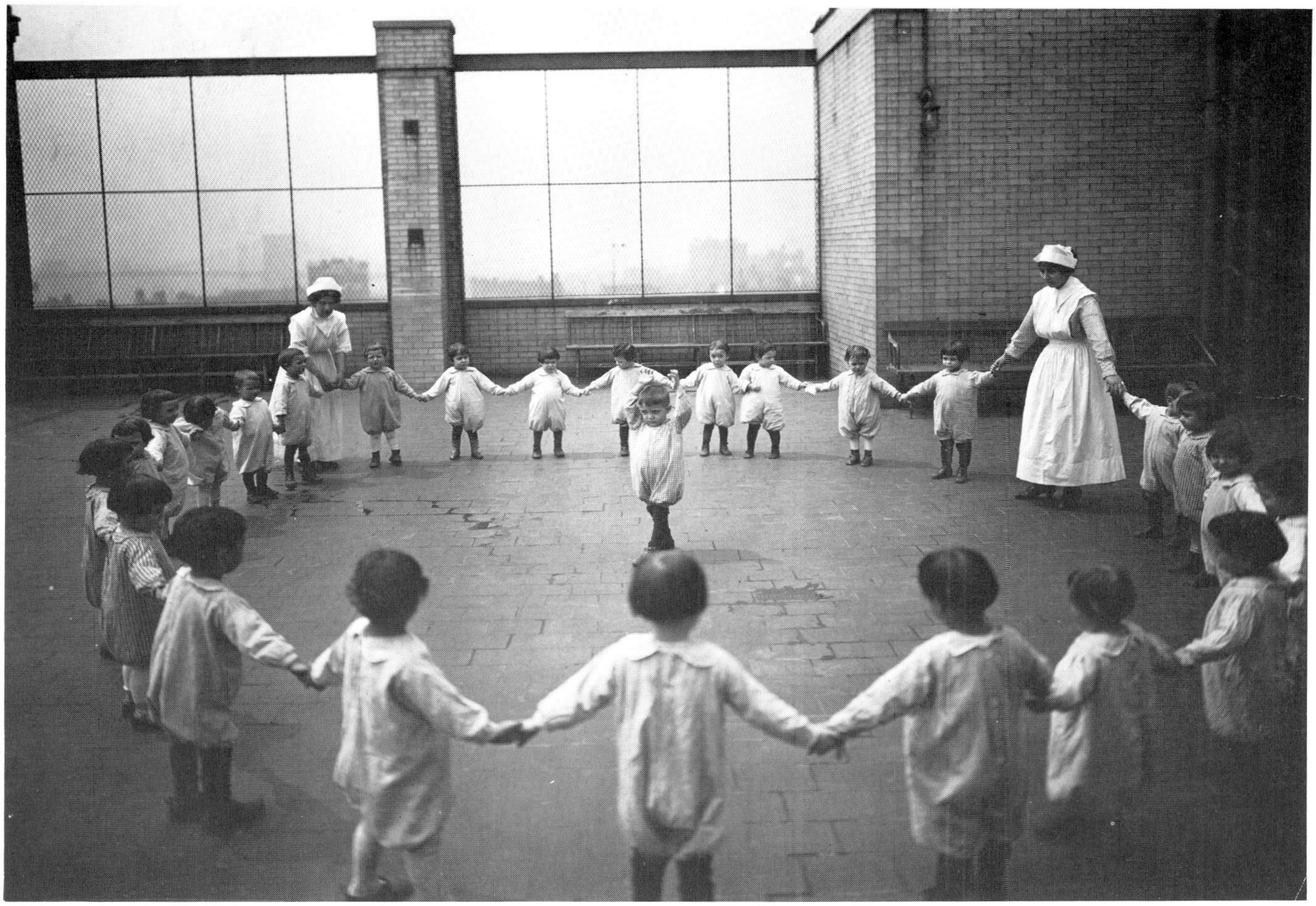

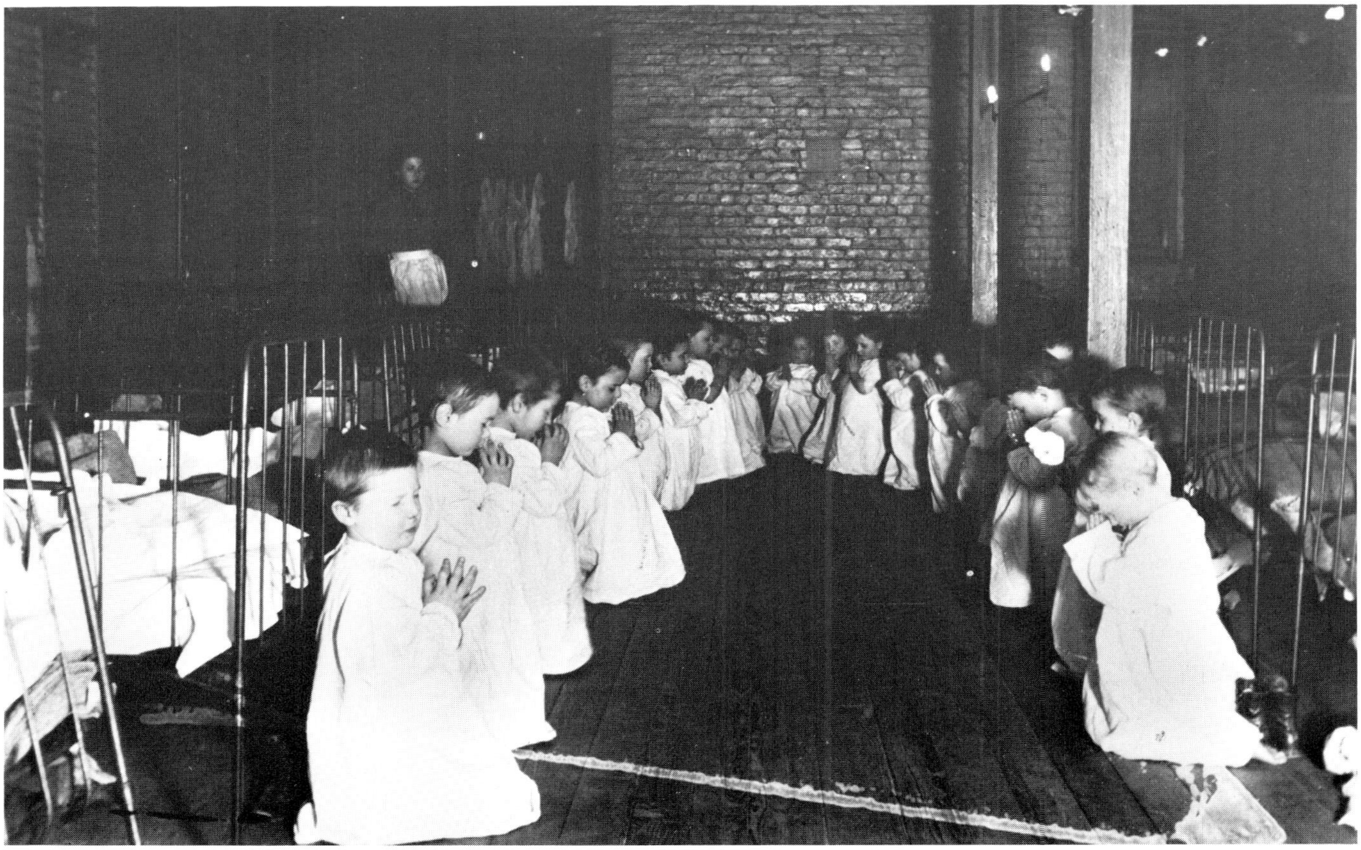

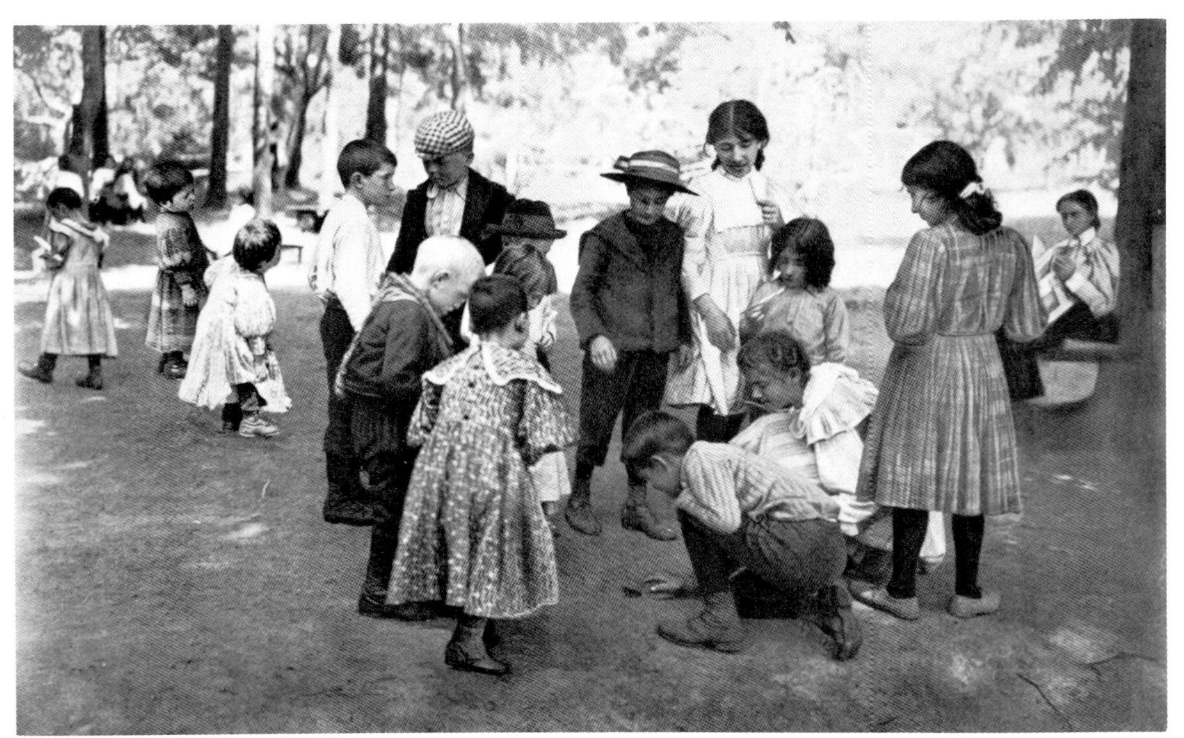

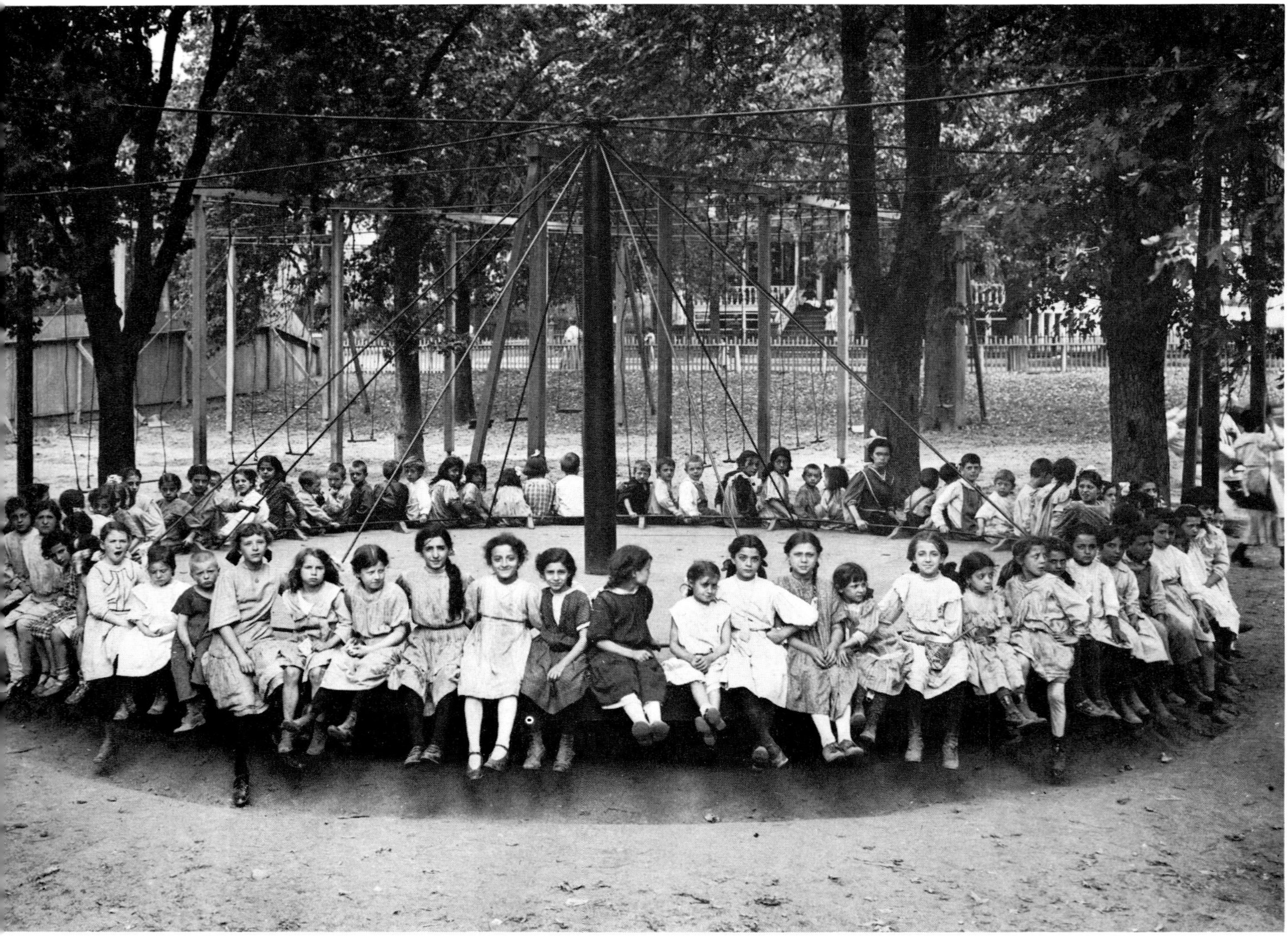

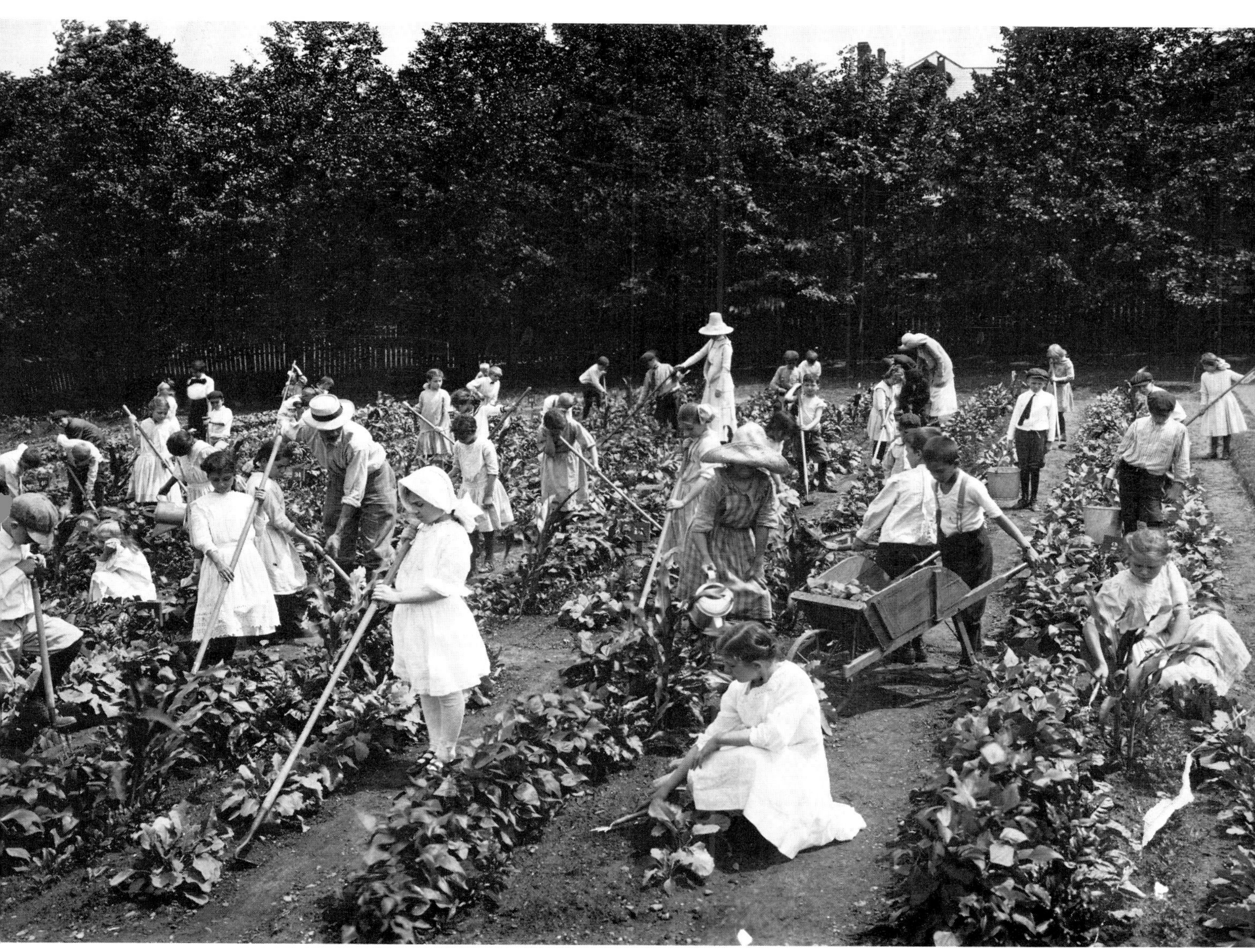

A CAS Country Outing [opposite, top]. Curious kids gather around a phenomenon of nature most have never before witnessed—a toad. The occasion was one of the regular summer outings in the country planned by the CAS to give kids a respite from the city heat. On these outings many slum kids saw cows, chickens, pigs and even growing vegetable gardens for the first time. **Children on a Merry-Go-Round** [opposite, bottom]. A playground at a CAS fresh-air center was built to accommodate crowds—and it got them. The CAS brought gangs of kids from the slum streets to give them a week by the water at its Bath Beach home in Brooklyn. The spacious home and grounds came into the possession of the CAS in 1875 and served as the first institutional fresh-air home for city kids on record. *(c.a.s.).* **Tending the Garden** [above]. In a scene so idyllic it might be posed, children from the city tend a vegetable garden at a CAS retreat on Staten Island after the turn of the century. The advent of the 20th century brought significantly changed attitudes toward street kids. Social scientists realized the wisdom of prophets like Brace and Riis, who had stated decades earlier that the way to defeat poverty and ignorance was to start with the children. Following the precepts of its founder, Brace, the CAS grew vigorously during this period, expanding the services and experiences offered street kids. The object was to give education and work to the children, not alms. And even city boys in hot knickers and ties learned the rewards—and toil—of working the land. *(c.a.s.).*

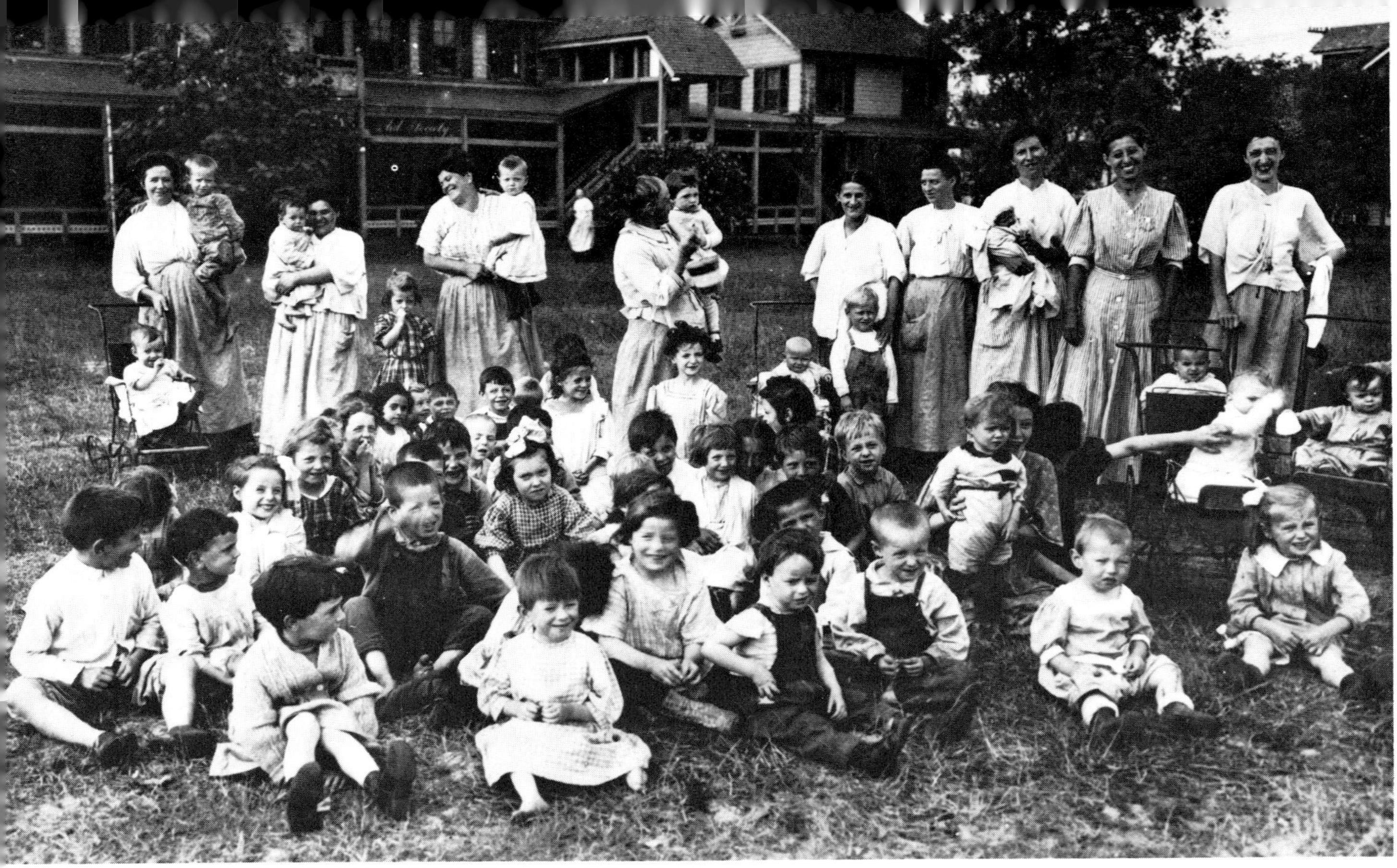

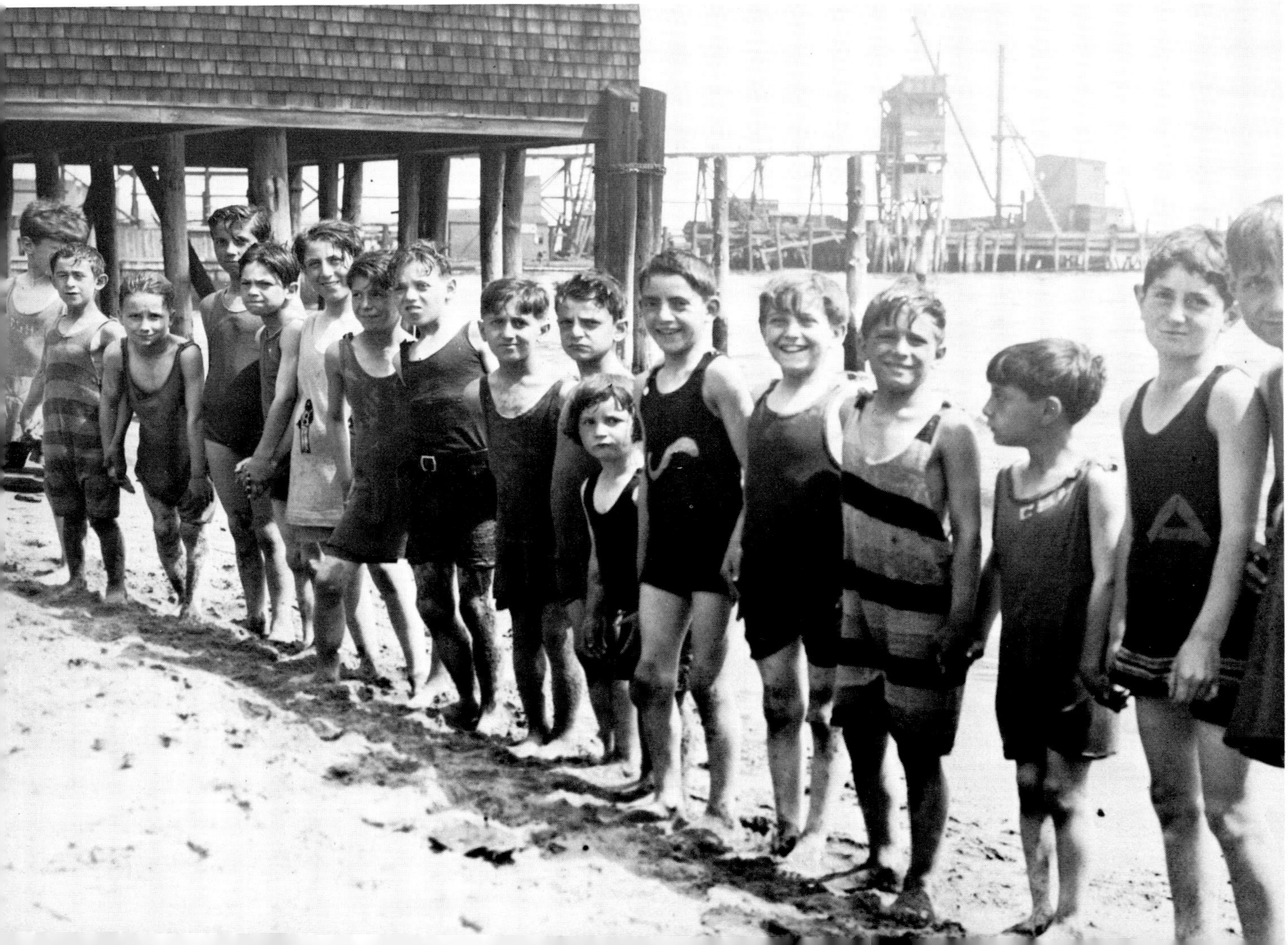

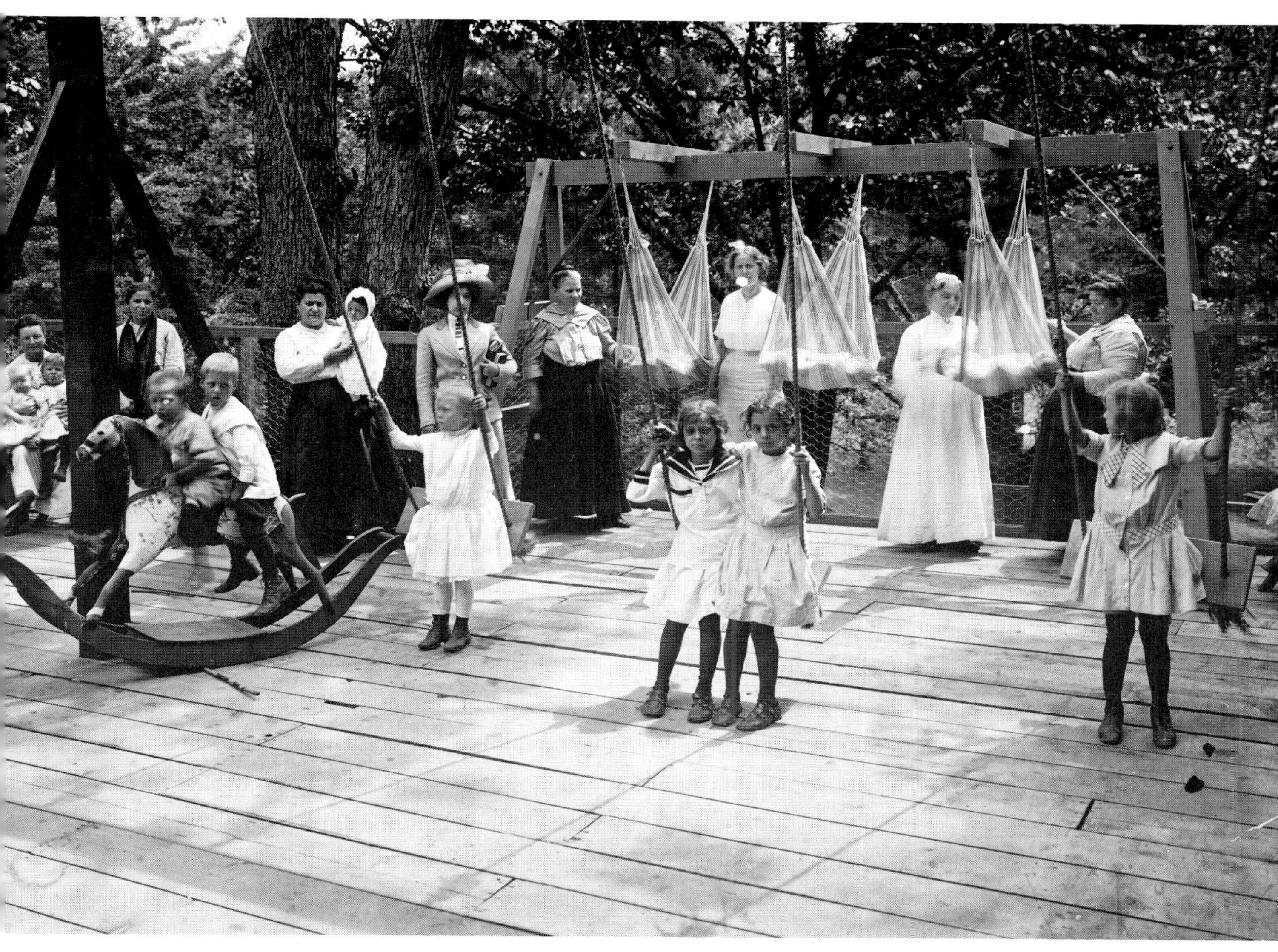

A Day Outing at the Health Home [opposite, top]. In the relative wilderness of a CAS health home at Coney Island, mothers and their charges escaped the deadly furnaces that tenements became in summer. The sun, beating down on the tightly packed buildings, along with the wood-burning kitchen stove, made the heat unbearable. Those kids lucky enough to dodge the germs that bred in the still, foul air risked suffocation or heatstroke. Babies were particularly vulnerable and infant mortality rates soared in summer. In desperation, families would drag mattresses out on fire escapes or up to rooftops to find relief in the night air. And after such hellish conditions a week in the country was a visit to paradise. *(c.a.s.).*
The Lineup [opposite, bottom]. The happy line of bathers on the beach at the CAS home on Coney Island in 1914 testified to the healthful effects of the outings on street kids. After viewing such dramatic results, the CAS became a leading advocate of fresh-air programs. At this time New York charities, including the CAS, sponsored 138 homes—30 in the mountains, 76 in the country and 32 at the seashore—with a capacity of 8095 beds. The most famous philanthropy associated with the movement is the Fresh Air Fund. Begun by the New York *Tribune* in 1882, the Fund continues to this day as an independent agency providing summer outings for city kids. *(Paul Parker. c.a.s.).*
Playground at Bath Beach [above]. The dress remains formal as befits the epoch, but children and their mothers glow with health at the CAS summer home at Bath Beach, Brooklyn, ca. 1905. Even the babes in arms have special hammocks so that they can take in the fresh air while their older siblings swing and rock at a platformed playground. *(c.a.s.).*

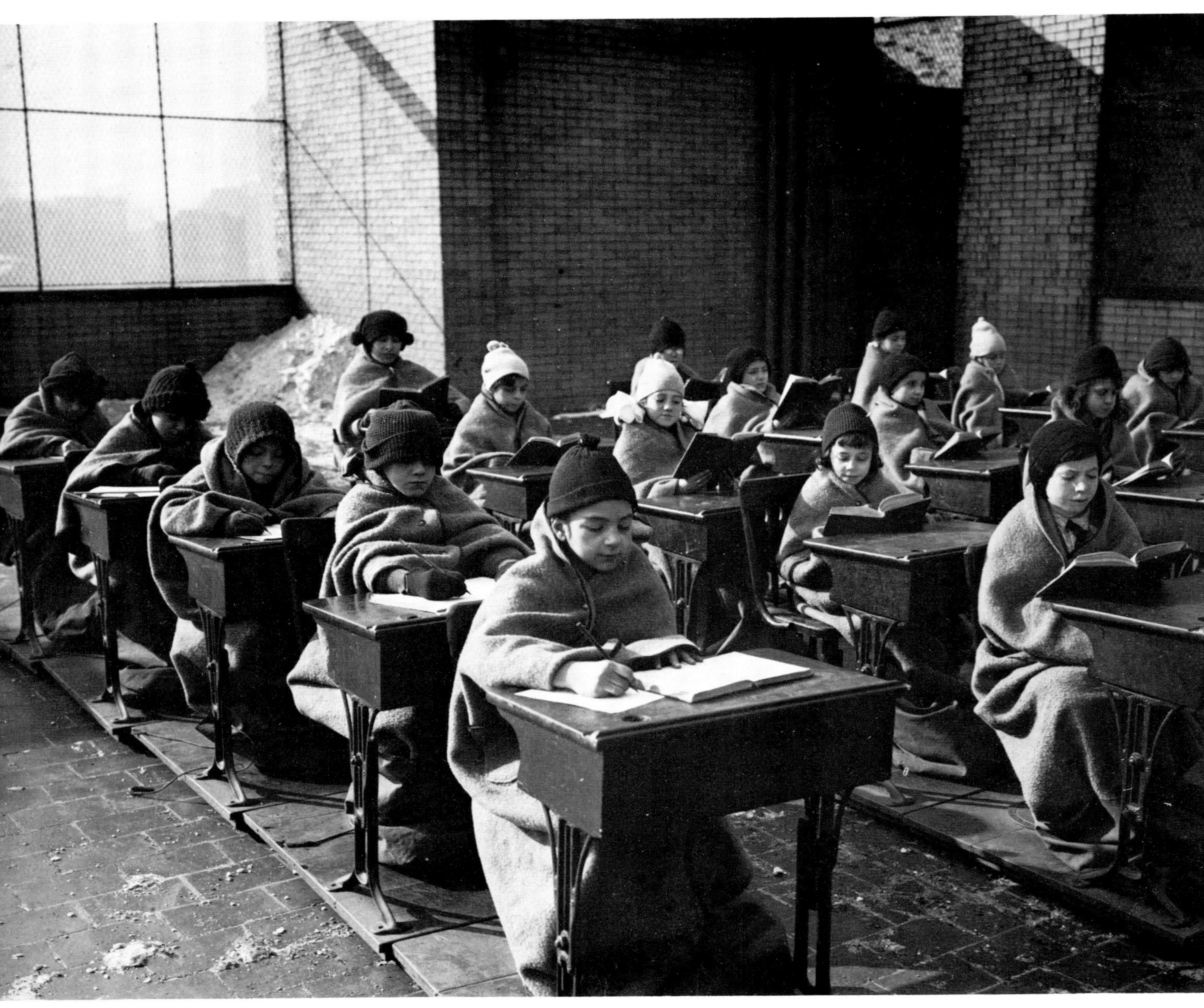

Outdoor Class for Anemic Children [above]. Seemingly oblivious of the freezing temperatures and the snow shoveled in the corners, anemic kids, bundled in blankets and wool caps, carried on their schoolwork at the James Center on Hester Street. These winter fresh-air programs complemented the summer outings to produce cures for the rundown children. *(c.a.s.).* **Nap Time, Outdoor Class** [opposite, top]. In 1915 the CAS established a special school on West 53rd Street for anemic children. "Anemia" applied loosely to kids weak and pale from improper diet and lack of fresh air; it also no doubt included children ill with tuberculosis, a disease usually affecting the lungs which no known drugs could cure. The prescription for anemia and tuberculosis was fresh air, nutritious food and plenty of rest. The school day, including nap time, was conducted outdoors. Nor did the CAS depend on parents to bring their kids to the school voluntarily. Young doctors were hired to scour the slums for anemic children, climbing flight after flight of narrow stairs to rap on old doors to inquire if there were sickly youngsters at home. *(c.a.s.).* **Roof Playground** [opposite, bottom]. Above the dangerous streets kids were free to romp in their games at the roof playground of the CAS West Side school. This refuge was the society's first venture into fresh-air work in the city itself. The roof playground, opened in 1909, led to a wave of outdoor educational and recreational activities designed to improve the health of kids who had been ground too long under the heel of poverty. *(c.a.s.).*

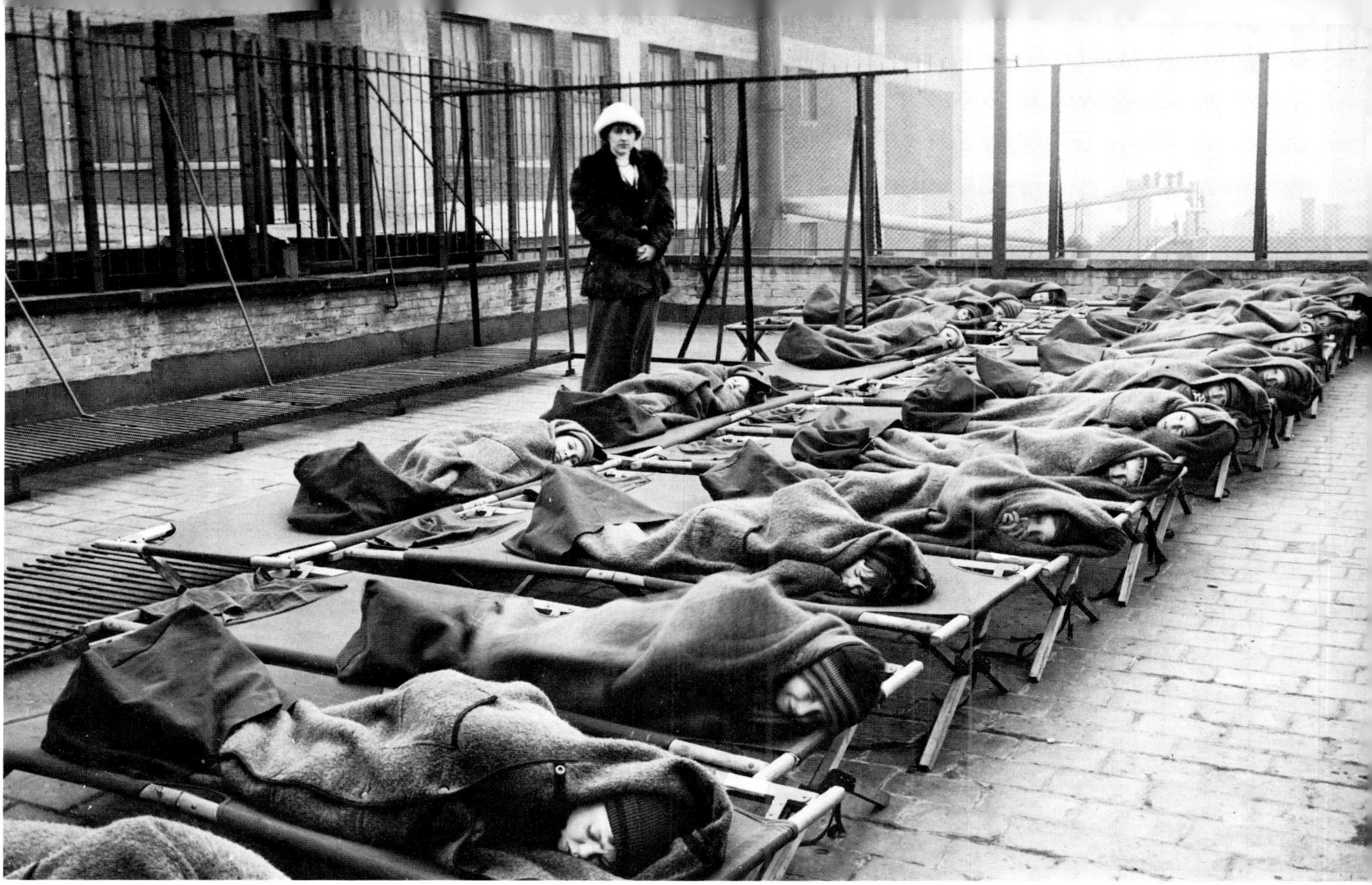

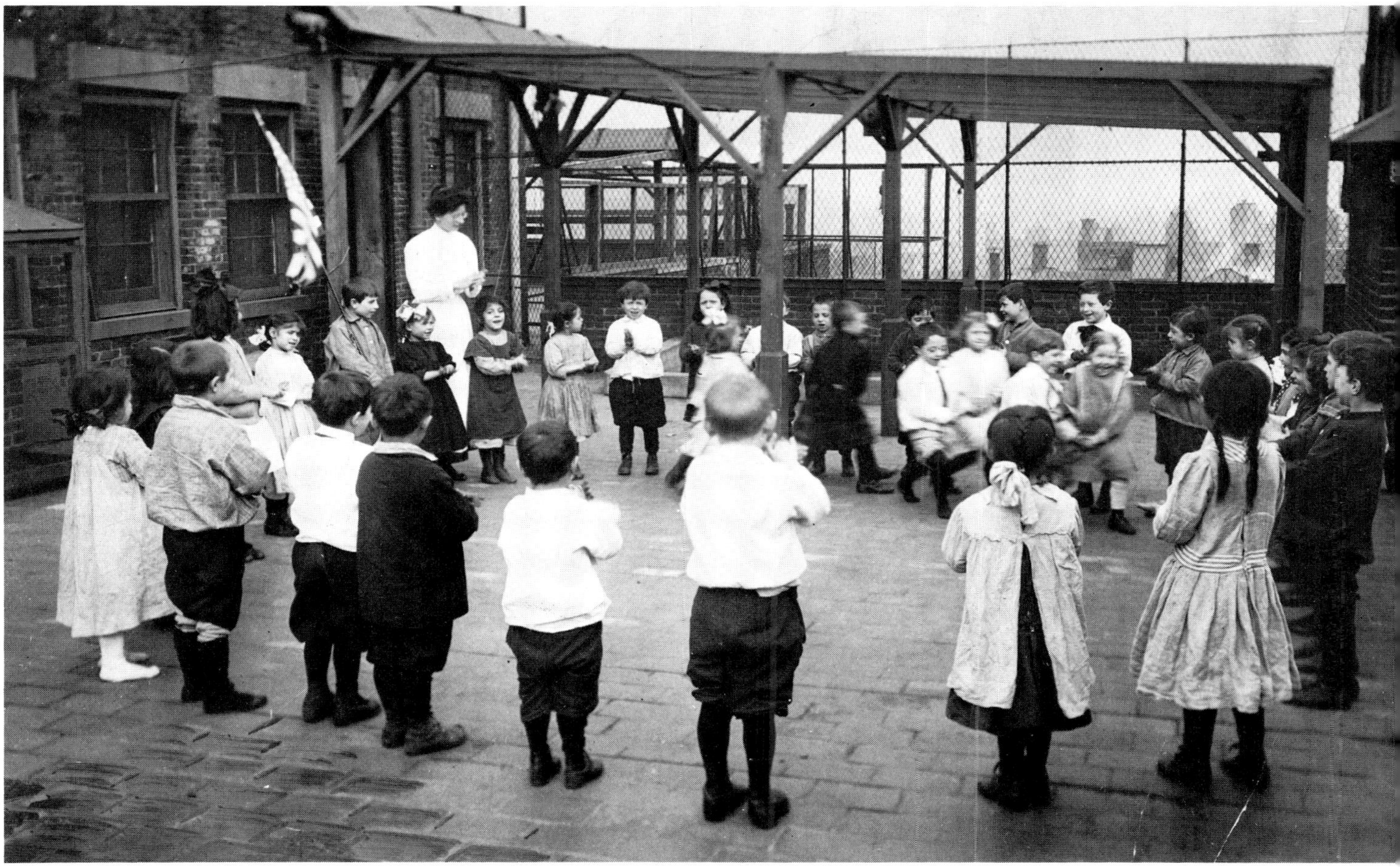

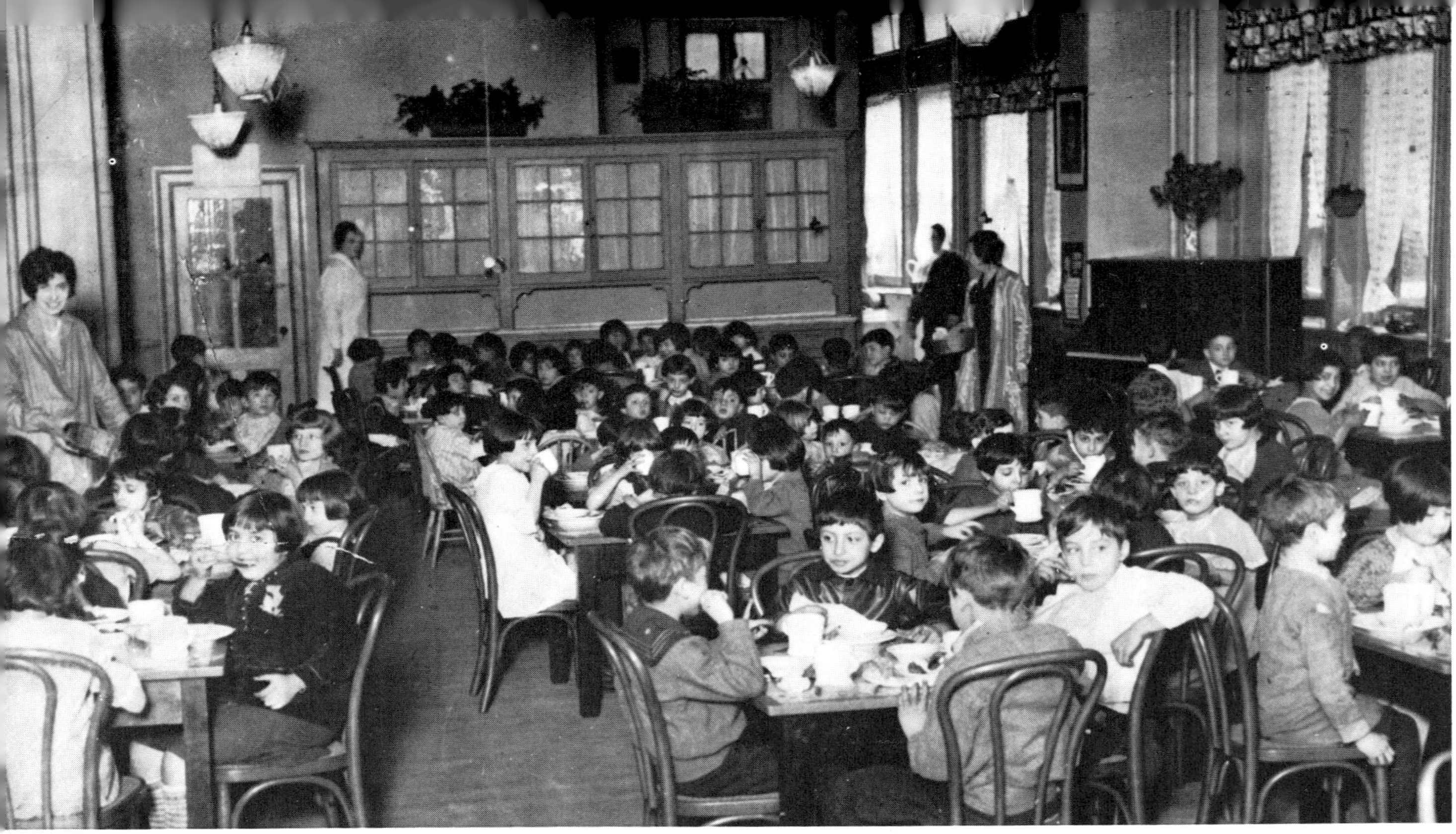

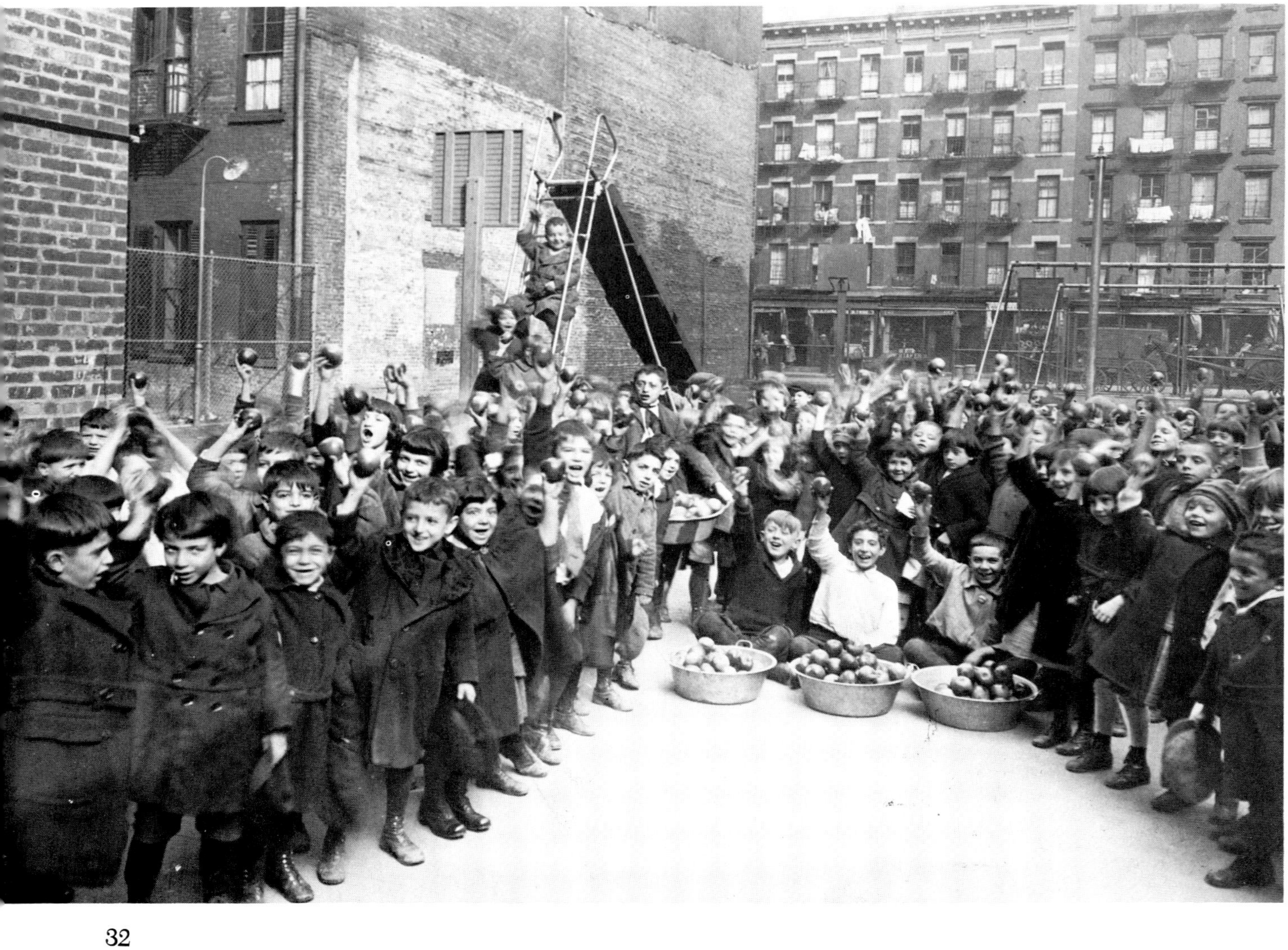

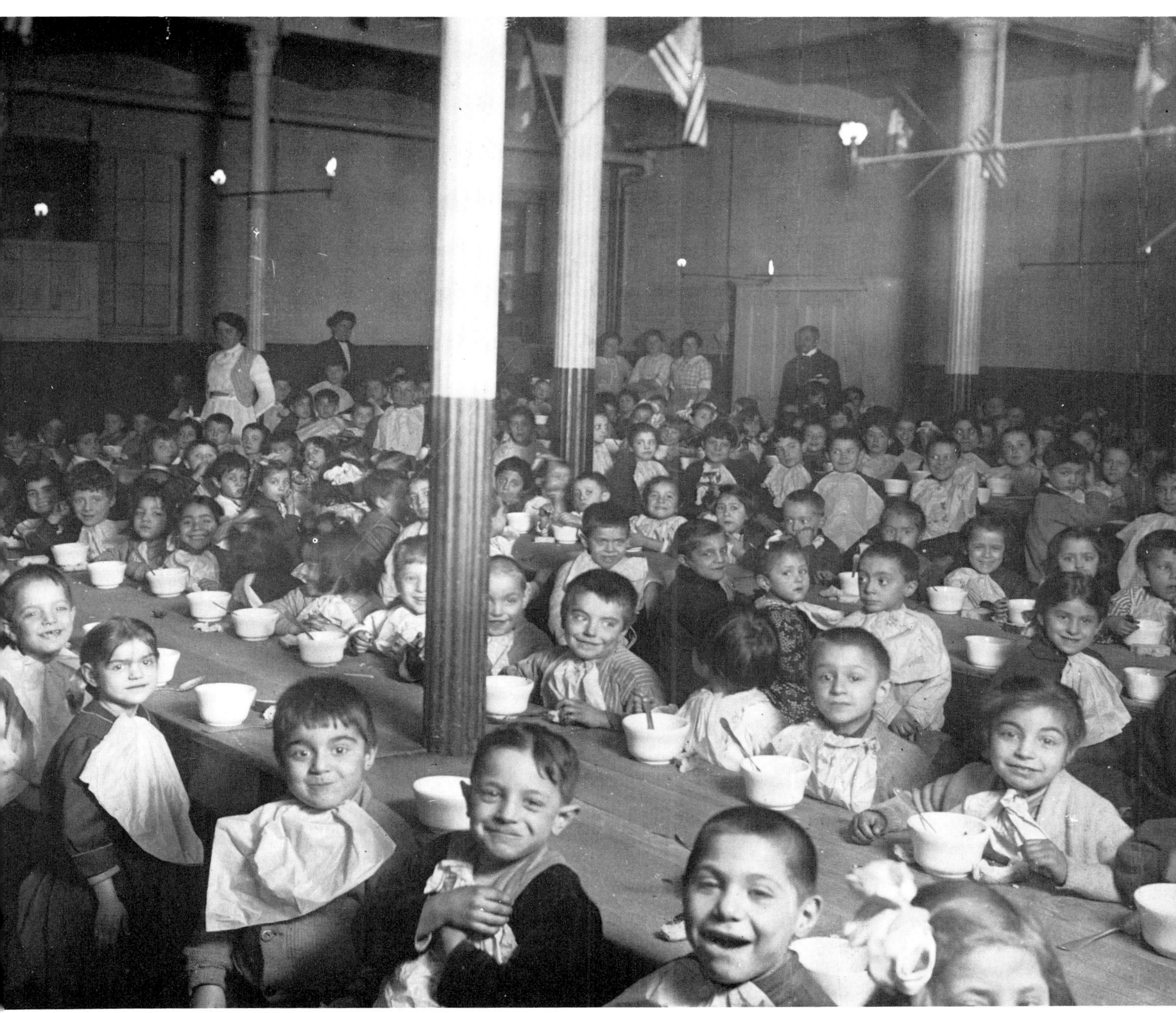

Eating Their Way Back to Health [opposite, top]. Undernourished kids are given hot meals at the CAS Sullivan Street Health Center. The CAS also composed and distributed pamphlets for the mothers on proper nutrition and child-rearing. Titled *Are You a Good Mother?*, the pamphlets were printed in English, Italian, Bohemian and Yiddish. They exhorted the mothers to feed their children plenty of fresh fruits and vegetables and to have them drink lots of milk and water (but no coffee or tea). They were also urged to bathe the children daily, to be sure they had plenty of sleep in well-ventilated rooms, to expose them to fresh air and sunshine as much as possible, to check their hair for lice and to have them brush their teeth daily. *(c.a.s.).* **Free Apples** [opposite, bottom]. An annual rite of autumn at the CAS centers was the distribution of free apples. In the days before packaging and rapid transportation made fresh fruit available practically year-round, the apples in autumn were a welcome relief in the dreary unbalanced diet. *(c.a.s.).* **Feeding Hungry Kids** [above]. A full youngster is a happy youngster, as may be seen from the faces of these children who have just polished off bowls of hot soup served at the James Center. Any neighborhood kid was eligible for the nutritious fare dished up at the CAS centers. For a nickel the child was given a hot lunch of beef stew, whole wheat bread, potatoes, onions, two glasses of milk and apple sauce. The payment was a continuation of Brace's conviction that kids should learn to pay their own way. However, a hungry child who lacked the nickel was never turned away. *(c.a.s.).*

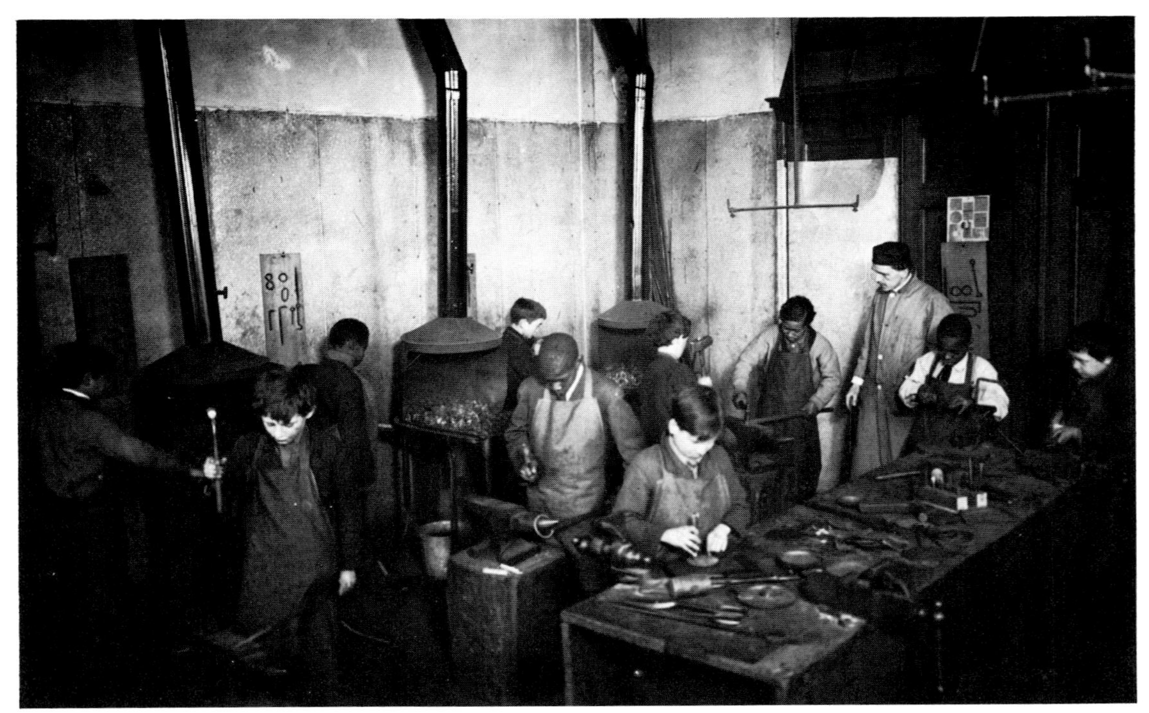

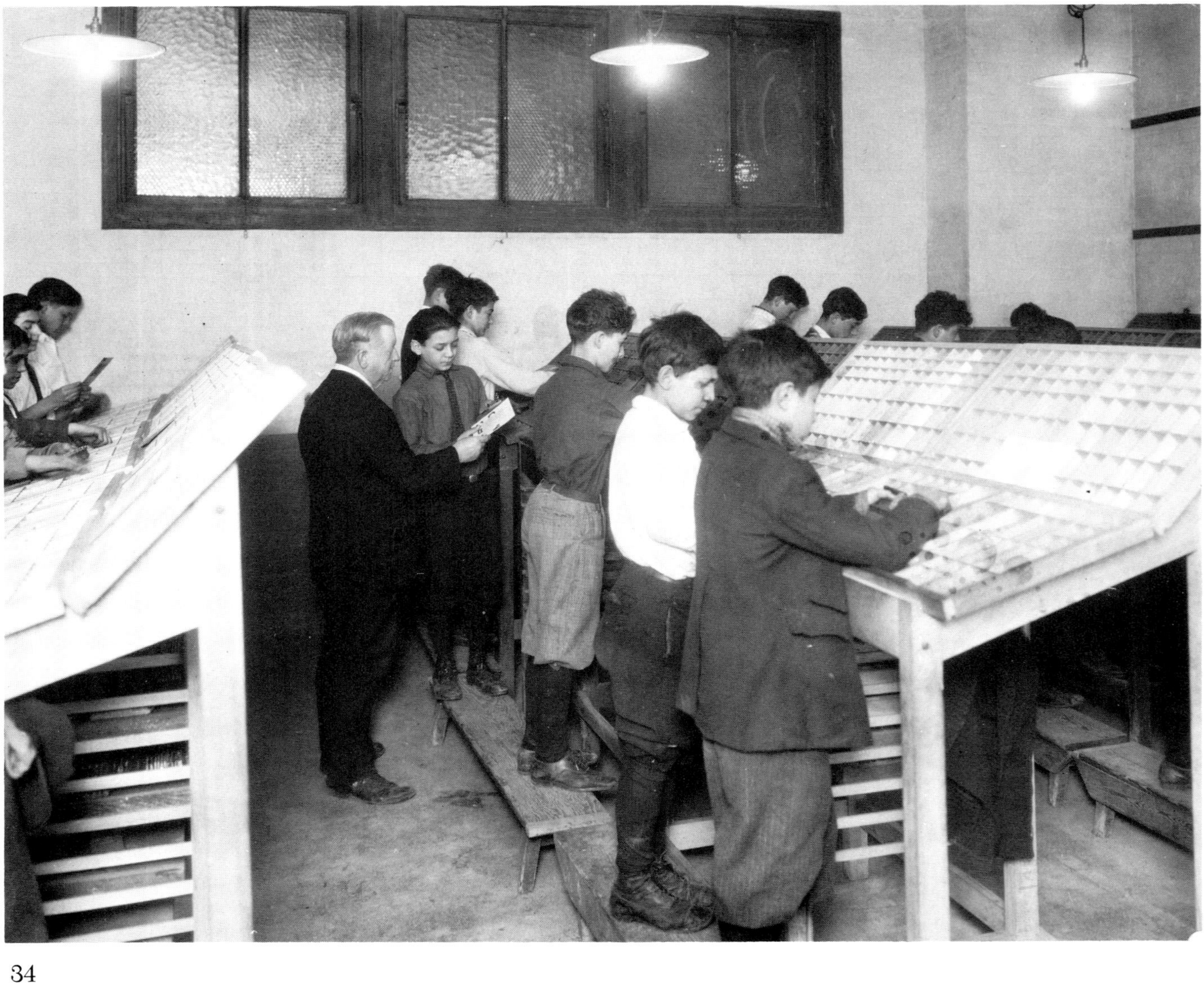

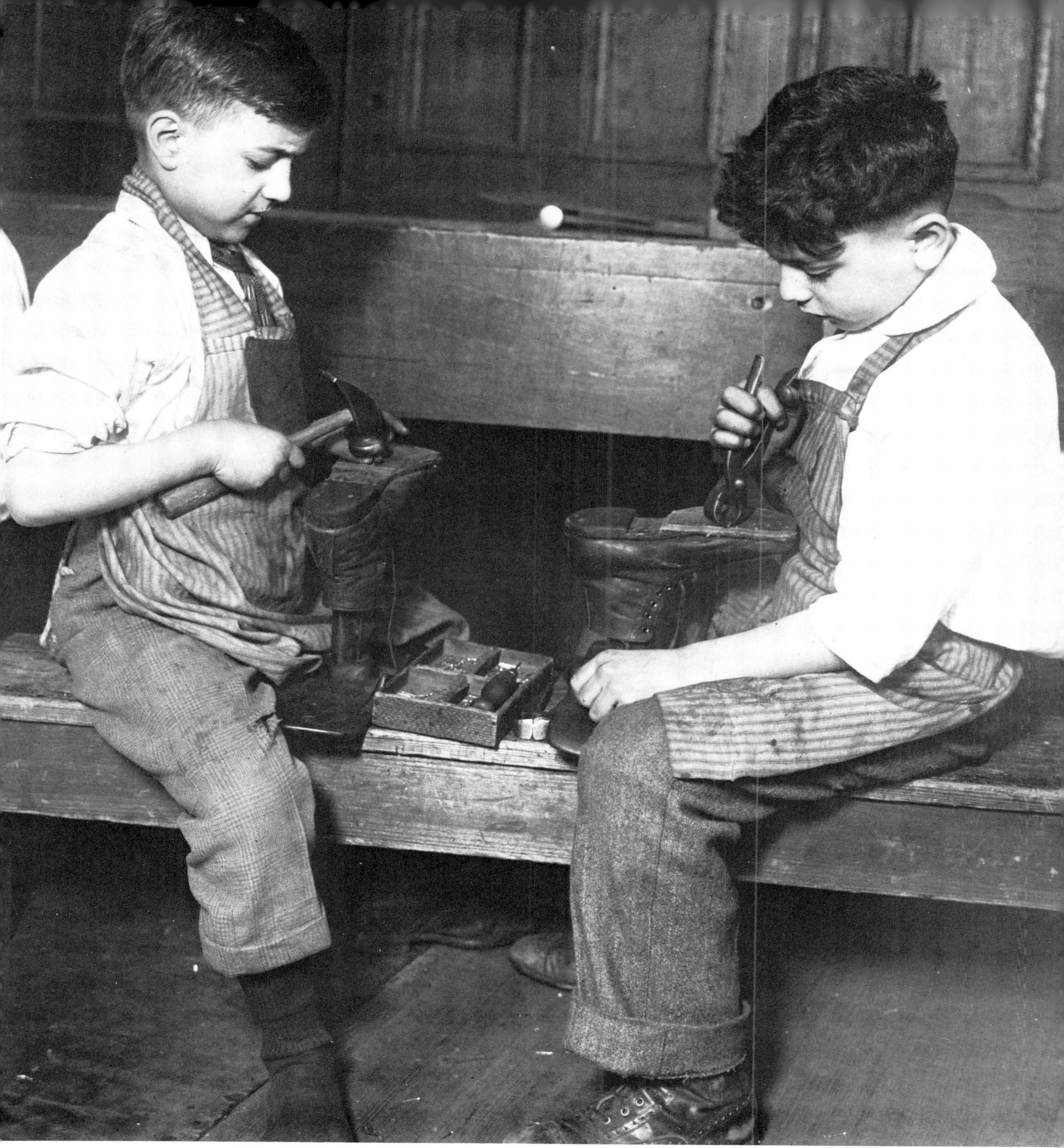

Blacksmith Class [opposite, top]. This class at the CAS West Side Industrial Center taught kids the mysteries of the blacksmith's forge, anvil and hammer. *(c.a.s.).* **Typography Class at James Center** [opposite, bottom]. One of the crafts taught at the CAS industrial schools was setting type by hand. *(A. Tennyson Beals. c.a.s.).* **Boys in Cobbling Class** [above]. The boys at the CAS industrial schools were taught many trades, including cobbling, carpentry, basketry, chair caning, sign painting, bookbinding, janitor work and printing. The girls attended classes in cooking, sewing, embroidery, dressmaking, millinery, stenography, typewriting and novelty work. In the entire CAS network of schools in 1910 there were almost 12,000 students, including 2700 in special night classes. *(c.a.s.).*

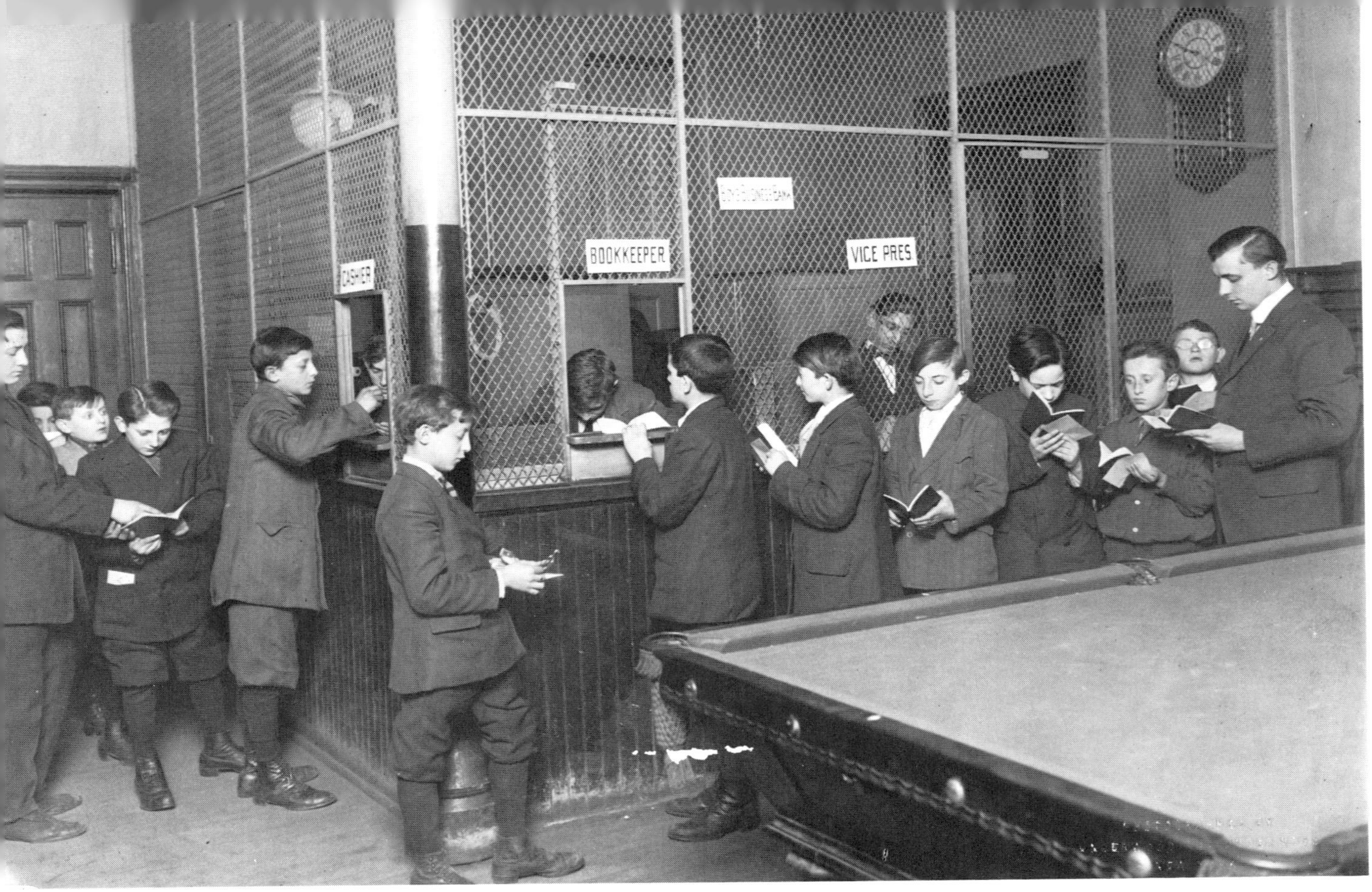

CASHIER
BOOKKEEPER
VICE PRES

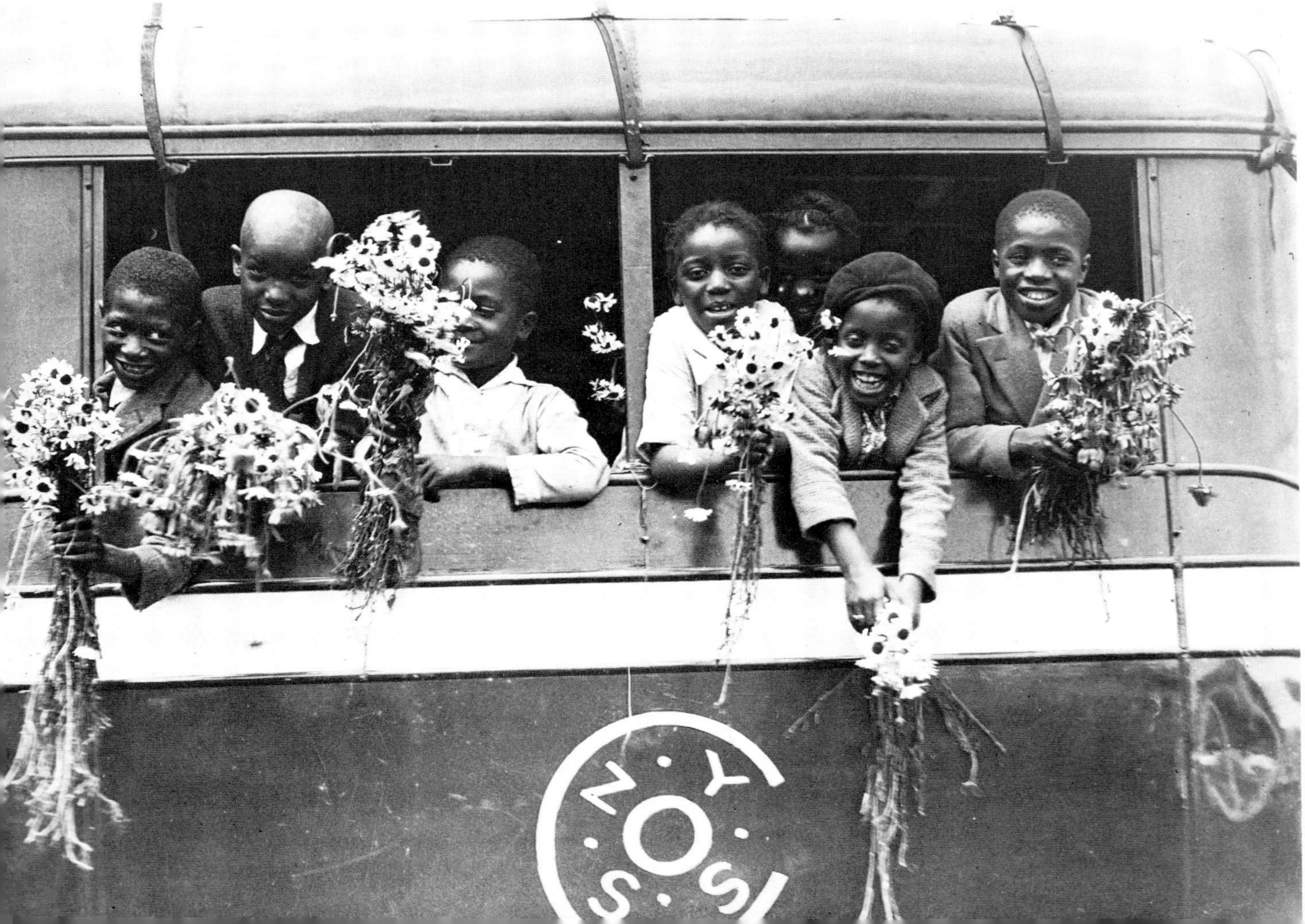

N.Y.S.I.

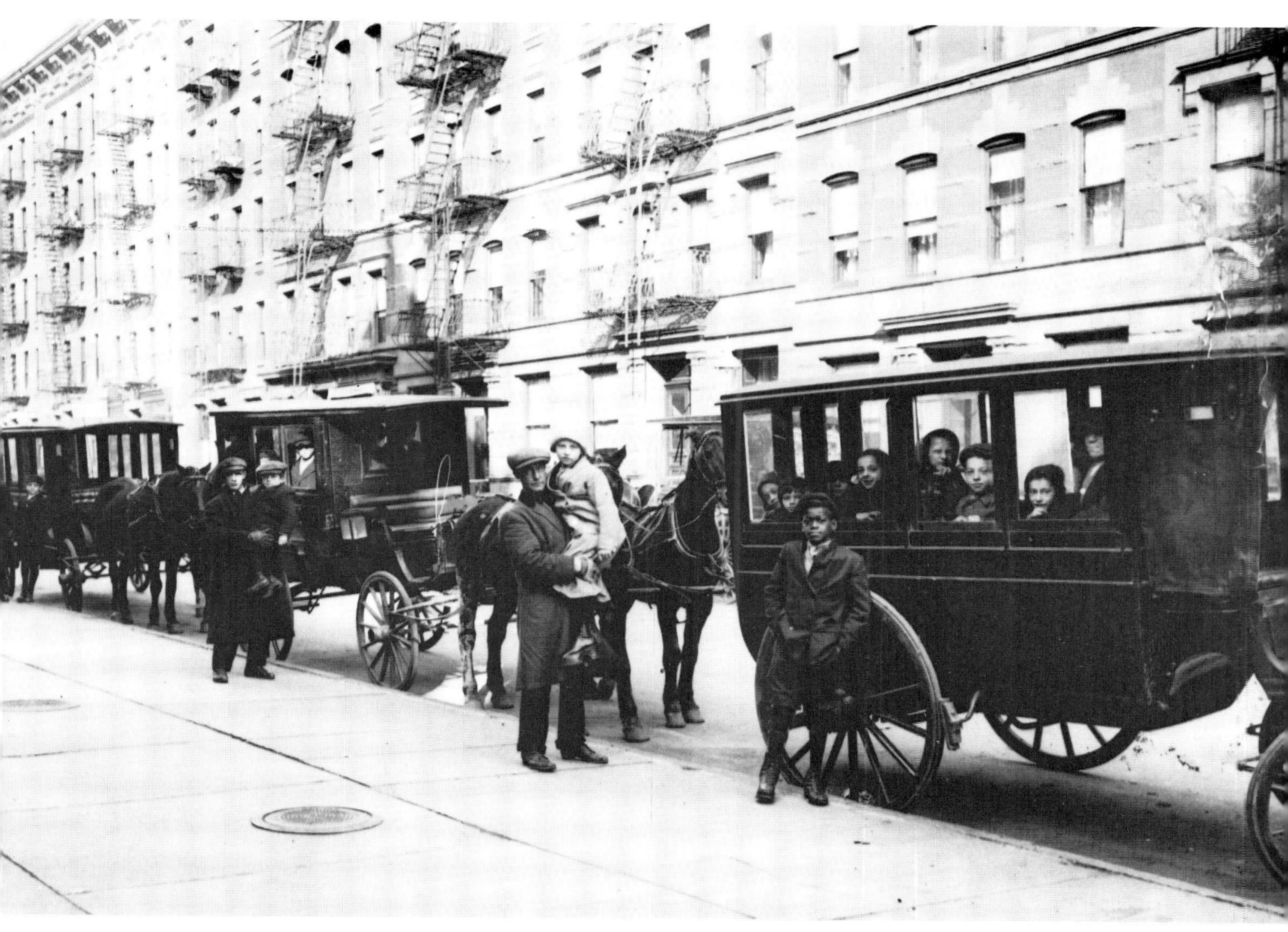

Boy's Business Bank, 6th Street School [opposite, top]. Future captains of industry were taught the intricacies of banking through experience at the Boy's Business Bank at the East 6th Street School of CAS. The bank was part of the Boy's Business Club, a program in which boys of 12 to 14 learned firsthand the ways of a commercial office. Operating the club like a business, the boys were drilled in the qualities that were considered necessities for success—honesty, neatness, politeness, the art of paying strict attention and obedience to orders. To cultivate the habit of saving, the bank was opened with individual deposits as low as a penny each. The boys acted as officers of the bank. While they learned about life in the teller's cage, their compatriots mastered the details of making deposits and withdrawals. *(c.a.s.).* **The Flower Mission** [opposite, bottom]. The kids from CAS centers take flowers to the halt and infirm, an act to brighten the day of the city's forgotten. The CAS custom began casually enough when the superintendent at the Rivington Street Lodging House built a small greenhouse to interest the children in plants. Good gardeners won their own potted plants as rewards. Soon extra plants and flowers were bestowed around the neighborhood as little gifts. Then sick children were singled out as recipients and finally shut-ins of all ages. The flower mission became so popular that a conservatory was constructed at the East Broadway building where enough plants and flowers could be raised for city-wide distribution. *(c.a.s.).* **Wagonette for Crippled Children** [above]. By cruel tradition with its roots in medieval superstition, the crippled child was a social stigma to a city family, an embarrassment relegated to a dark back room away from the public eye. Left to themselves, these forgotten city kids never experienced the challenges of school or the streets. To change such heartbreaking practices, the CAS in 1900 initiated classes for the crippled and even sent horse-drawn wagonettes to fetch the new students. The program started modestly with only three kids. By 1905 there were 240 in studies, learning such handicrafts as making brushes and lampshades. Six horse-powered vehicles transported the youngsters, most of whom had never left the house before. The CAS also mounted a companion educational program for the parents, counseling them at meetings and opening their world through parties and country outings. *(c.a.s.).*

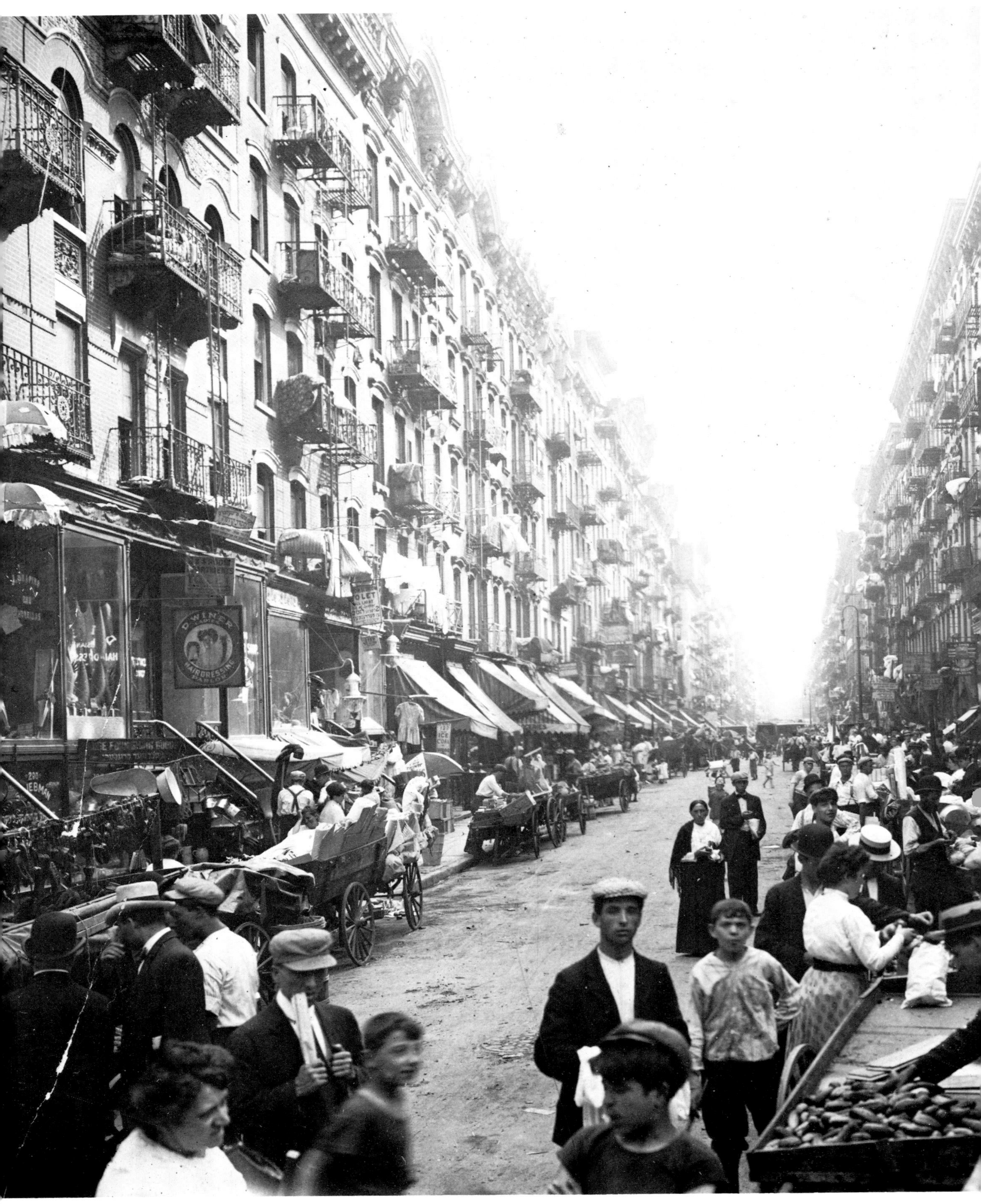
D. WINER
HAIRDRESSING

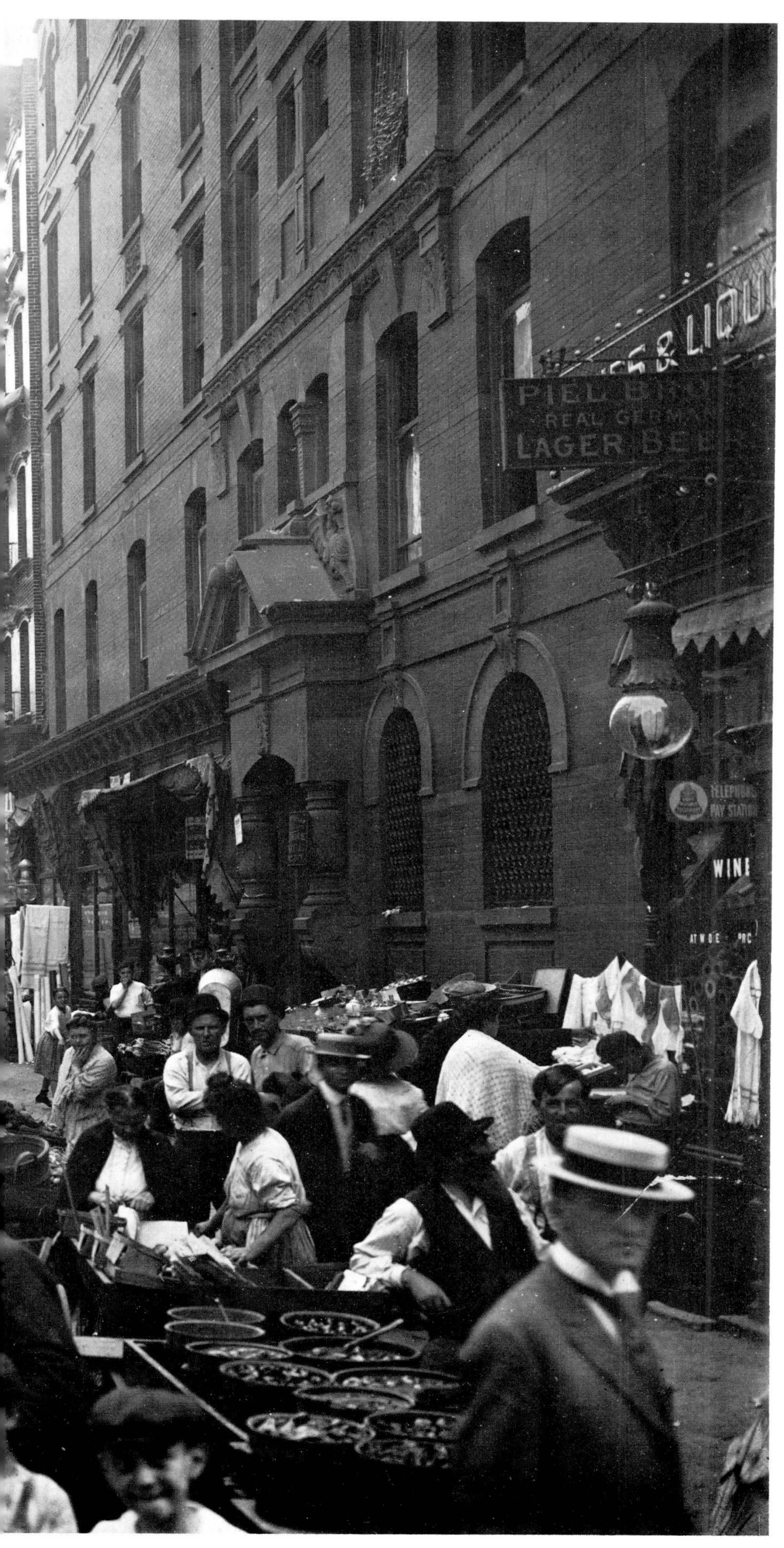

Street Scene. Early in the 20th century even more kids were dumped into the slums of the city as waves of fresh immigrants washed in from the Old World. From 1900 to 1914 some 14 million immigrants arrived in the United States, most of them unskilled, non-English-speaking farmers or laborers from southern and eastern Europe —Italians, Poles, Russians, Romanians and Jews. The vast majority of these settlers remained in Manhattan, which was probably then the largest manufacturing center in the nation. These immigrants became virtual prisoners of Manhattan, clinging to the slim hope of jobs while lacking the mobility of spreading out into the boroughs or other regions of the country. They clustered with their own kind, speaking their native languages and continuing their old-world customs. Thus they continued the traditions of previous urban pioneers by transforming whole neighborhoods into replicas of the mother country—Little Italy, Little Bohemia, the Jewish shtetls. Many immigrants would remain in these neighborhoods for their entire lives, as did their children and even their children's children. *(c.a.s.)*.

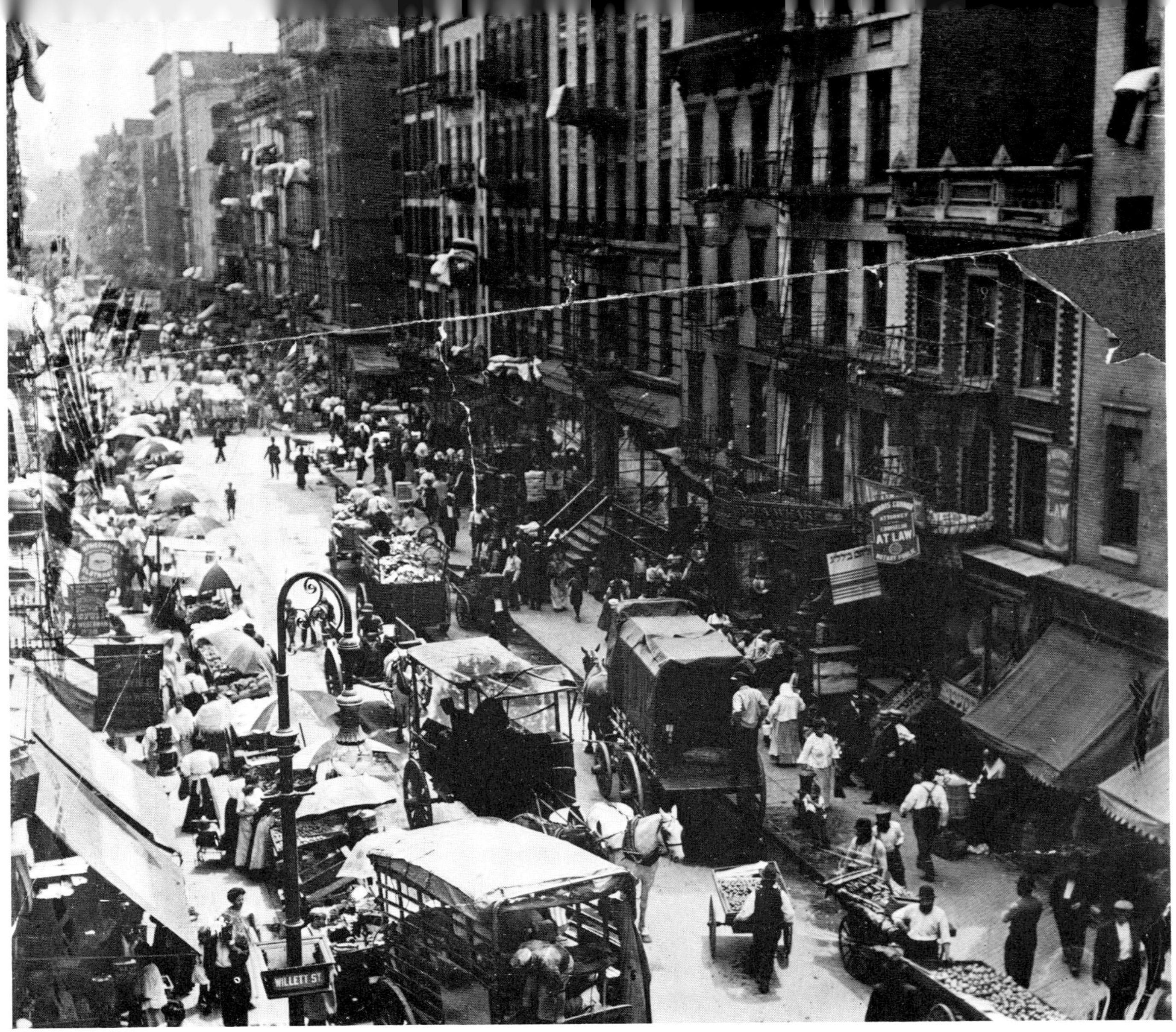

Willet Street [above]. No group of immigrants took a stronger hold on an area than the arriving Jews did on the Lower East Side. They displaced established immigrant families—Irish or German—in many tenement neighborhoods. They set up stores and shops on busy thoroughfares such as Willet Street and manned pushcarts that transformed the streets into bazaars. Under these tumultuous conditions, immigrant kids found little that was stable or comforting. Many were forced by their parents to work hard in school and pore over books in the library as a way to break out of the slums. Many more were forced to fight for jobs in the city's lofts where everything from toys to dresses was manufactured. The weather in the slums was no kinder to the new arrivals than it had been to the old. The summer heat threatened the very lives of the young stacked in the tenements and the winters were just as fierce, when "slack time" idled the garment workshops, and the money slowed or stopped. While the bitter winds whipped through the leaky old tenements, kids competed for bits of coal or collected sticks around the city as fuel for the aging kitchen stoves. *(c.a.s.).* **New York City, 1912** [opposite, top]. The young girl carrying home piecework from a garment workshop was a common sight during this period. The mass of immigrants caused a glut of workers on the labor market. To exploit this excess, clothing manufacturers let out jobs by the piece. Children were pushed by their parents to tackle this work since it could be done at home before chores and school. To many, however, piecework was just another phrase for regular employment at starvation wages. Kids were particularly vulnerable because there were no state or national laws prohibiting child labor. Efforts by Congress to protect the child-worker were systematically overturned by conservative U.S. Supreme Courts. In 1918, for example, the high court declared a child-labor regulation unconstitutional because it infringed on states rights and "denied children the freedom to contract work." It would be 1938 before the Supreme Court finally upheld a law protecting children from unscrupulous employers. *(Lewis Hine. The Edward L. Bafford Photography Collection, University of Maryland, Baltimore County)* **Street Trades** [opposite, bottom]. One of the oldest professions in the city is that of delivery boy. Indeed, foot power was all important, for these were the days before the networks of private transportation, particularly the subways and els. *(Lewis Hine. The Edward L. Bafford Photography Collection, University of Maryland, Baltimore County)*

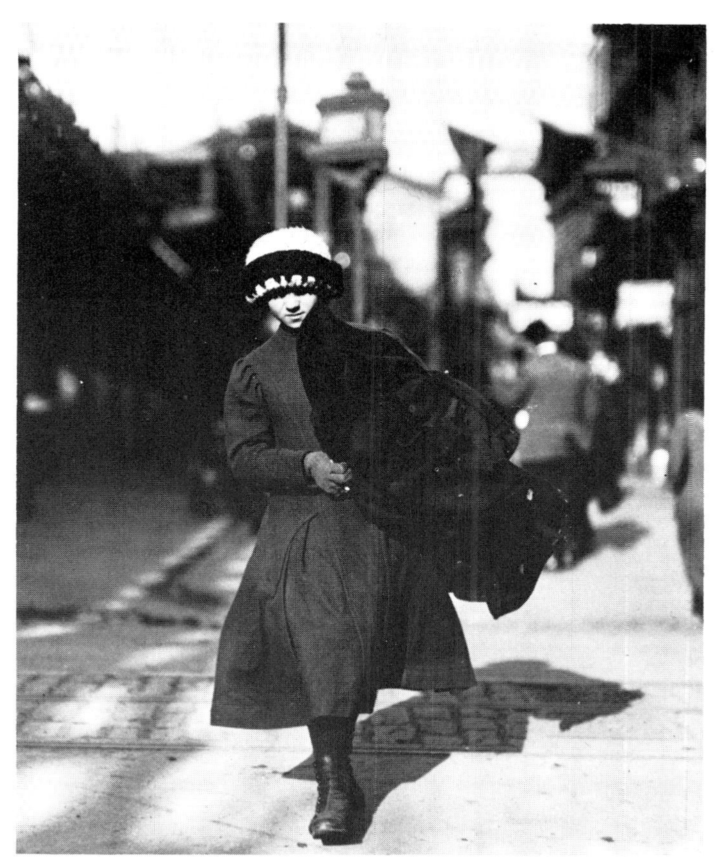

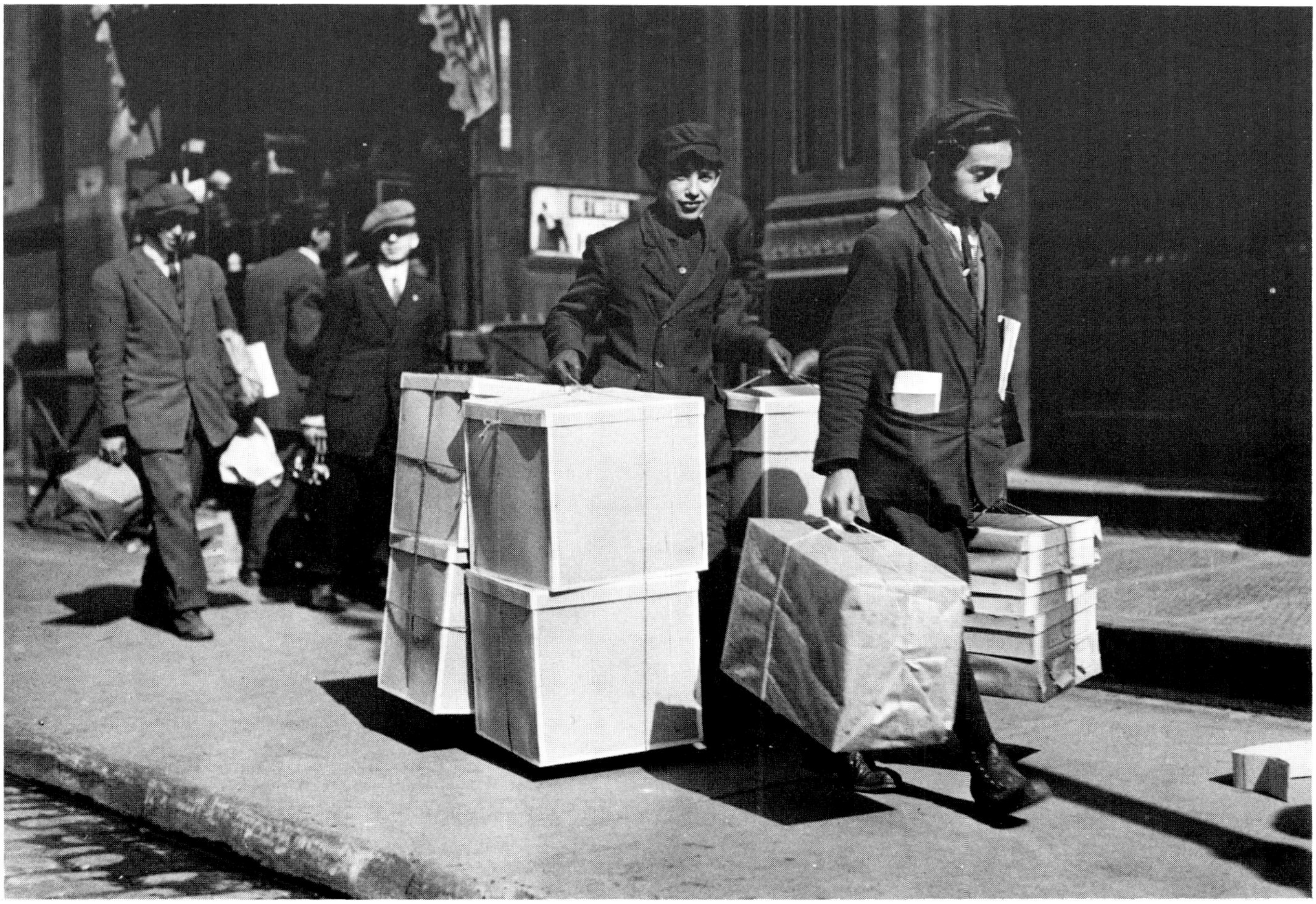

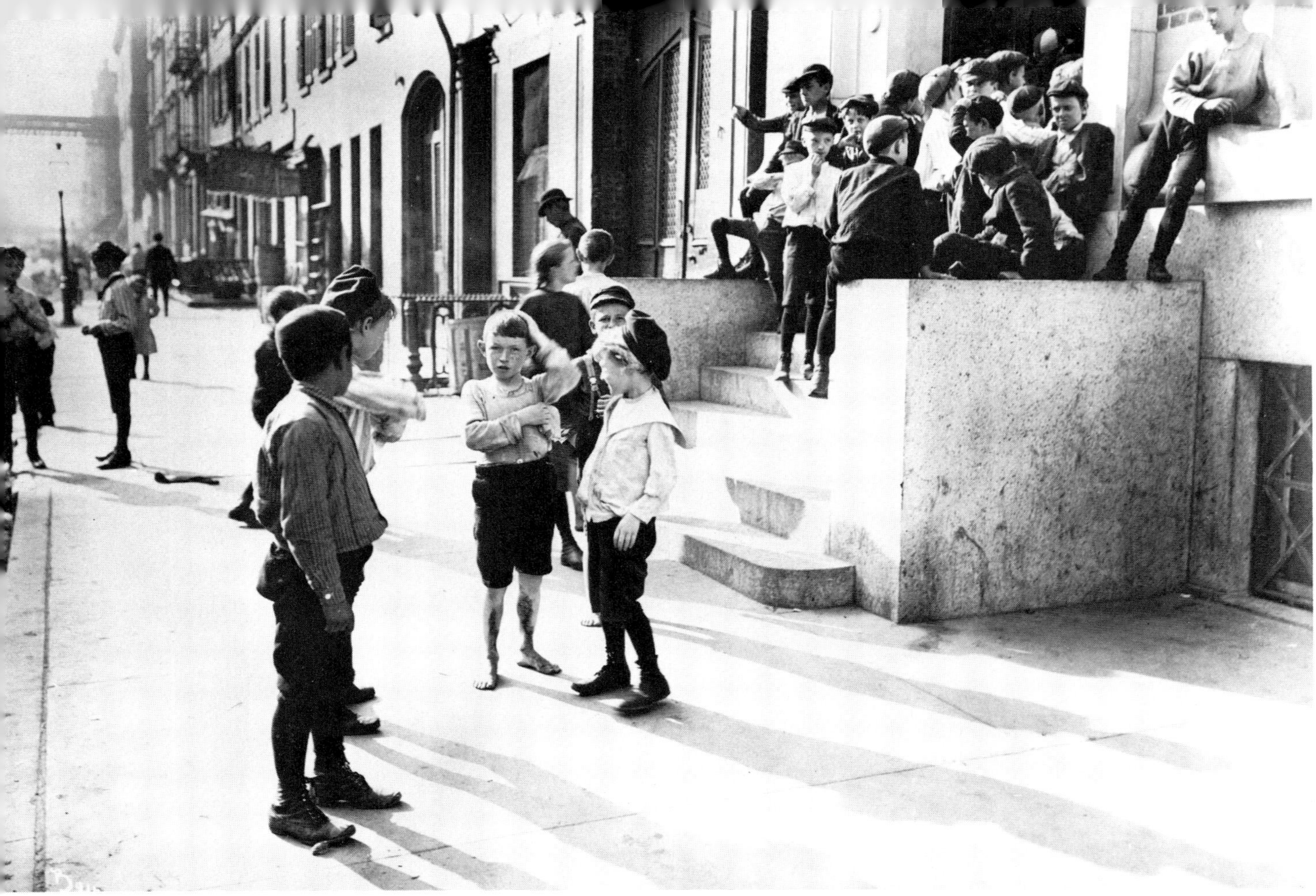

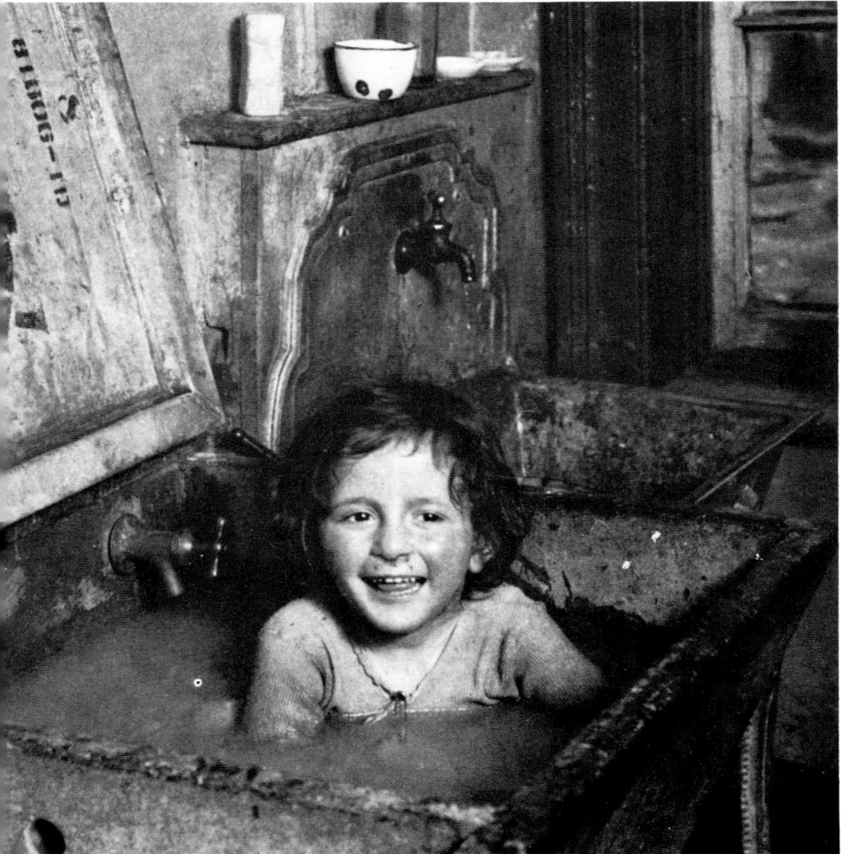

Children Outside a Municipal Bath on East 38th St. [above]. To compensate for limited bathing facilities at home, the city built public baths with showers, swimming pools and even gymnasiums. Many were impressive structures built in the striking Beaux-Arts style of the period. The baths were immensely popular with the children. The 15-cent admission fee provided a few hours of swimming and frolicking and, almost as a side effect, the kids came out clean. *(The Byron Collection, Museum of the City of New York)* **Combined Bath and Laundry in a Tenement Sink** [left]. The kitchen sink was the only tub in the tenement apartment and served to wash dishes, clothes and kids—sometimes at the same time. *(Lewis Hine. International Museum of Photography, Rochester, New York)* **Tompkins Square** [opposite, top]. For the kids in the blocks of surrounding tenements, Tompkins Square, in what is now called the East Village, was one of the few places to play in safety. With playgrounds nestled among lofty trees—many as tall as the tenements themselves—the kids found a patch of greenery and fresh air amidst one of the city's most crowded and noisome areas. *(The Byron Collection, Museum of the City of New York)* **New York City East Side Kids** [opposite, bottom]. Aggression is no stranger in New York. As one boy raises his shovel to make a point, another readies a snowball in retaliation. *(Brown Brothers)*

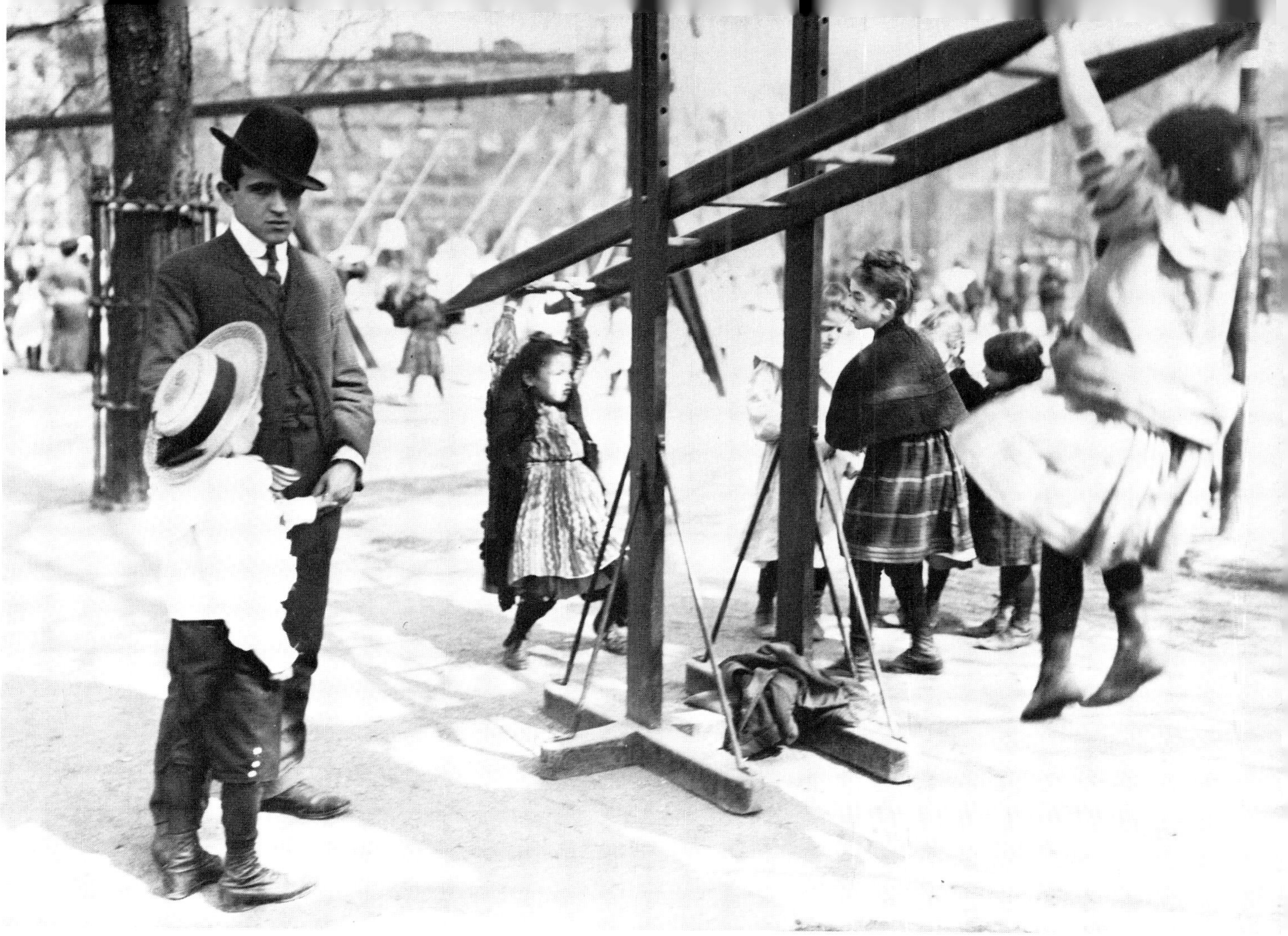

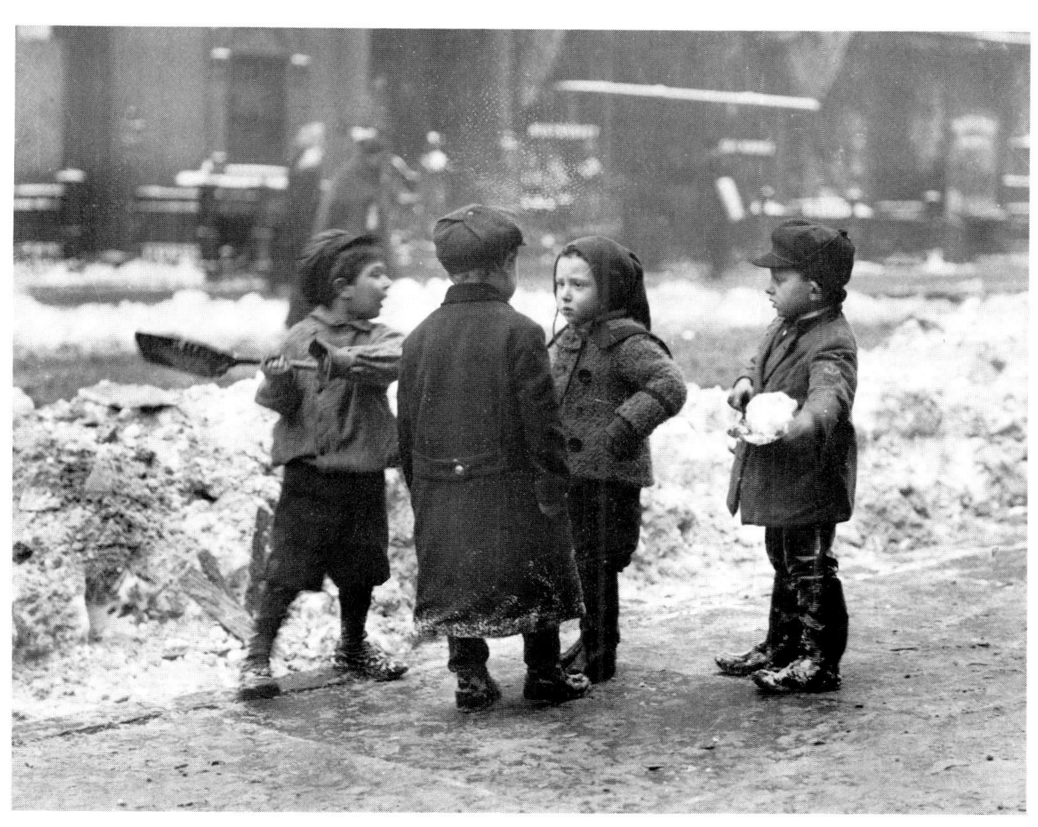

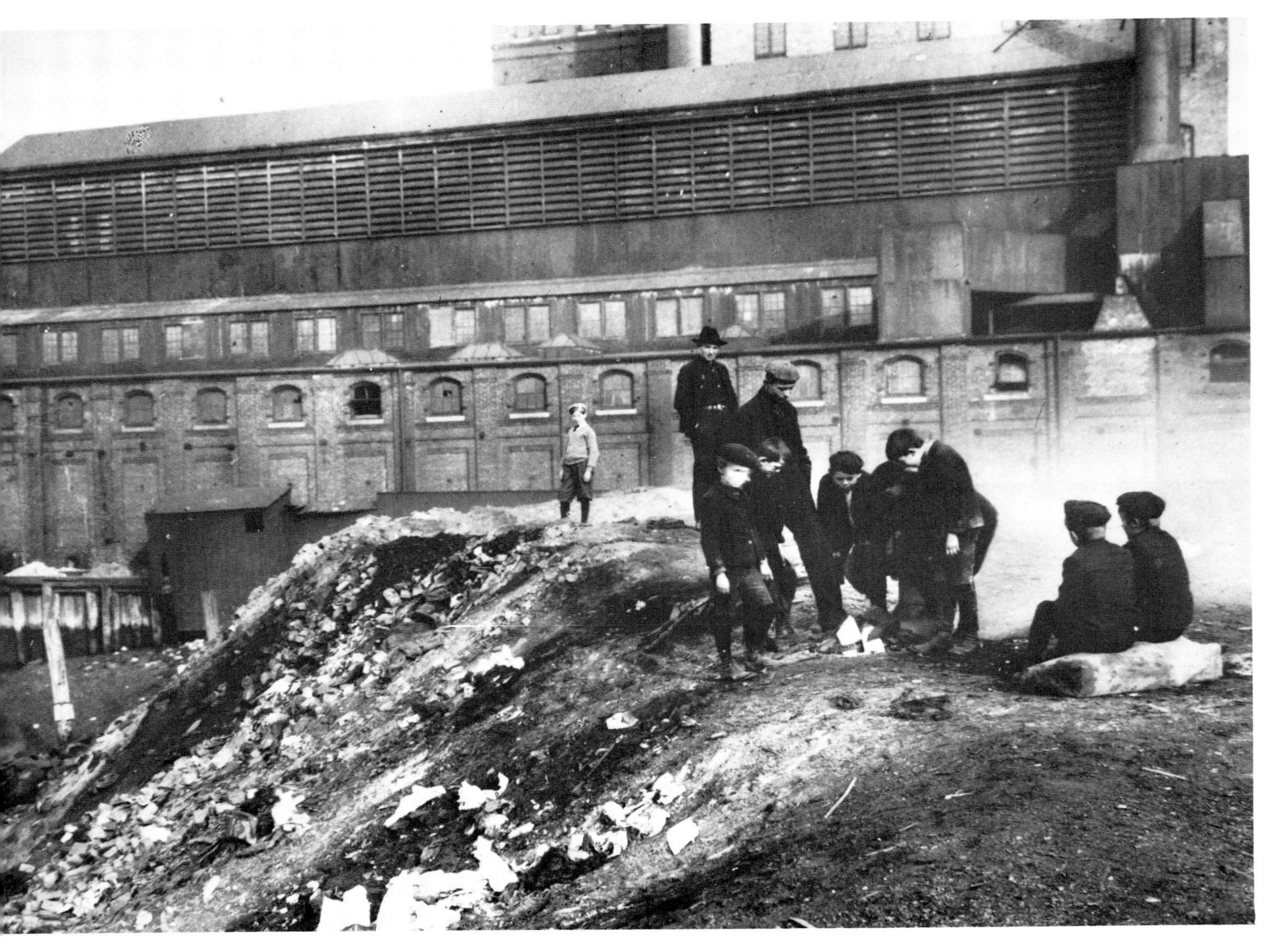

Rendezvous of Yonkers Gang. City kids find dumps a natural meeting ground. Here are the remains of civilized life, things that have been unceremoniously discarded, things that can be collected or burned with impunity or further destroyed for fun. It is a place where kids can start a warming fire or throw rocks at old bottles without raising the ire of property owners or cops. *(Lewis Hine. International Museum of Photography, Rochester, New York)*

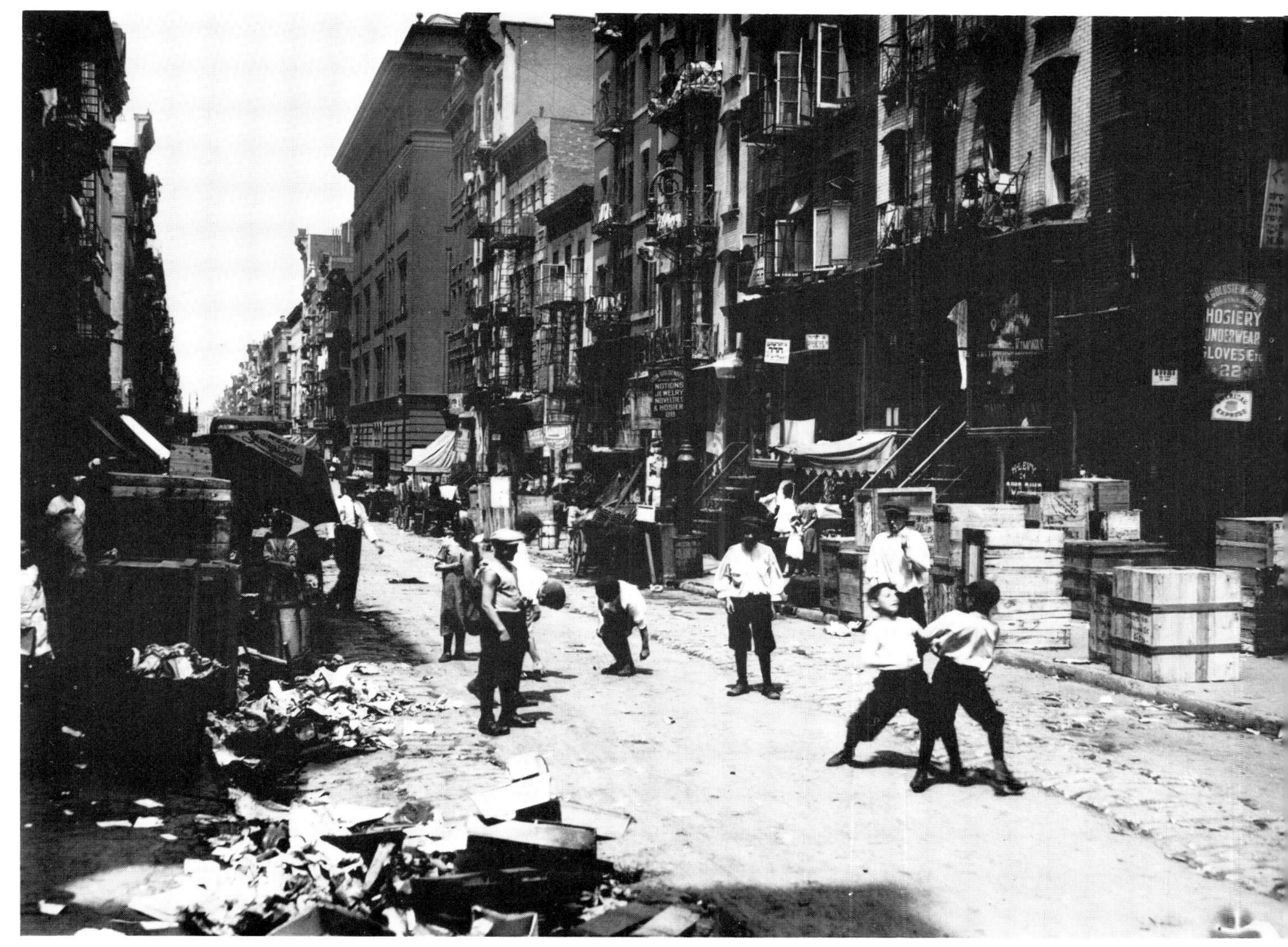

New York, East Side. No city kid grows up without fights; they are part of the urban experience. Sometimes these fights are playful encounters that release the hostilities inherent in street existence. Often, the fights are aggressive displays, more strutting and posturing than actual hitting. On more somber occasions, the street kids will go at one another punching, kicking and wrestling until one of them cries "Uncle." *(Lewis Hine. International Museum of Photography, Rochester, New York)*

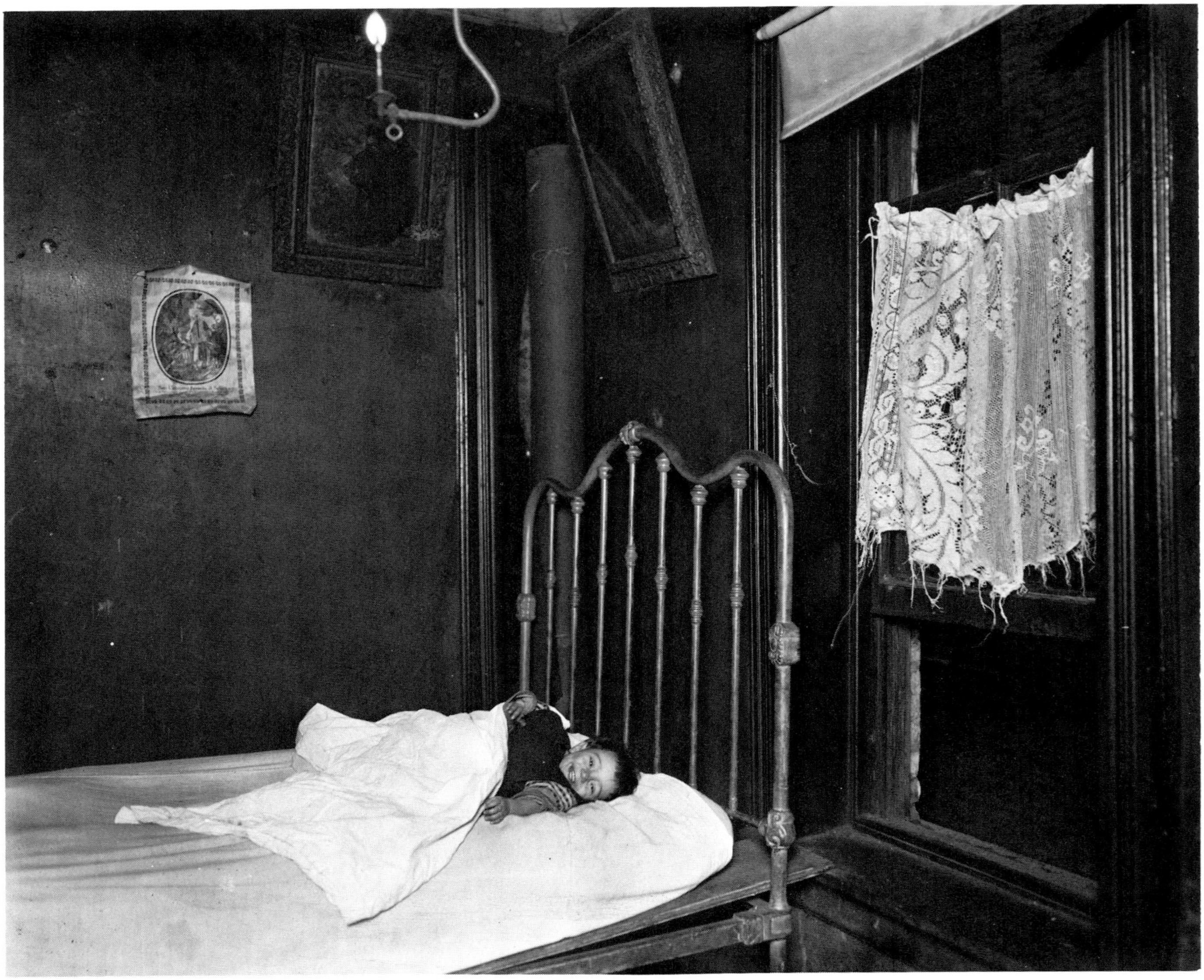

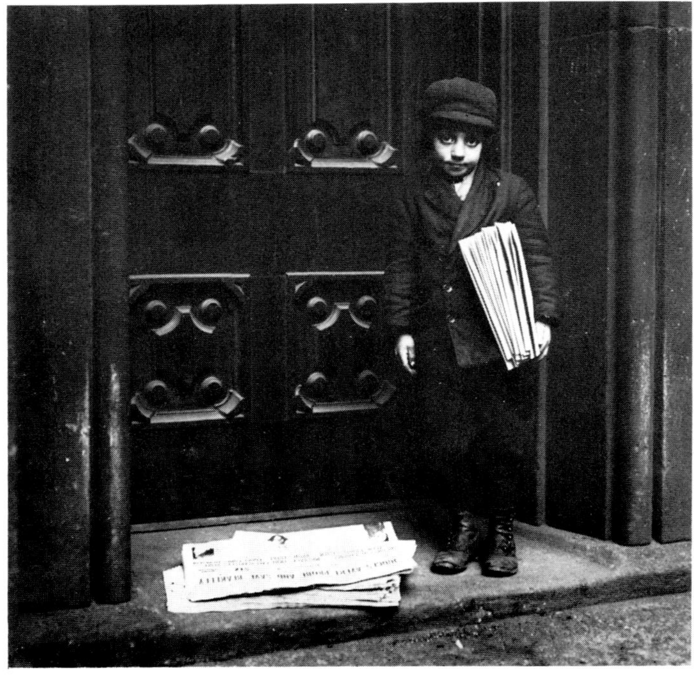

Tenement Interior [above]. Such scenes of contentment—a baby luxuriating in a full-size bed—were rare in tenement apartments. Children were usually tucked together three and four to a bed like so many dolls with their parents sharing a mattress in the same room. Privacy was for the rich. Despite the poverty, the accoutrements of better classes are there—a lace curtain, decorative brass bed and the reproduction of a work of art. *(c.a.s.).* **Small Newspaper Boy** [left]. The cry of "Wuxtry, Wuxtry," from kids hawking the latest lurid headlines was as much a part of the city's atmosphere as the squeal of trolley-car wheels or the rattle of the el. However, shy old-world kids patiently standing on corners to earn an occasional penny were also part of the newspapers' large distributional network. *(Lewis Hine. The Edward L. Bafford Photography Collection, University of Maryland, Baltimore County)* **Third Floor Front** [opposite]. To escape the sweltering heat of August in an Allen Street tenement, these kids pitched their own sleeping tent on the fire escape. No one could blame them for trying to catch the faint stirrings of air. But bedding down on the fire escape posed its own hazards: the passing el created an ear-splitting roar and kids had been known to fall from the tenuous perch during a restless night. ***(Museum of the City of New York)***

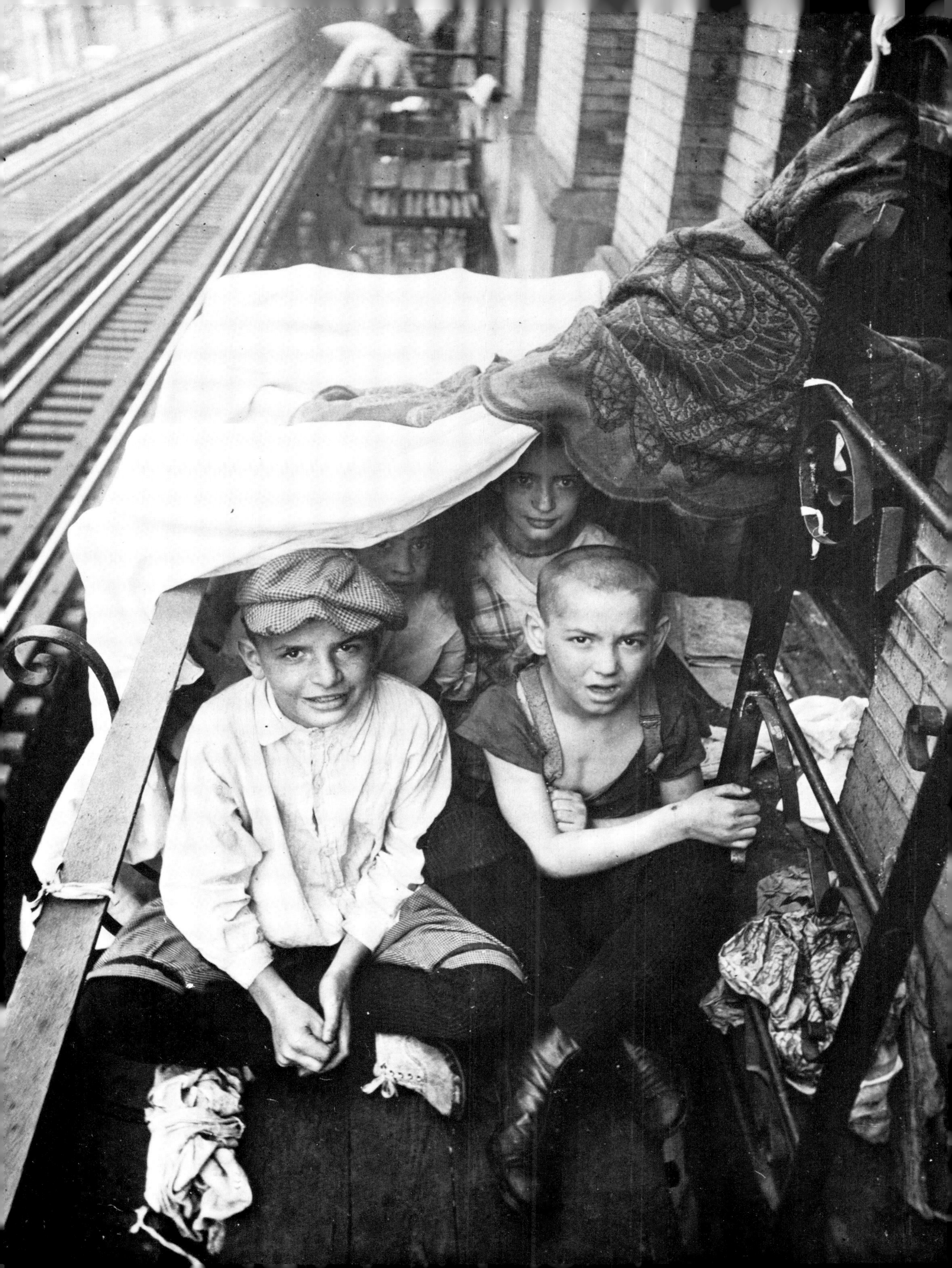

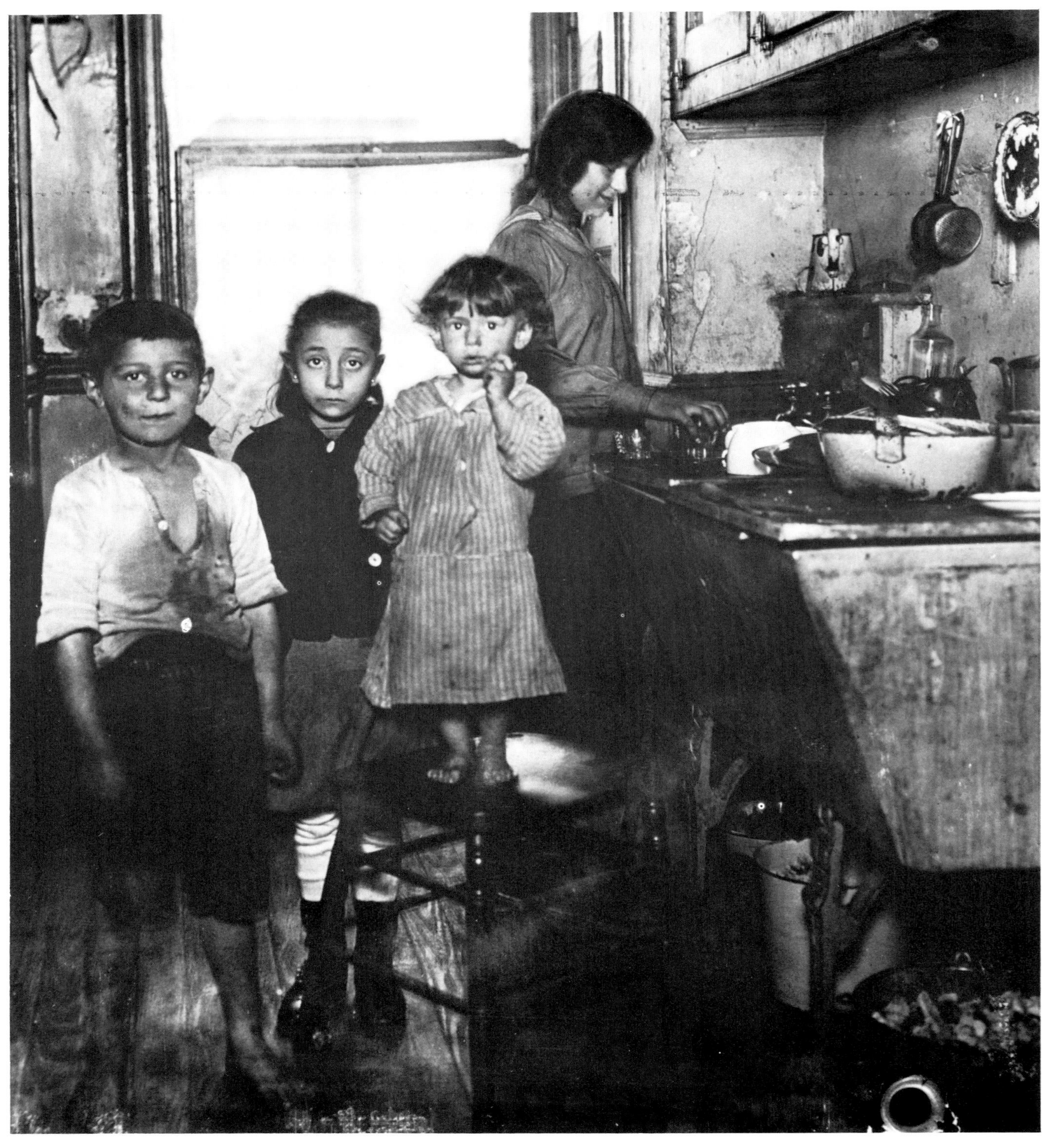

Family in Tenement Kitchen. Although conditions in tenement apartments were appalling, the rents were far from cheap. Most families paid a week's earnings every month, about $8 or $10. Of course, the rent was due even if there was no work. And in these days before welfare and unemployment insurance, eviction followed quickly on the heels of skipped rental payments. A common sight was a family's belongings—furniture, clothing, utensils—dumped on the street along with the children awaiting some belated help. To reduce the inexorable demands of the rent, many families shared apartments with relatives or even with other families. Some rented beds or mattresses to roomers. Crowded together with virtual strangers, kids were often subjected to adult depravities committed in their own beds. *(Community Services Society of New York)*

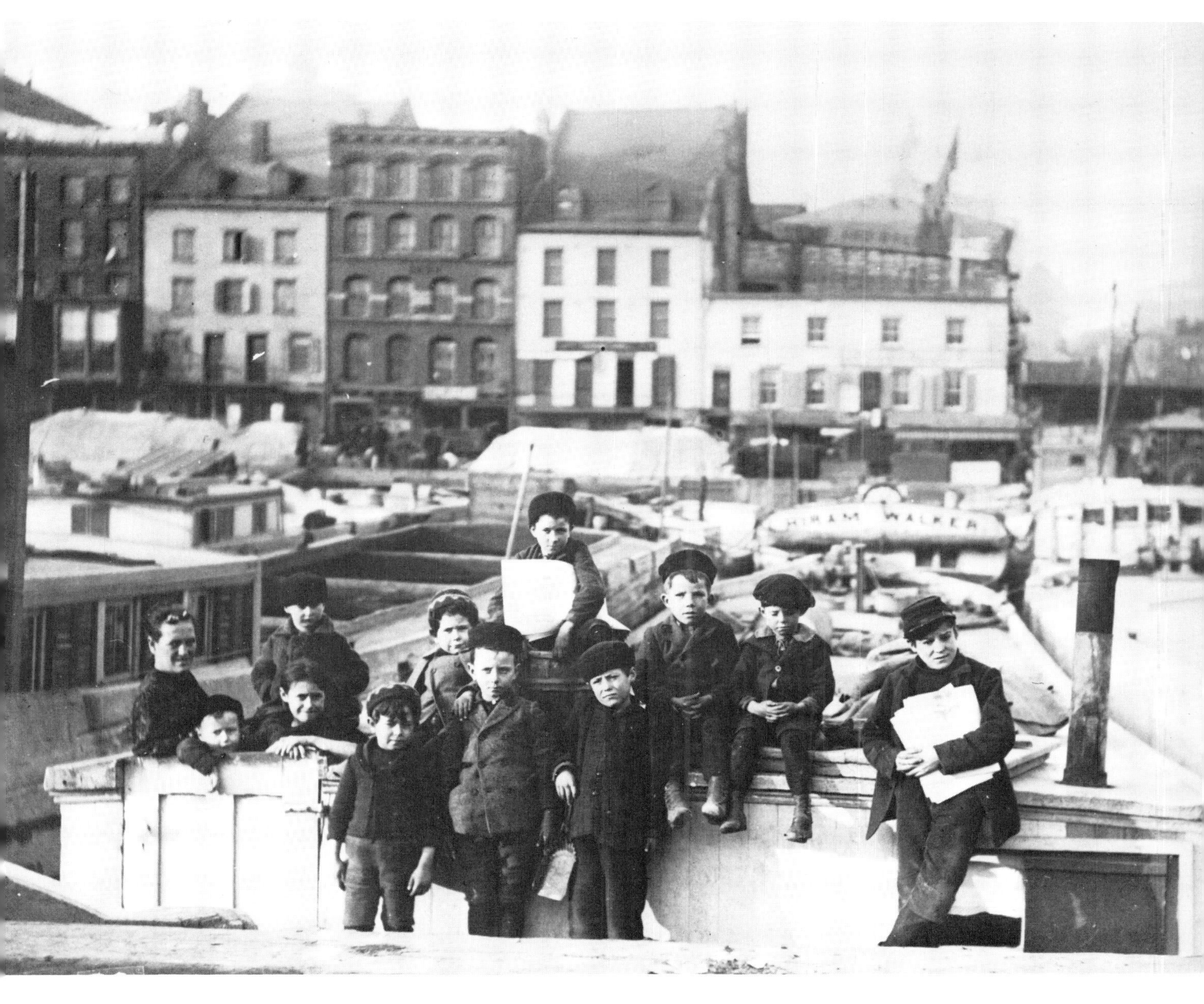

Children on Scow at Coenties Slip. The East River waterfront was an exciting place of escape for kids. Away from the mean streets and tenements they could inhale some salt air and mix with sailors who told of wondrous places beyond the horizon. Even a local scow that probably never went much farther than Staten Island was a magical place where newsboys and street urchins could take a break from the competitions of the street. *(The New-York Historical Society)*

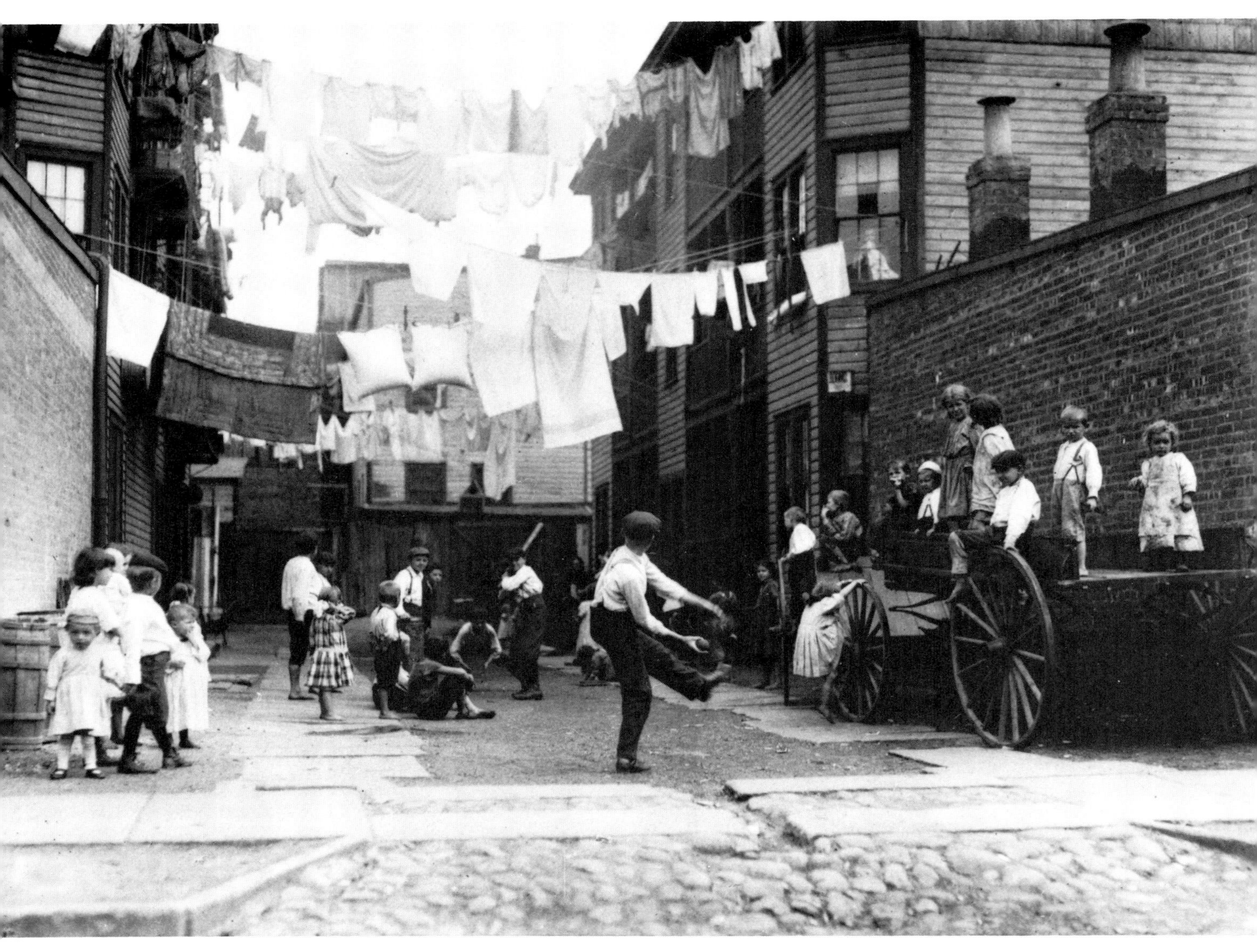

Playground in Tenement Alley [above]. No area was too cramped for a game of baseball. At the time, the local New York Giants were being led to pennants by John McGraw. Elsewhere, Ty Cobb was burning up the American League in Detroit and a young pitcher was making his name known around Boston—Babe Ruth. The excitement of baseball soon permeated the young immigrant's life. Through a child's imagination the cluttered yard or busy street became Ebbet's Field. Even Abraham Cahan responded to the national craze with articles on baseball in the Yiddish paper the *Forward. (Lewis Hine. The International Museum of Photography, Rochester, New York)* **Brooklyn Pier** [opposite, top]. The street kid's private swimming pools were the city's rivers and bays. Using an old pier as his diving board, the urchin discovered in the waters a welcome break from the blistering streets and a chance to display his diving or jumping form. Swimming from the piers was illegal, but unpreventable. Not only was the water polluted by sewage; the currents were so treacherous that drownings were frequent. *(Brown Brothers)* **Garbage Cleaners** [opposite, bottom]. Going through the garbage was not the work of eccentric old folk during this era but part of a kid's struggle for survival. Kids were dispatched to bring home whatever leavings they could scrounge, including unburned coal for the fire. Those without homes had to subsist on whatever they could rummage from the garbage pails. Nor were the children without competition from adults. Many unskilled immigrants became the city's rag-pickers who sorted through the trash for bits of cloth which were later sold to rag dealers. *(Lewis Hine. The International Museum of Photography, Rochester, New York)*

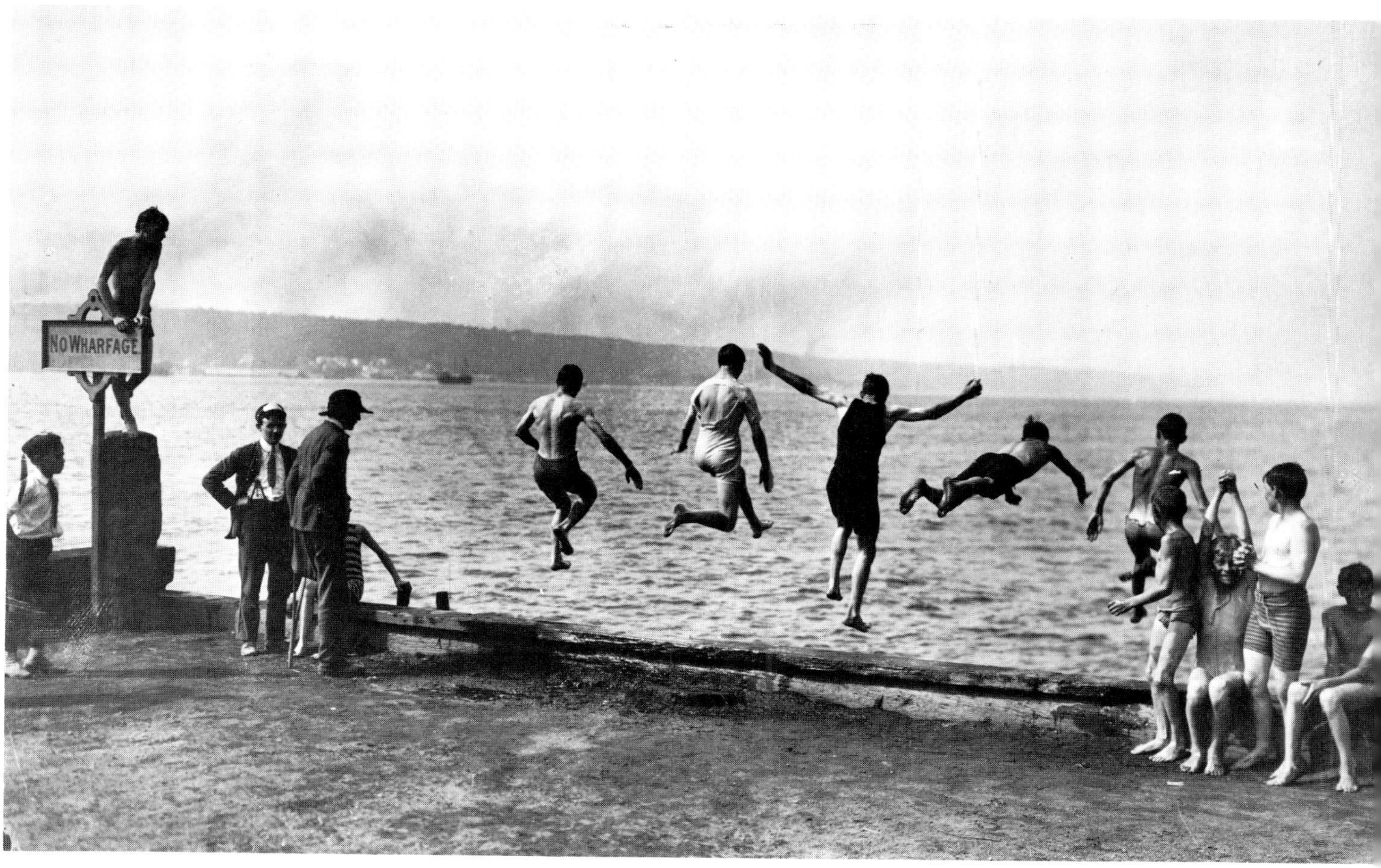

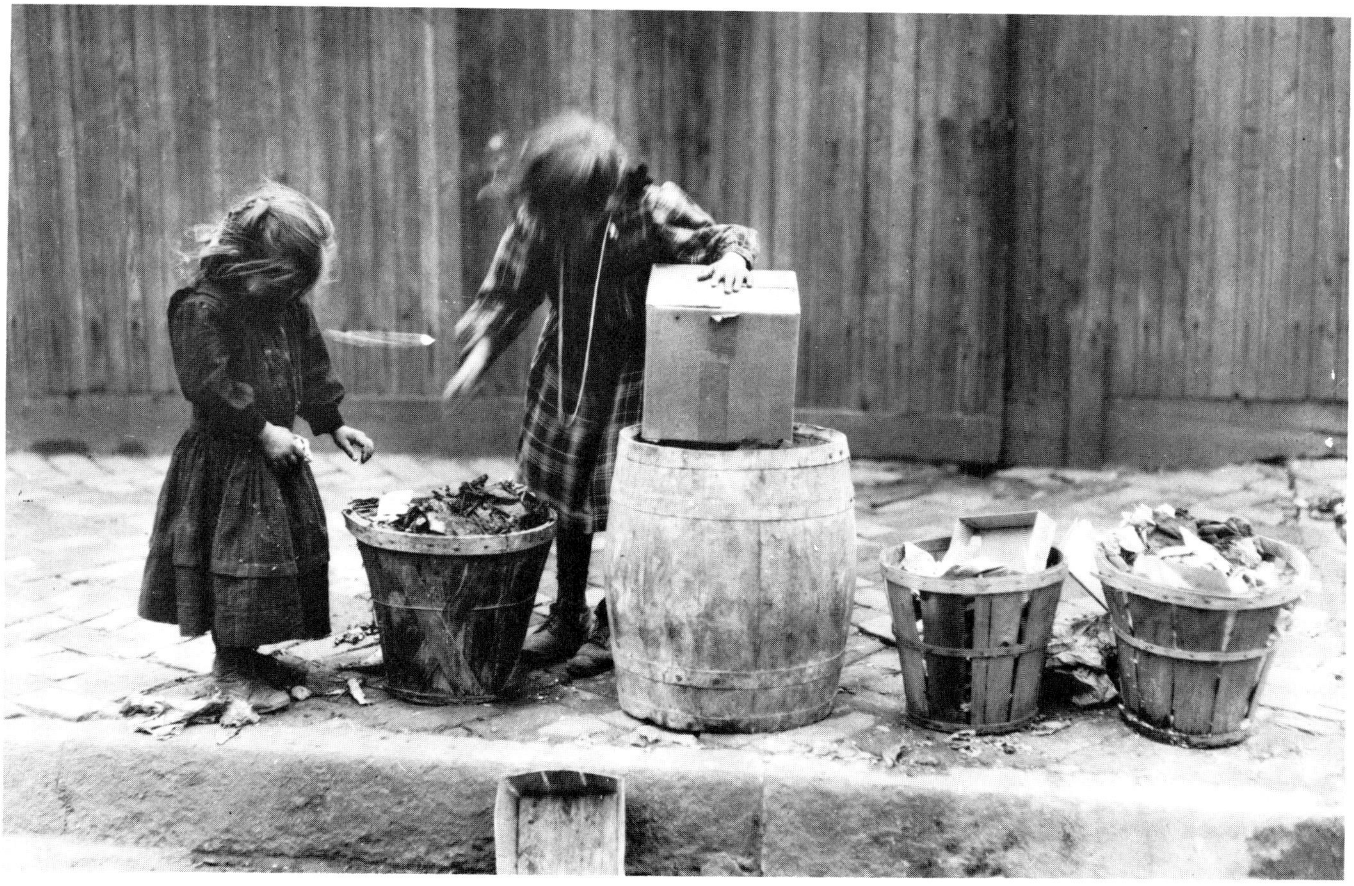

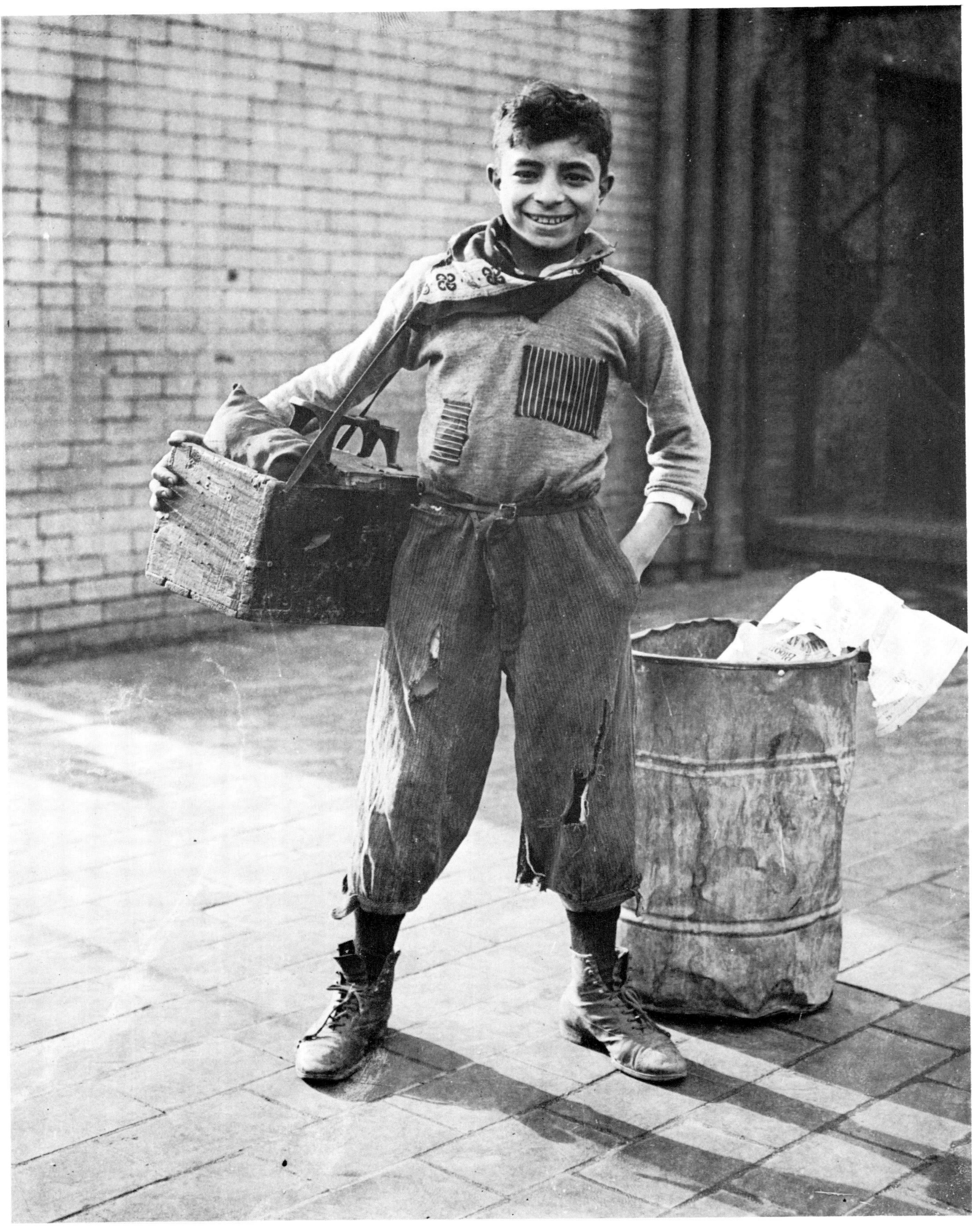

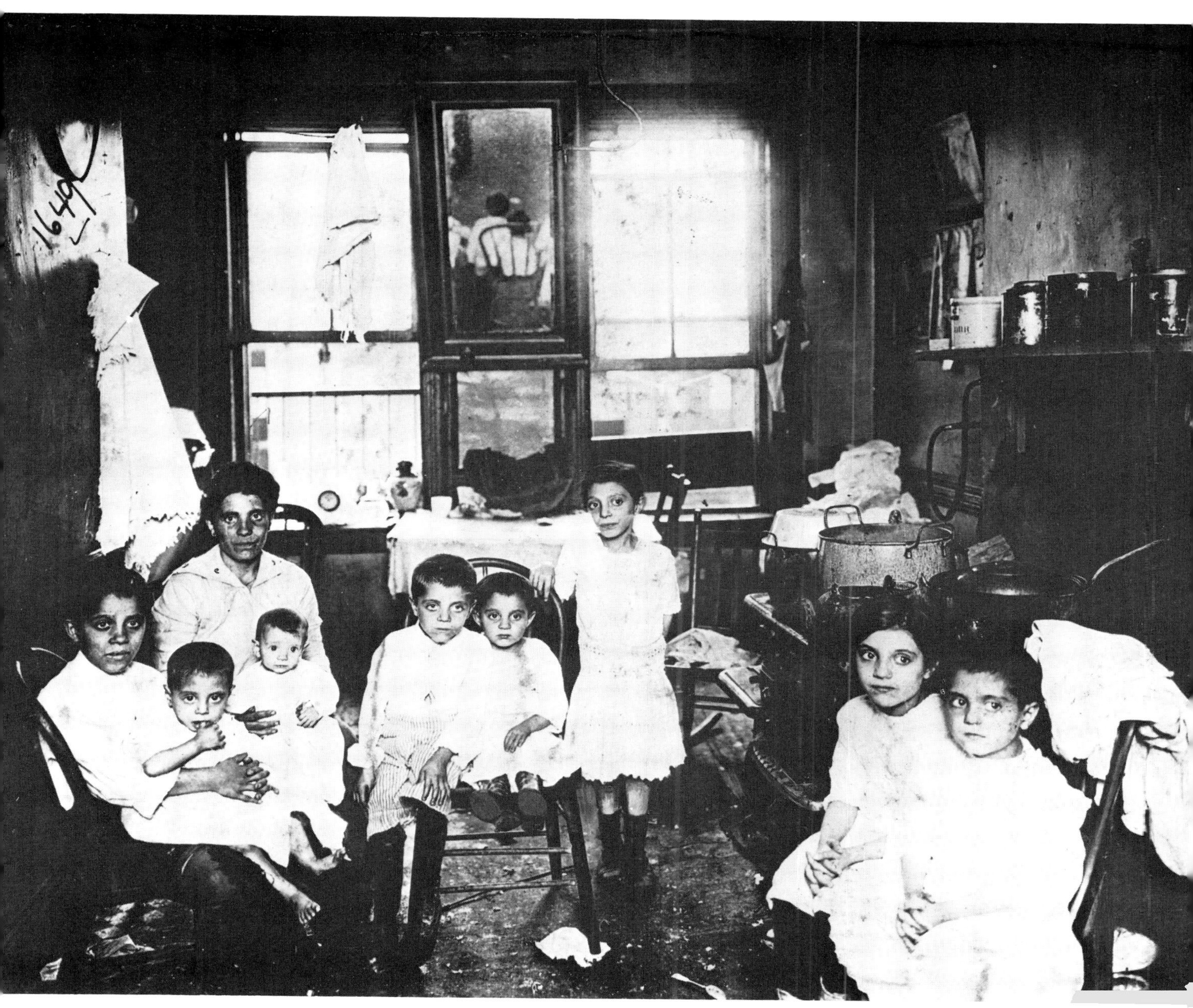

Shoeshine Boy [opposite]. Brimming with confidence, a smiling bootblack in his clean but tattered clothes sets forth on his daily rounds. This lad was but one of the thousands who lived at lodging houses run by the CAS, for which he paid a nominal rent taken from his earnings. While the CAS ran clean and warm lodging houses for the homeless, its stated purpose was always to help the child with parents through difficult times so that he or she could enjoy a more settled home life. *(c.a.s.).* **Poor Family with Eight Children** [above]. The 1920s witnessed the end of the massive immigrations as Congress passed restrictive laws and quota systems. These laws were probably unfair but they did give the city a chance to try to absorb the new arrivals. For some kids, however, life remained dismayingly familiar. Tenement rooms already stuffed with humanity were pushed beyond their capacities by the growing families of the poor. During the 20s birth control and abortion were luxuries of the rich. One of the city's grisly phenomena was the number of unwanted babies found stuffed in garbage cans or floating in the rivers, cast off by desperate mothers unable to bear the burden of another mouth to feed. *(Community Services Society of New York)*

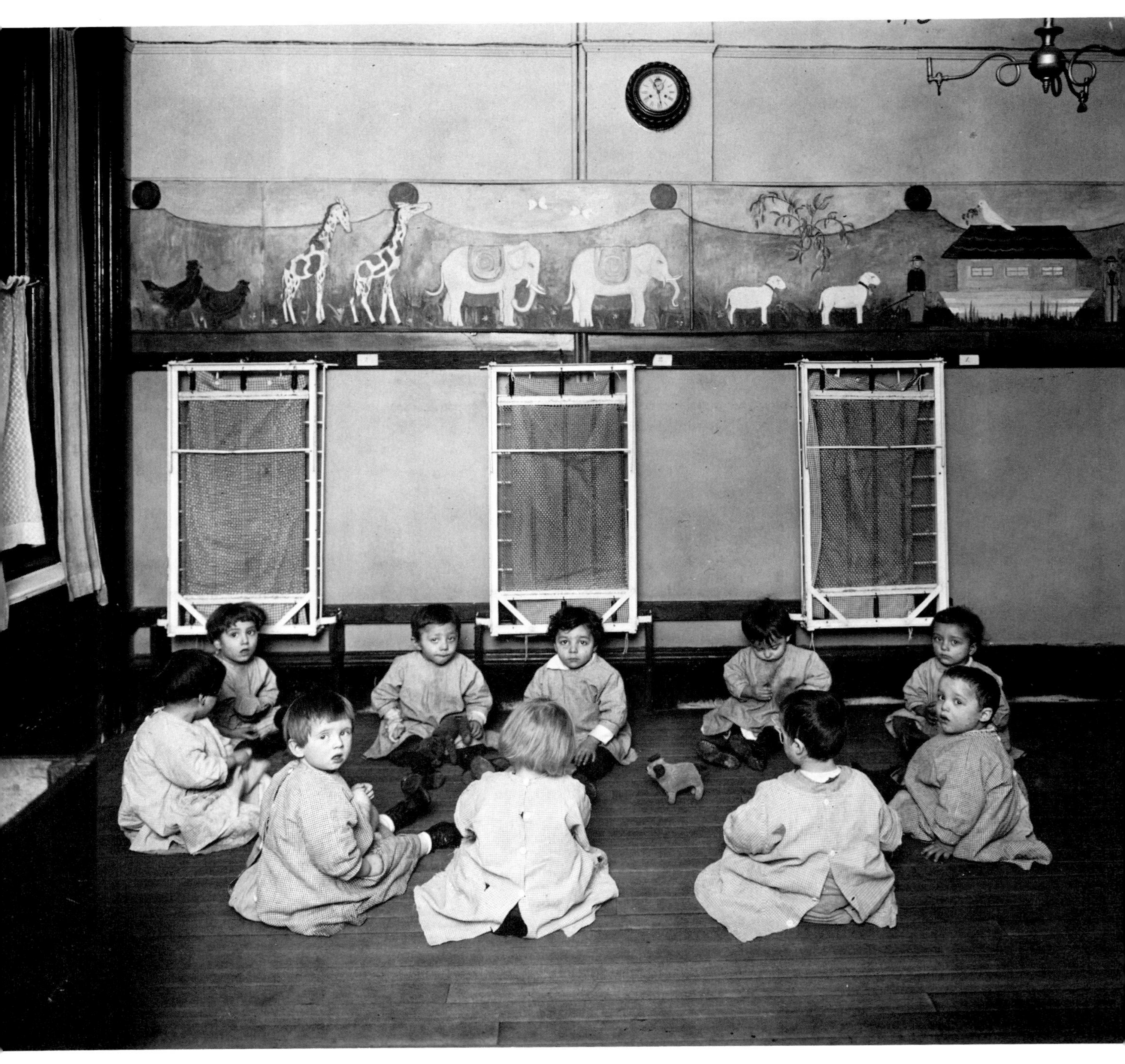

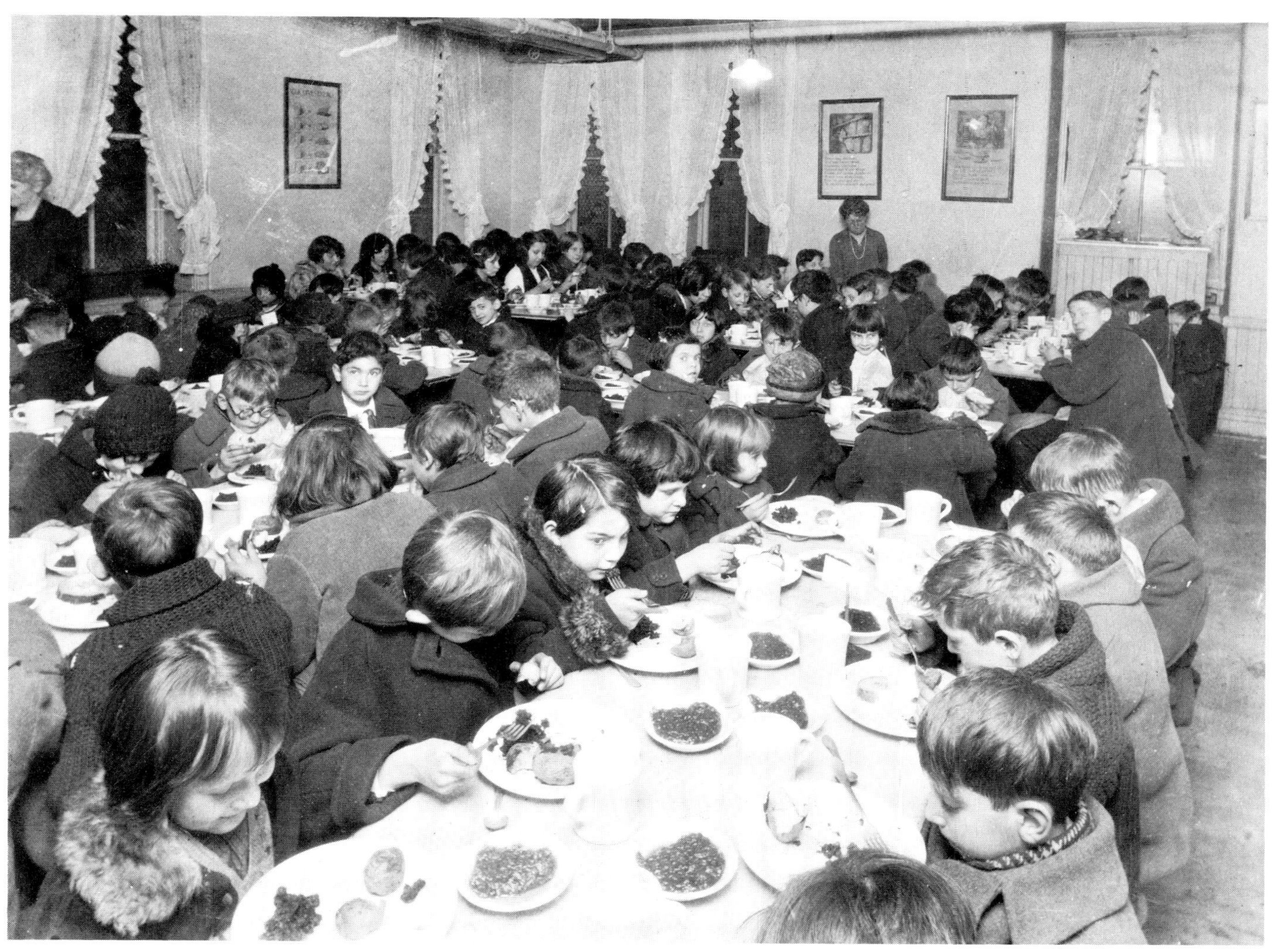

CAS Kindergarten at the Rhinelander School [opposite]. In clean smocks and with plenty of room, kids in a CAS kindergarten enjoy group experiences under supervised care for the first time. *(c.a.s.).* **Malnourished Children Have Lunch at a CAS Center** [above]. Still bundled up against the chill of outdoor class, these underfed children are typical of those who ate nutritious meals at the CAS centers. In one poor district a survey showed that 67 percent of the children were malnourished. In their effort to combat this state of affairs, the Society served 1600 meals daily at 10 health centers. The Society backed up its hot meals with admonishments to the mothers through pamphlets: "Nourish them that they may grow strong and straight and happy." It also attempted to steer mothers away from junk food. The literature claimed that a lack of intelligent buying was almost as great a cause of malnutrition as a lack of money. Ironically, although food is more plentiful today, the problem of poor nutrition may even be greater *(c.a.s.).*

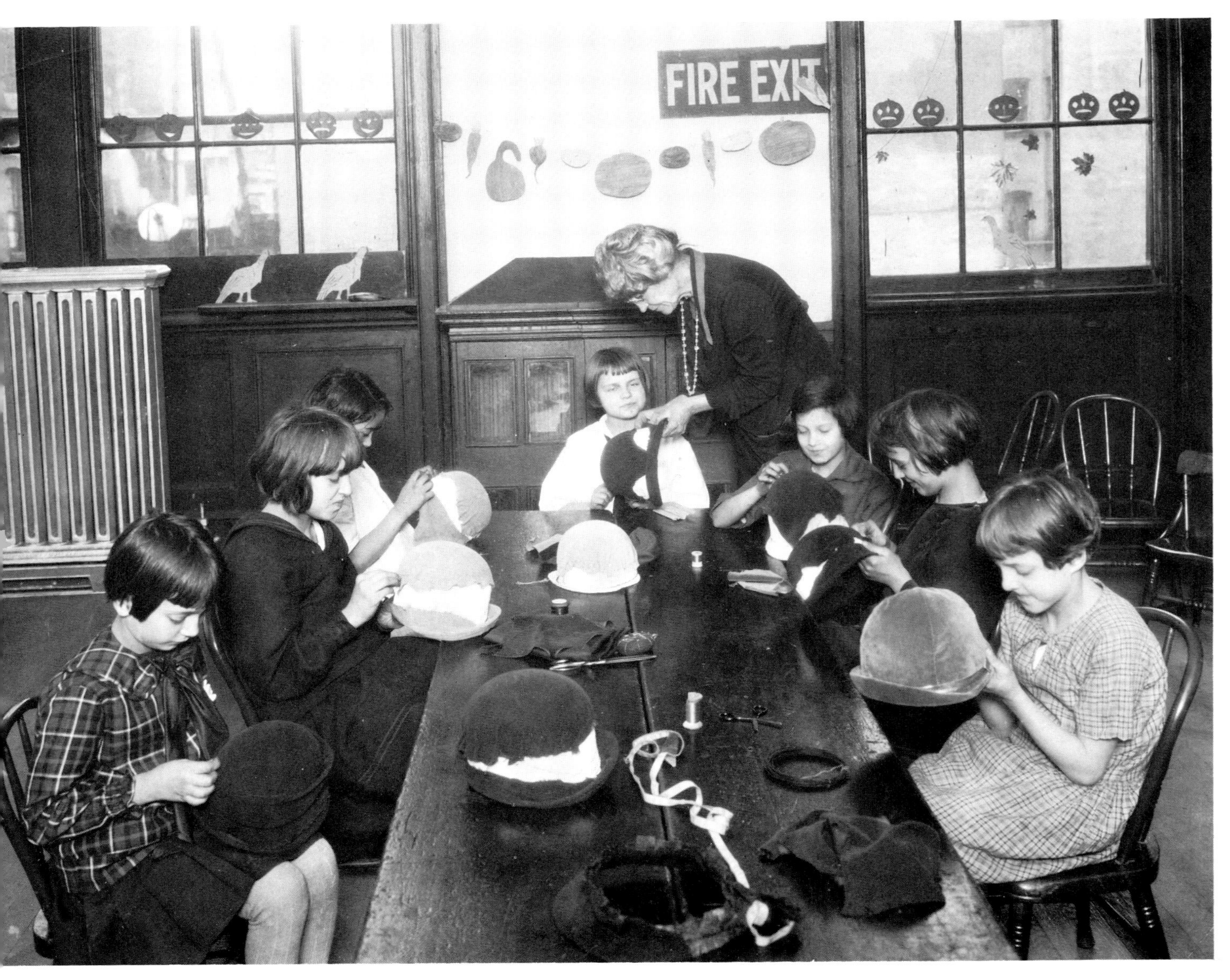

Millinery Class at a CAS Center. The Society stressed self-help to the kids by teaching them trades and crafts they could use in later life. Hatmaking was definitely a marketable profession for girls willing to work in the garment industry. *(c.a.s.)*.

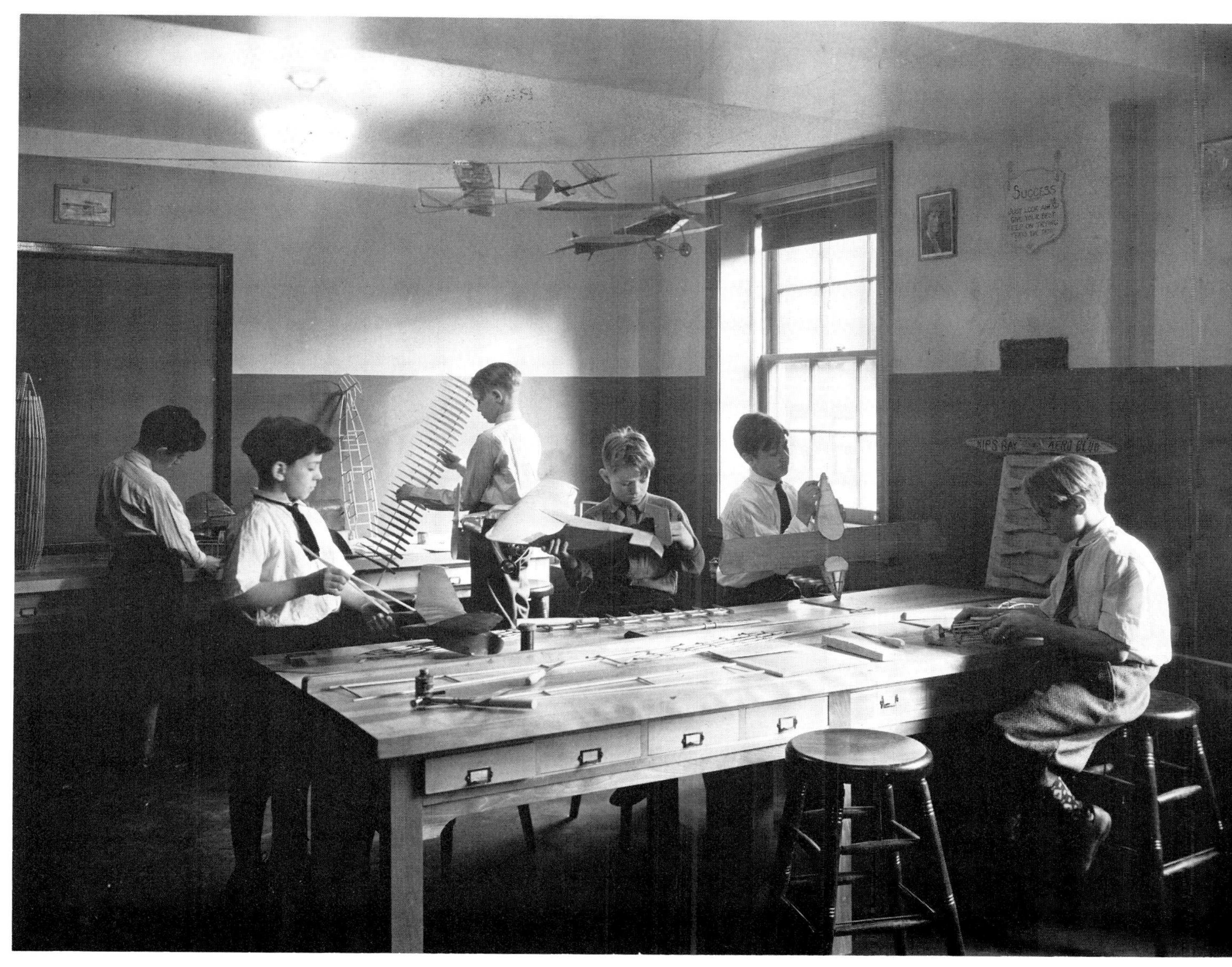

Model Building. Not everything the kids at CAS picked up had strictly practical applications. Clubs promoted hobbies as a respite from the daily grind. In the 20s, the airplane was still in its infancy and boys with manual dexterity were intrigued with model plane building. Working with care and patience, the boys cemented the balsa-wood braces and struts in place, then covered this lightweight skeleton with rice paper. *(Paul Parker. c.a.s.).*

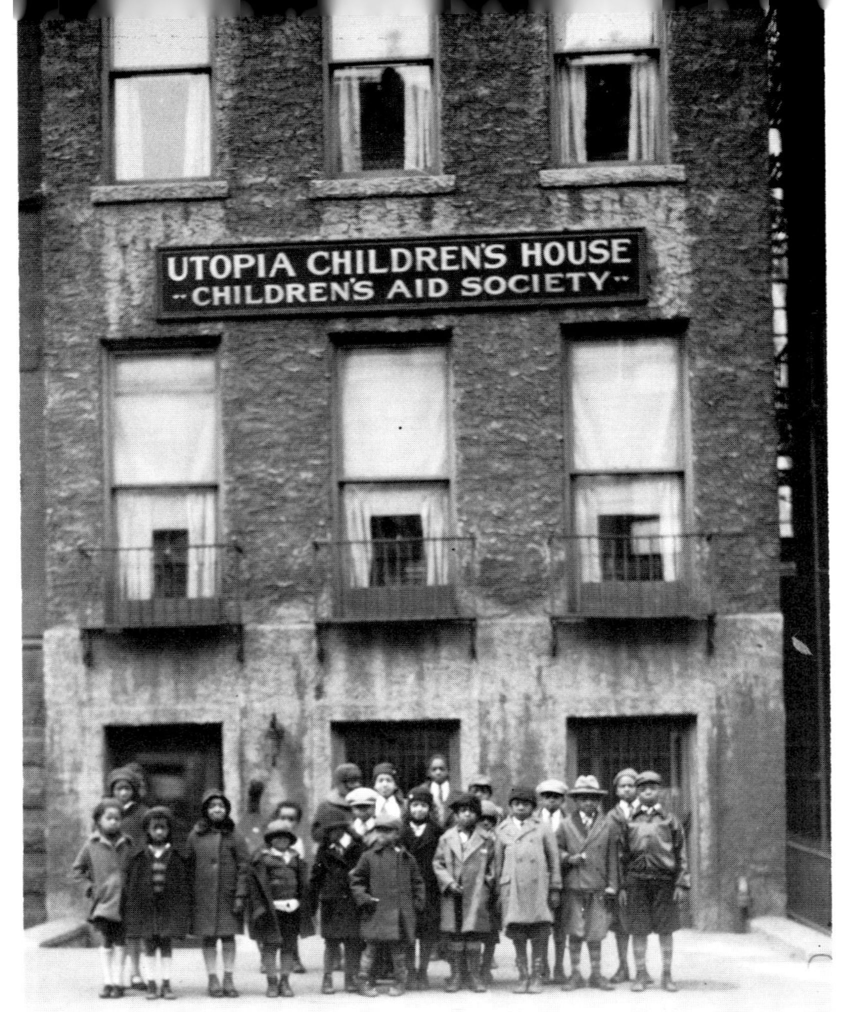
UTOPIA CHILDREN'S HOUSE
-CHILDREN'S AID SOCIETY-

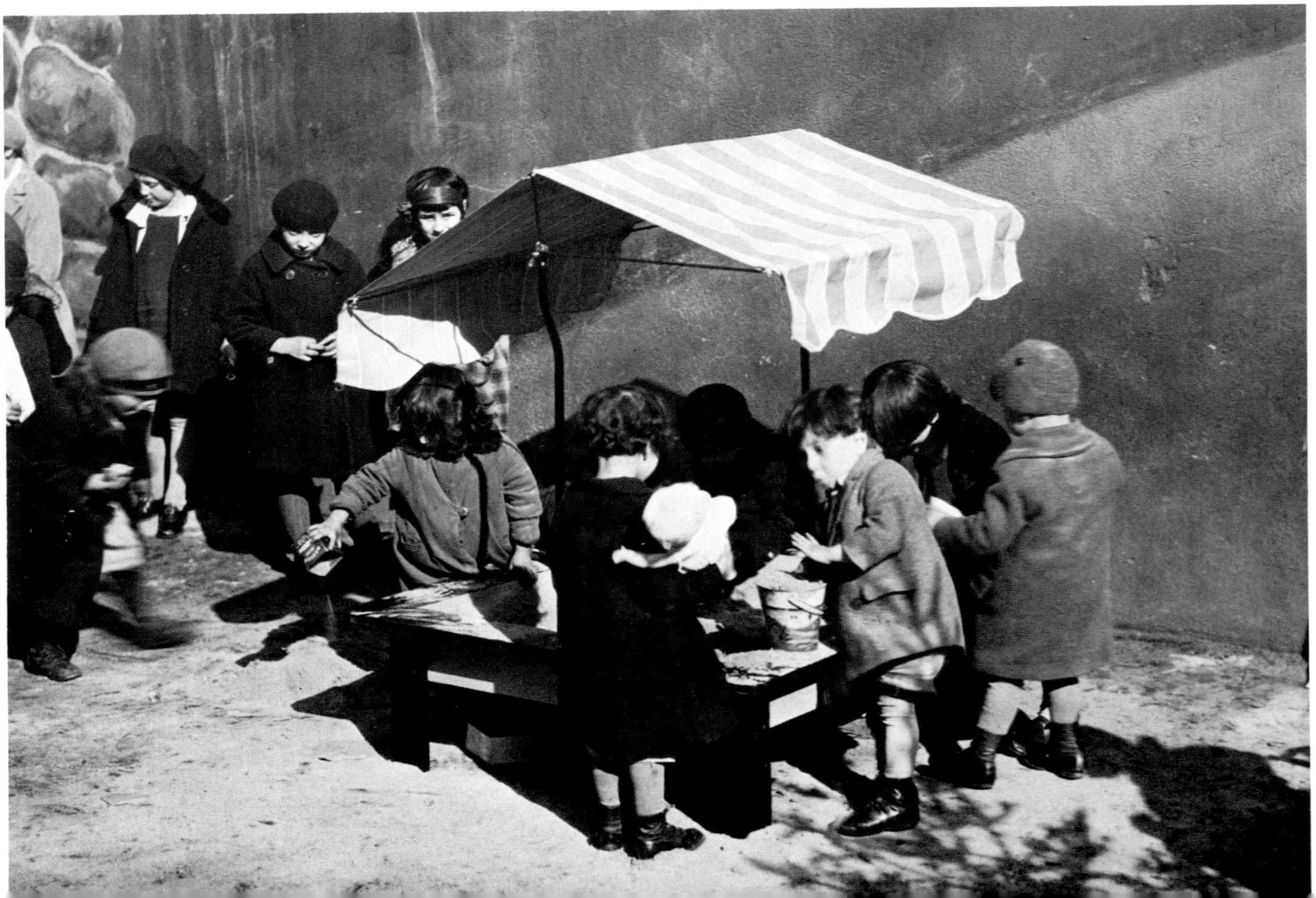

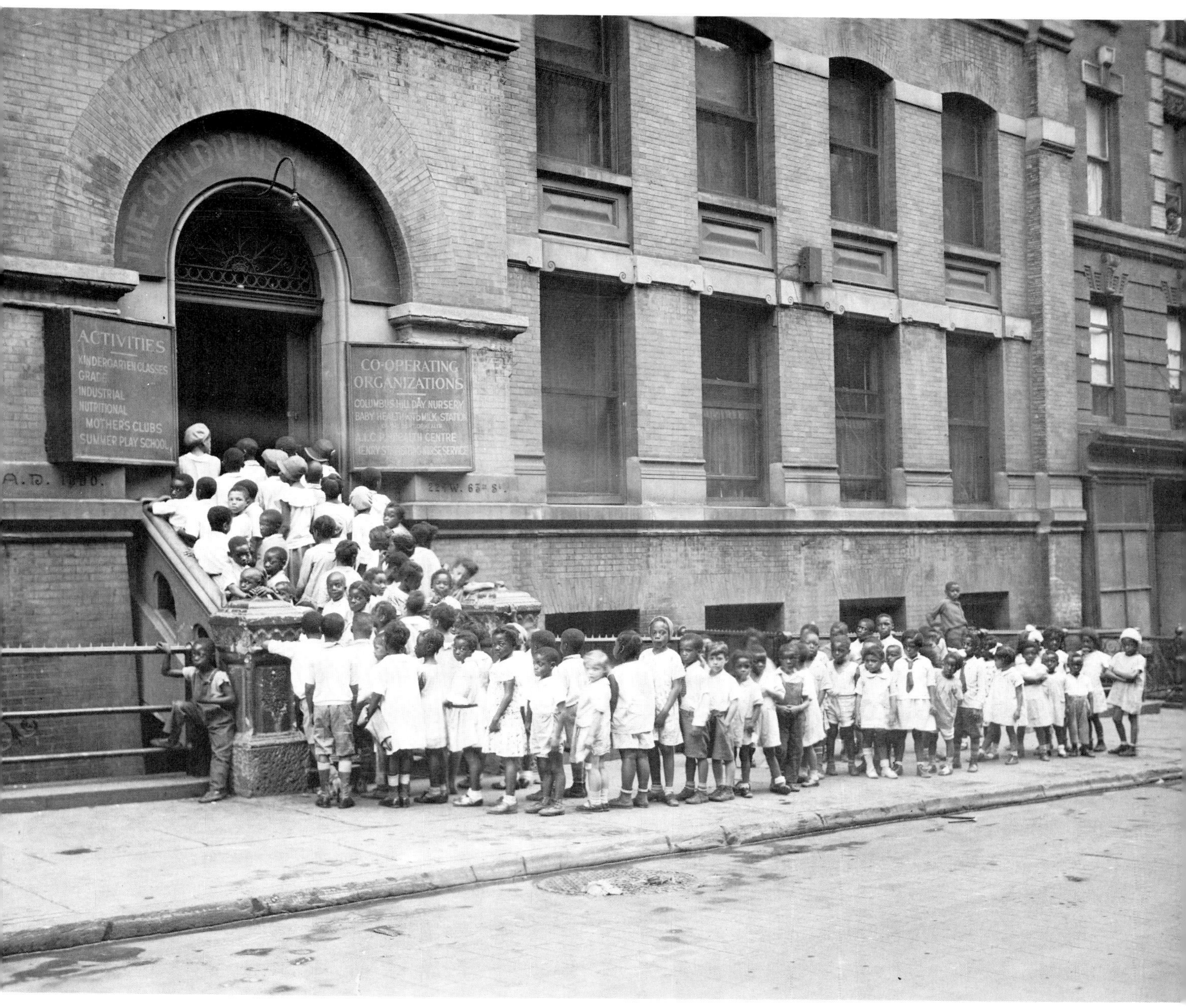

Utopia Children's House [opposite, top]. No kids needed the helping hands of the CAS more than New York's Blacks. According to one survey, five times more Black mothers were forced to work outside the home than were White mothers. More than 400 children were registered at the Utopia center on West 130th Street while 100 school children suffering from malnutrition were fed daily. *(c.a.s.).* **Sandbox at West Side Center** [opposite, bottom]. Charles Loring Brace was one of the first social reformers to recognize the value of play in the life of a street kid. Beginning with the Schermerhorn Playground, seen here after its inauguration in 1923, the CAS opened a series of playgrounds throughout the city. Through its efforts, playground facilities like the sandbox became part of the heritage of every city kid. *(c.a.s.).* **Columbus Hill Center** [above]. The Columbus Hill Neighborhood Center opened in 1928 as a recreational establishment for Black children and their parents. Located on West 63rd Street, it offered 18 clubs concerned with a range of activities from homemaking to swimming to the formation of an orchestra. *(c.a.s.).*

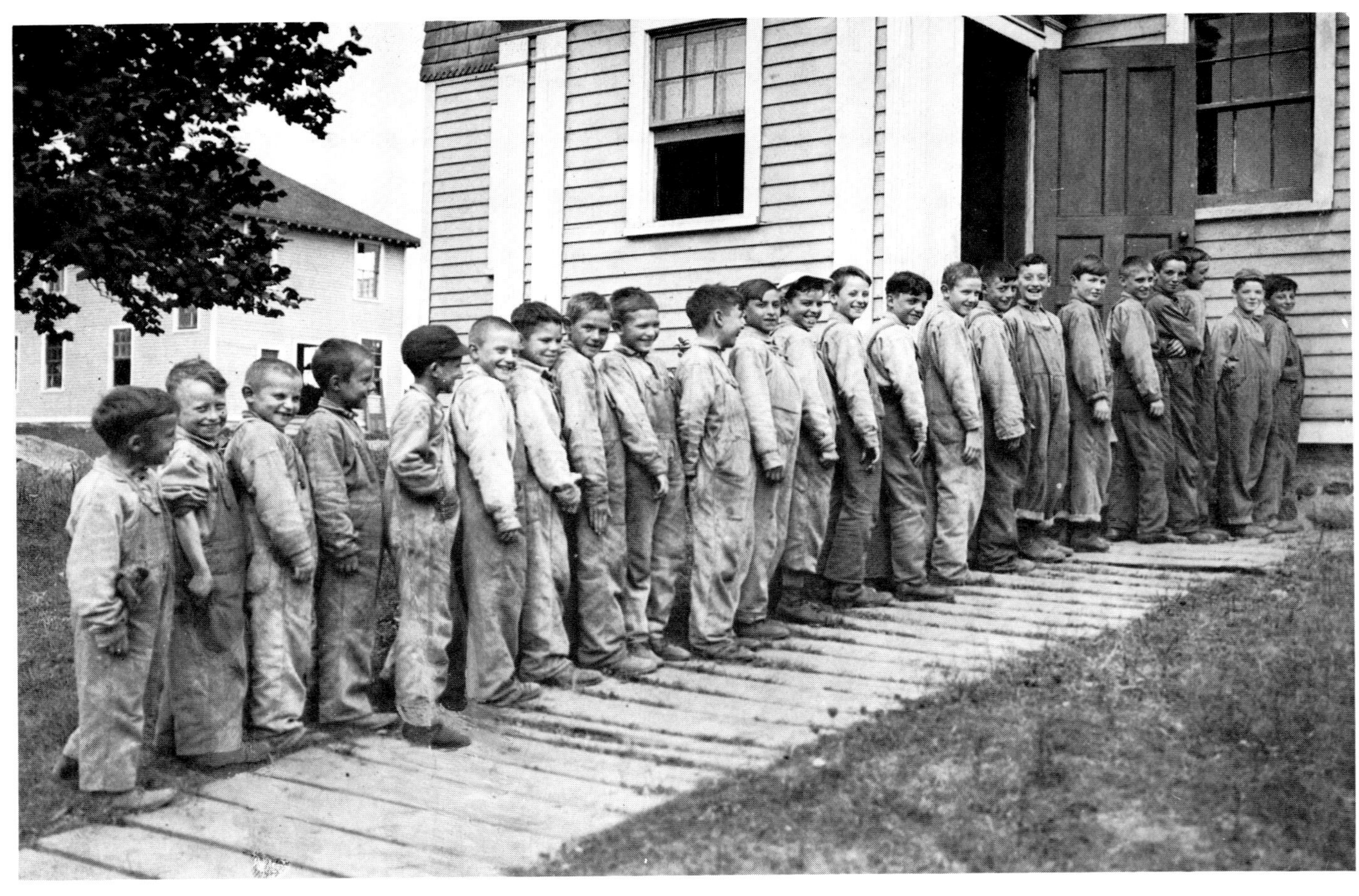

Bowdoin Farm School [above]. Prospective farmers, these street boys received extensive training at the Bowdoin Farm in Dutchess County, New York. The 300-acre working farm was donated to the CAS by a gentleman farmer, George Temple Bowdoin, in 1929. City boys who volunteered for the program were schooled in the fundamentals of farming during summer stays. When they were old enough, they were placed on private farms to work for wages. The grounds also served as a coeducational camp during the summer. *(c.a.s.)*. **Bus Service to**

School for Handicapped [opposite]. The work of educating the handicapped, begun at the turn of the century by the CAS, continued through the 20s under the public school system. The children's willingness to attend school is in marked contrast to their outcast state just a few decades before, when families hid them with shame from common view. These well turned-out kids are headed for the Rhinelander School for Handicapped Children on East 88th Street. *(c.a.s.)*.

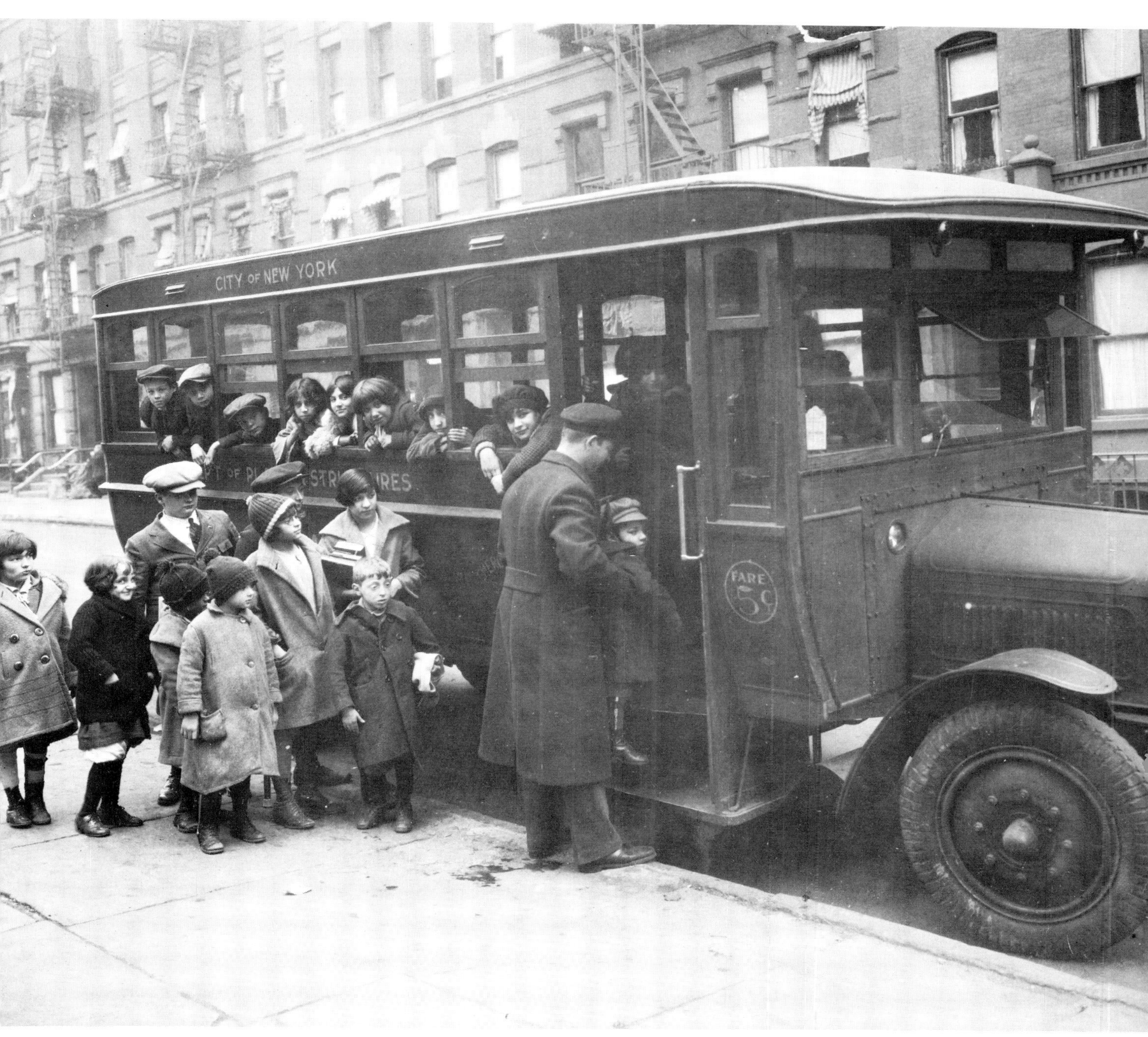
CITY OF NEW YORK
FARE 5¢

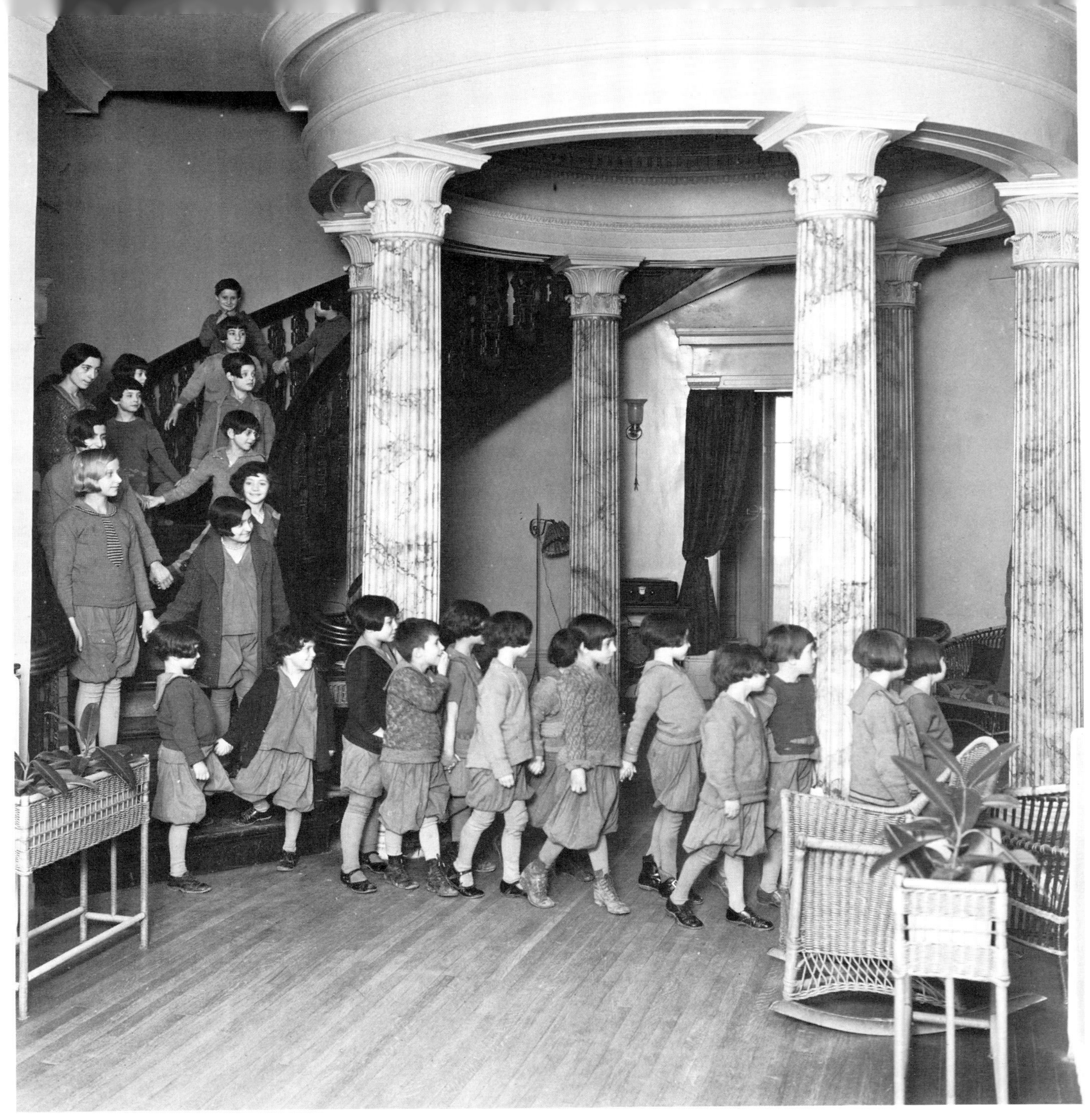

File Out Two by Two [above]. Neatly coiffed and dressed, pairs of city girls file down the main stairway of the George Bowdoin mansion at a summer camp run by the CAS. The Bowdoin Farm, overlooking the Hudson River 68 miles north of the city, provided two-week vacations to kids between the ages of 7 and 20. Since the cost to each child was only $2 weekly, the grand total for each vacation was $4. Impressing self-sufficiency, the CAS advised children to tuck their extra pennies and nickels into special savings cards during the year to pay their own way to the camp. *(Paul Parker. c.a.s.).* **Learning to Cook in a CAS Kitchen** [opposite, top]. *(A. Tennyson Beals. c.a.s.).* **Apple Week at a CAS Center** [opposite, bottom]. The custom of passing out fresh apples to needy kids continued through the 30s, when kids could use all the free food they could get. With the country in the grip of the Great Depression, some 200,000 young workless drifters, all of them under 21, wandered aimlessly in search of employment. More than 5000 found their way to New York, where they swelled the already teeming ranks of unemployed kids. The CAS tried to help by pushing its services to the utmost: CAS aid increased 86 percent. But the relentless numbers of rootless kids finally prompted the officers of the Society to make radio pleas for would-be wanderers to stay at home. *(c.a.s.).*

Children Under Hydrant [over]. Hot kids and cold water from fire hydrants is a classic urban matching. While the stronger kids hold a board or tin can over the mouth of the hydrant to create a plume of water, the others dance and squeal in the spray. *(Weegee)*

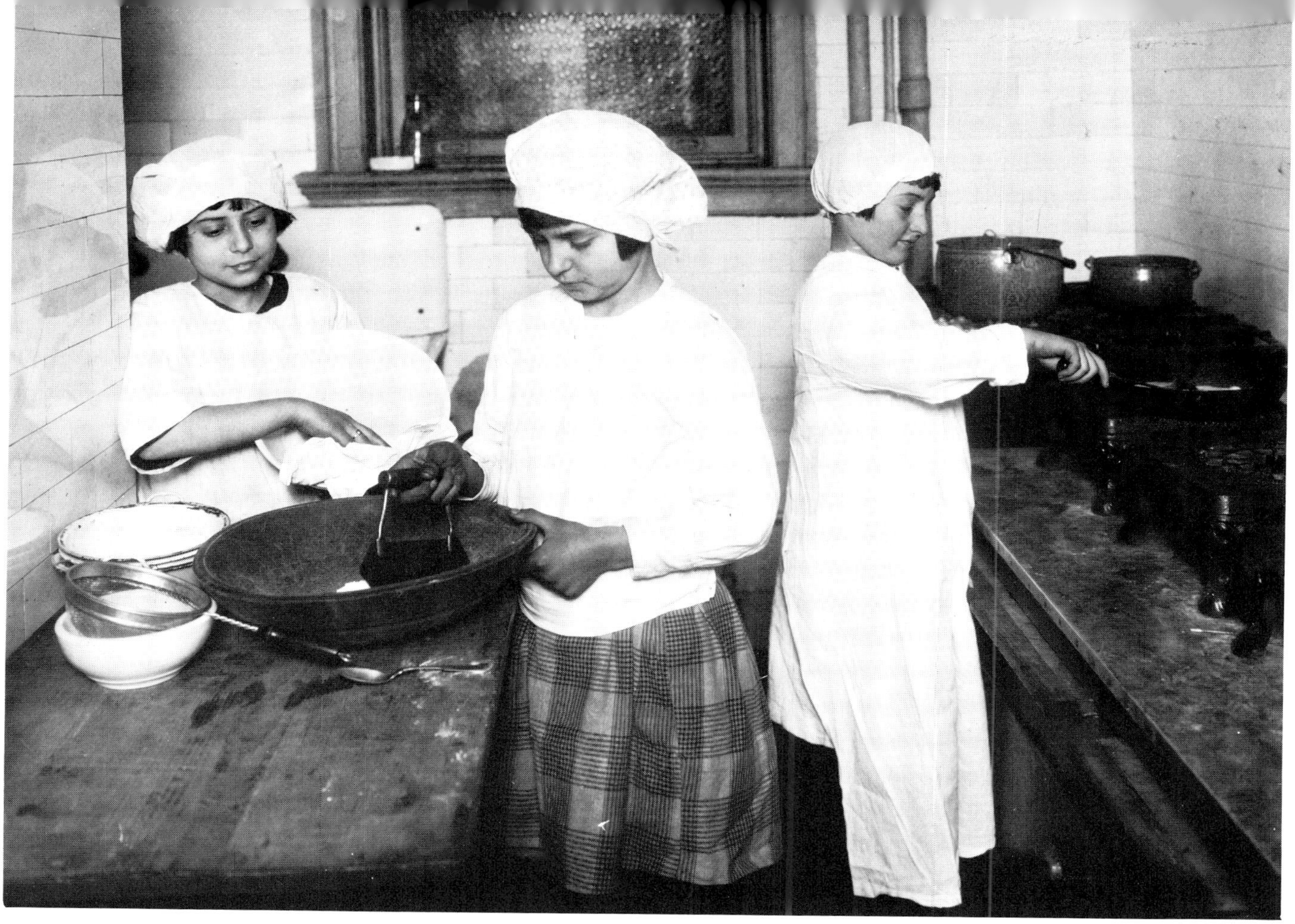

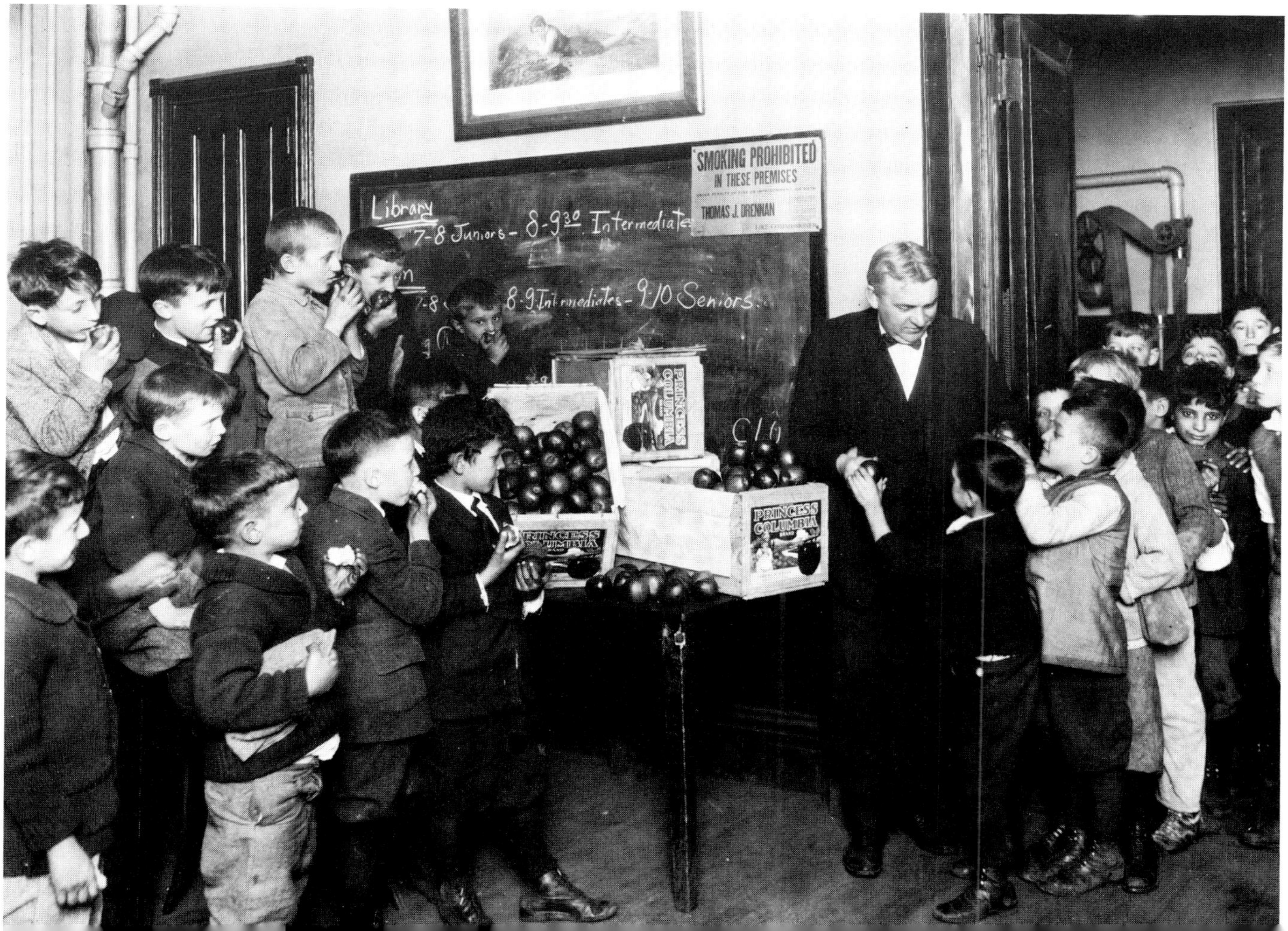

SMOKING PROHIBITED
IN THESE PREMISES
THOMAS J. DRENNAN
Library
7-8 Juniors - 8-9 30 Intermediates
8-9 Intermediates - 9-10 Seniors.
PRINCESS COLUMBIA

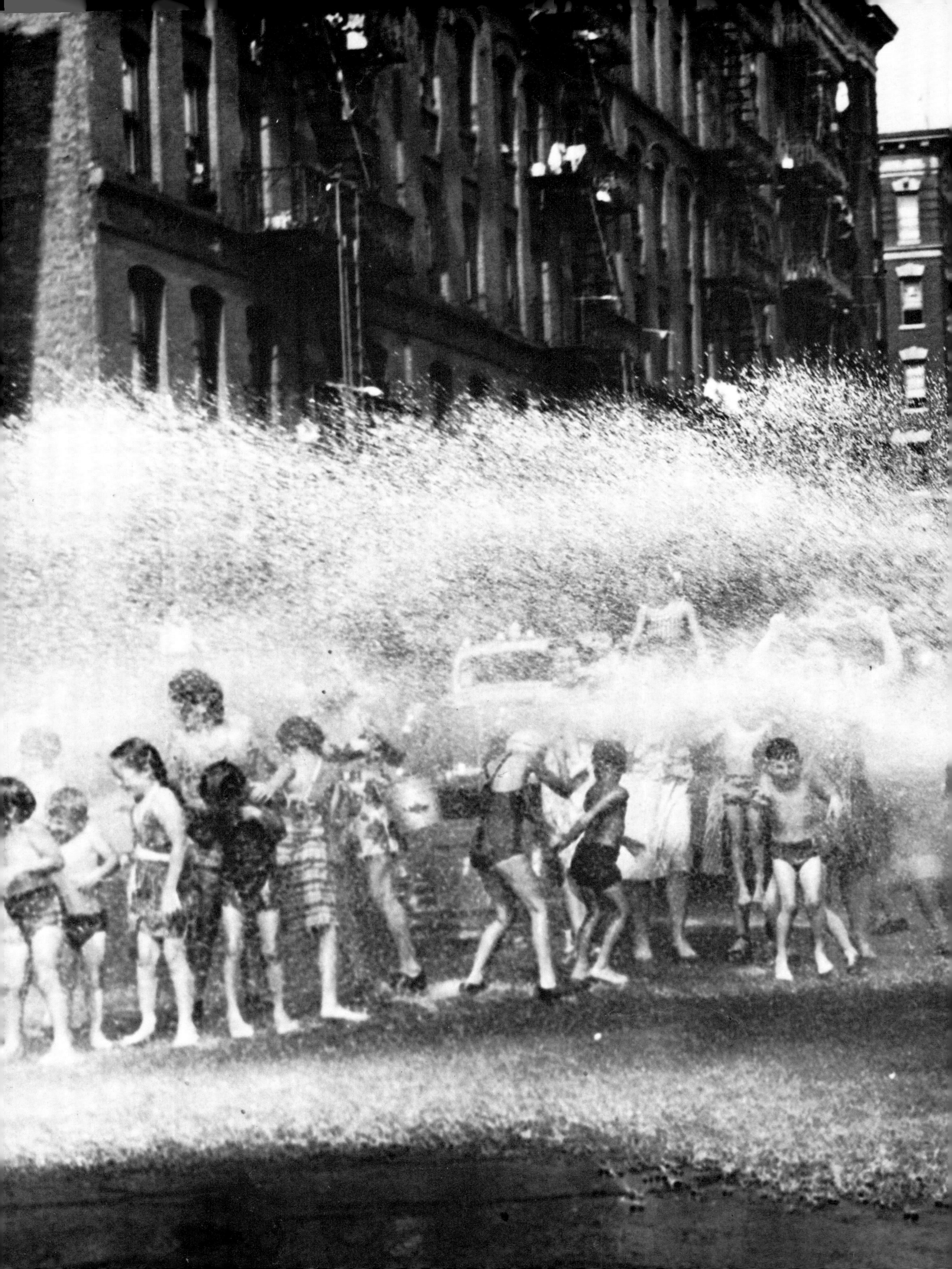

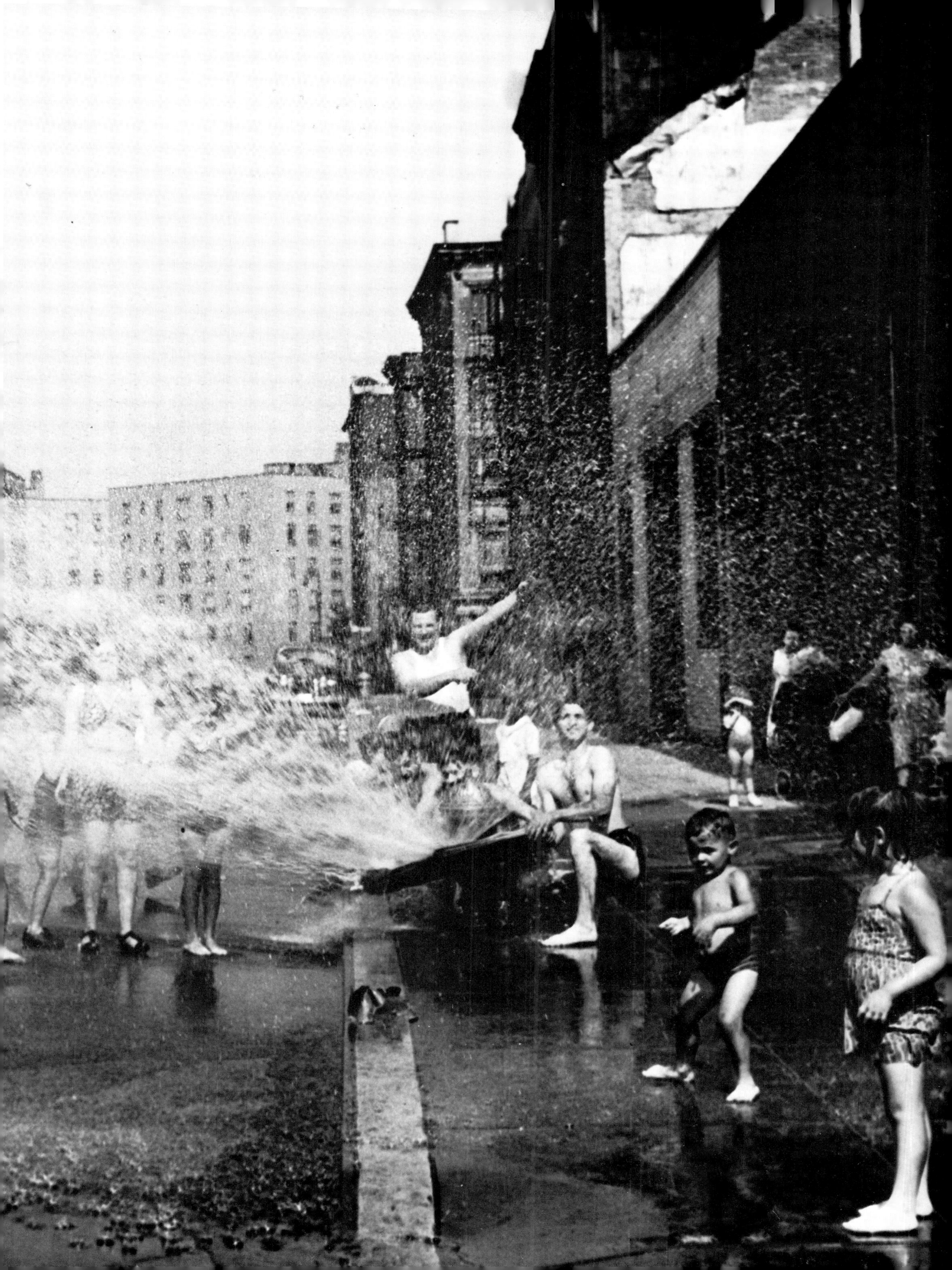

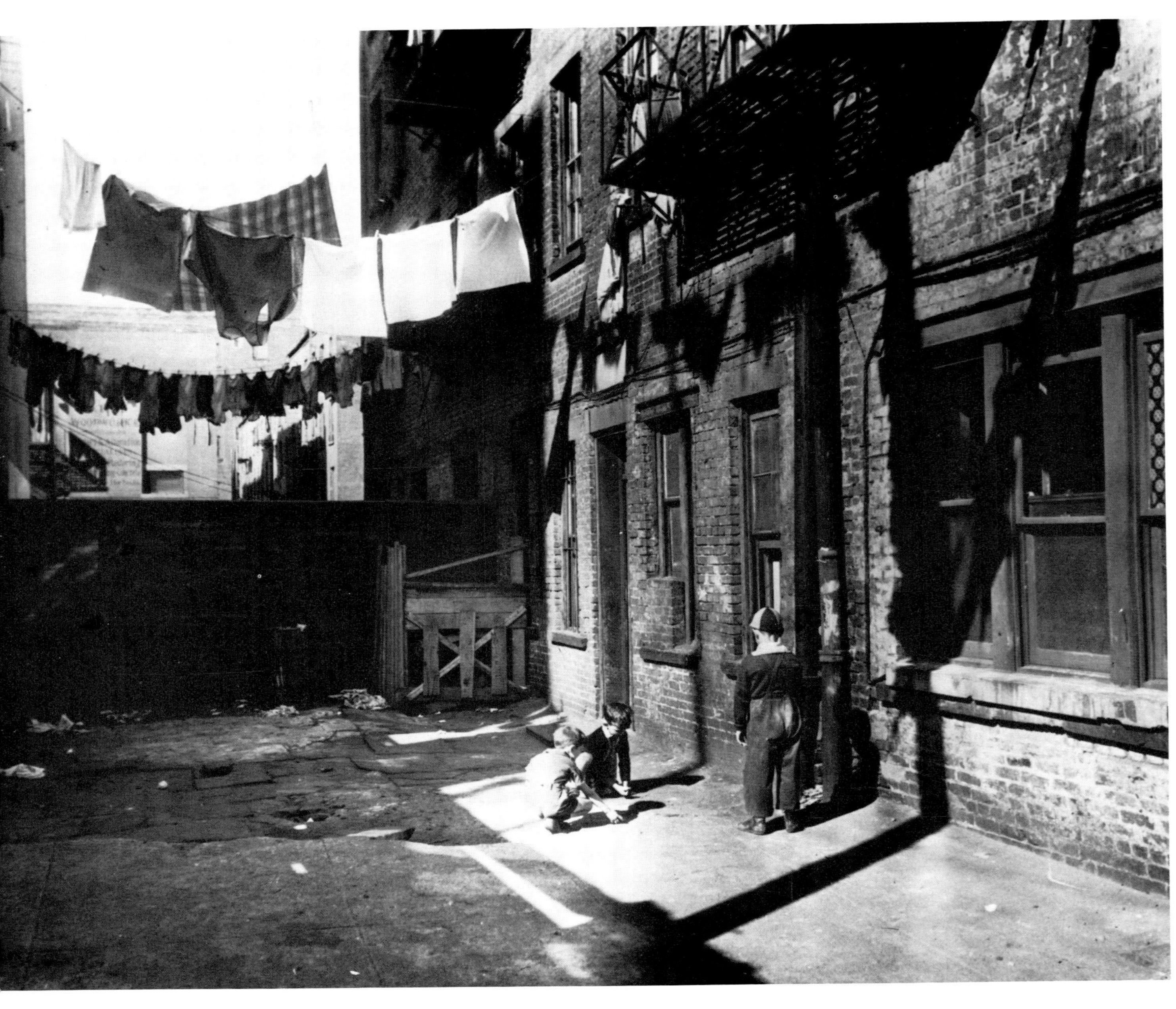

Outdoor Recreation To document the plight of the city kid, the WPA sent out photographers to record the children at play. As the picture demonstrates, kids continued to find as their preferred habitat back alleys under the strings of laundry. The site, however, is clean and airy compared to the alleys of earlier decades. *(WPA Photo No. 69-N-16192, The National Archives)*

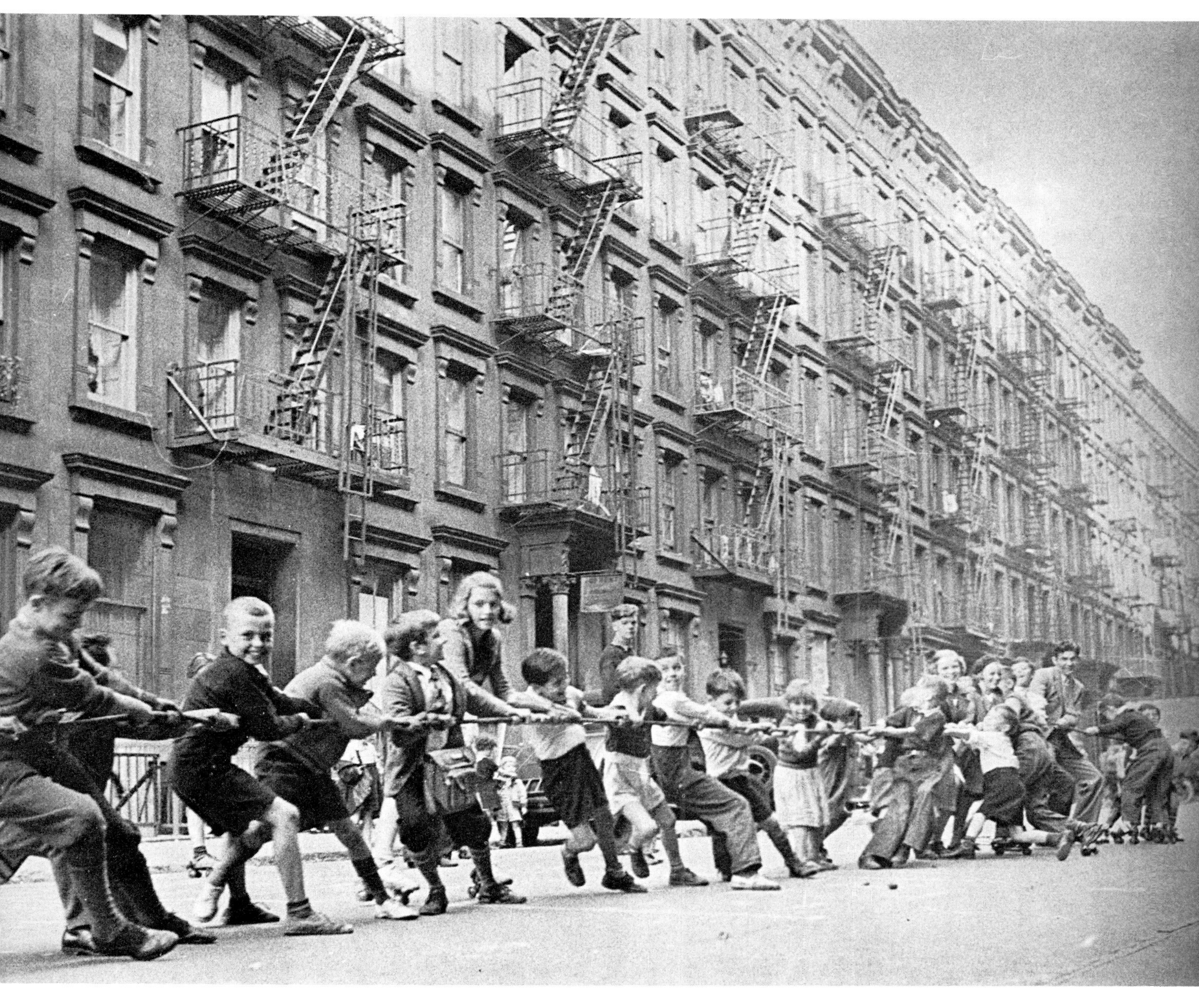

Tug of War. In the 30s many streets and school yards were designated as play areas for the local kids. Government agencies and other groups like the Police Athletic League (PAL) sponsored games and contests to let kids burn off their energies in lawful ways. The games were usually impromptu like the tug of war. Here, kids in school clothes and encumbered with book bags compete with others still on roller skates. The repetitious fire escapes form a complementary backdrop to the lineup of contending kids. These straightforward documentary photographs often contain more artistry than those of popular salon photographers. *(Pollard. WPA Photo No. 69-N-16235D, The National Archives)*

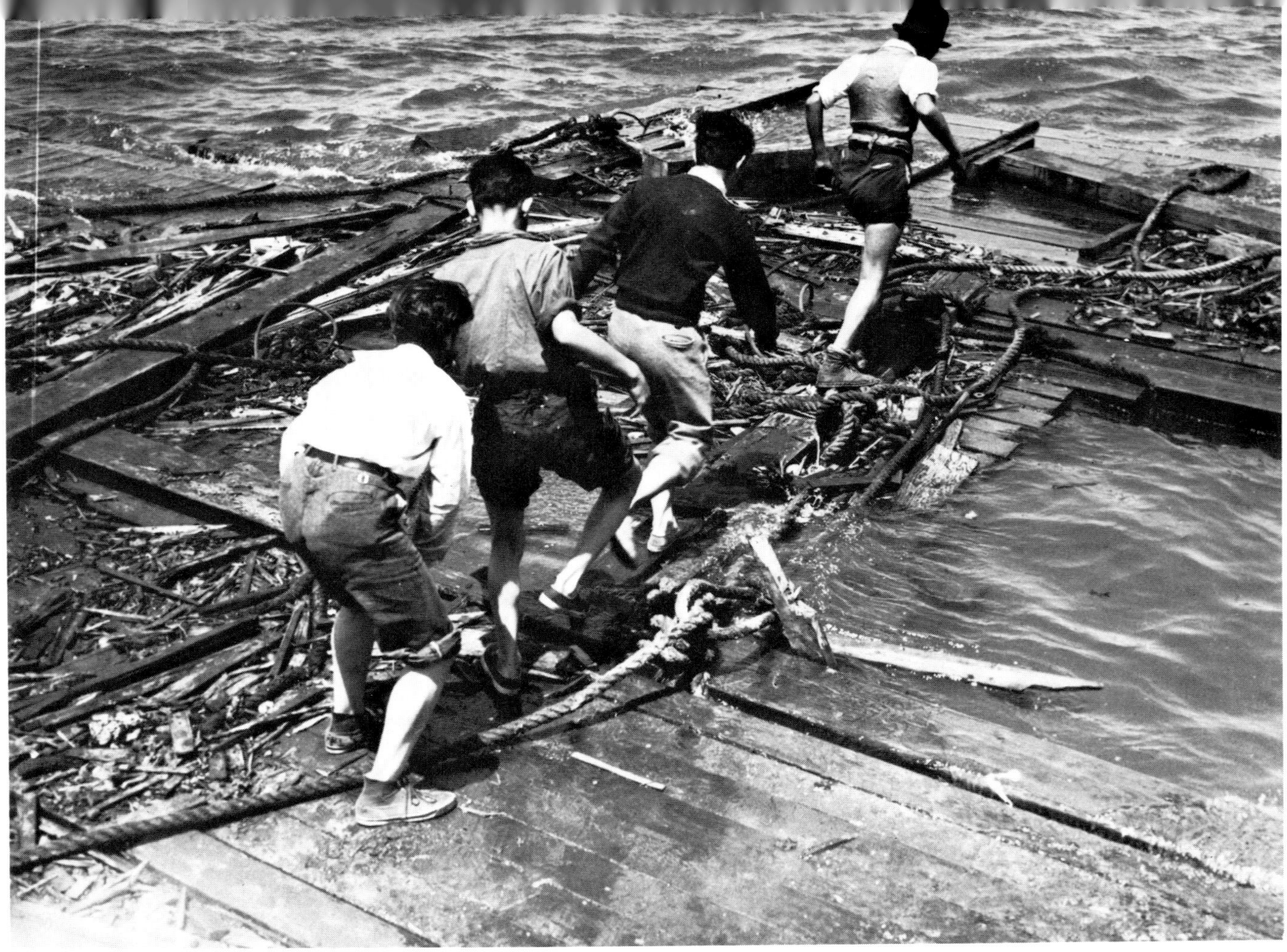

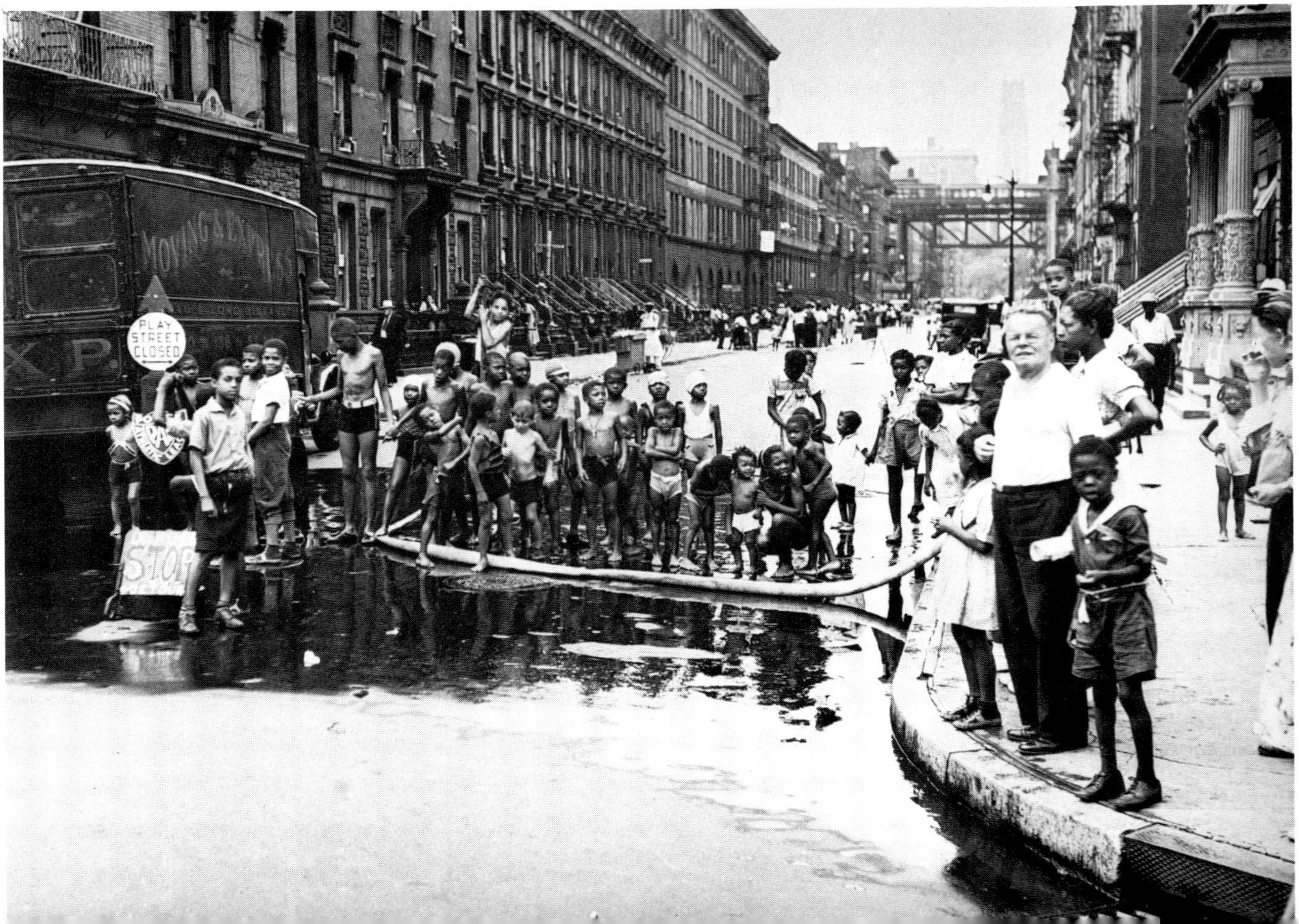

MOVING & EXPRESS
PLAY STREET CLOSED
STOP

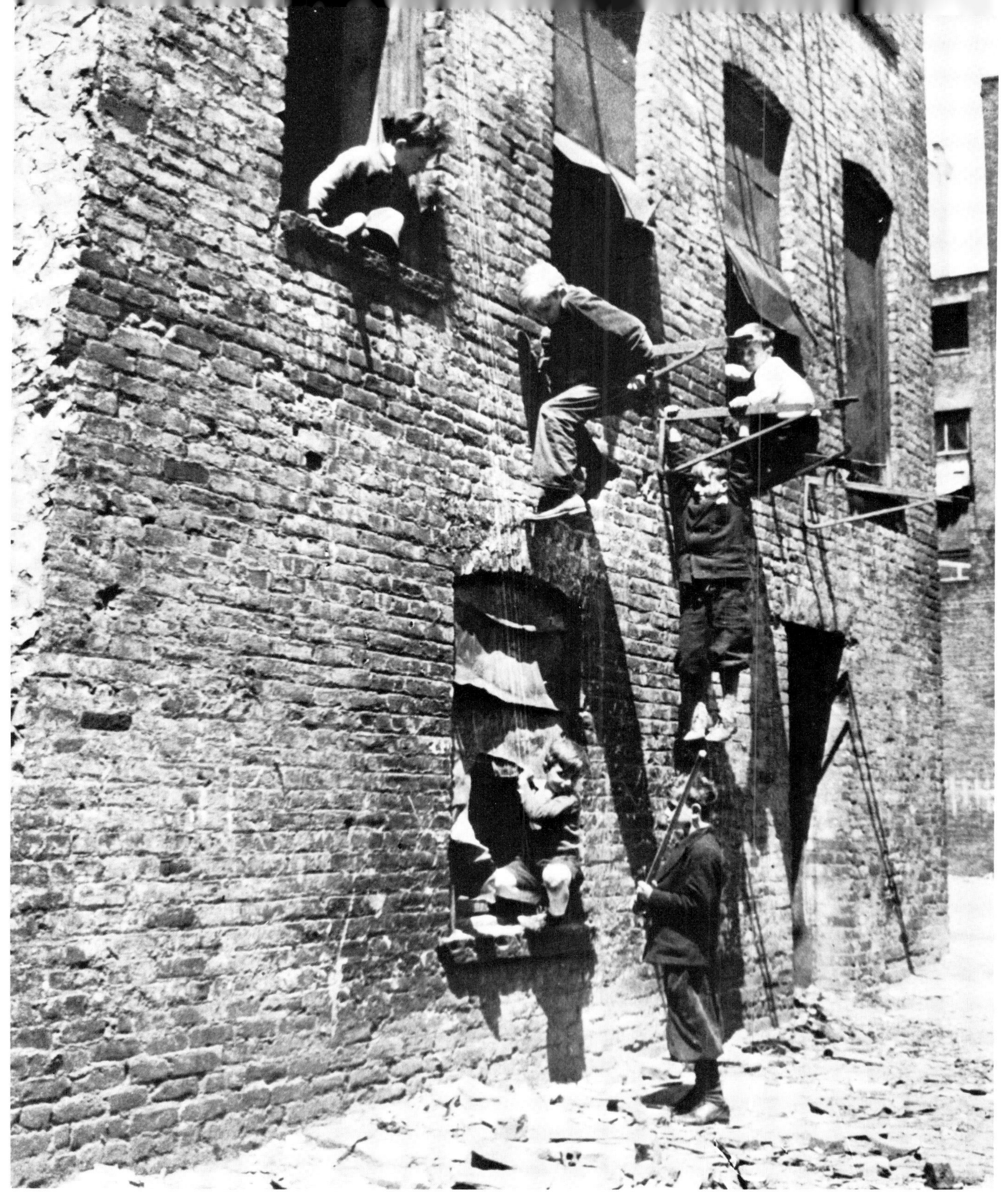

Seeking Adventure [opposite, top]. A wrecked pier awash with jetsam is a place most humans would avoid. But to the city-bred teenager, it is a risky challenge, a fulfillment of the street bravado that contends nothing without peril is worth attempting. *(Pollard. WPA Photo No. 69-ANP-IN-8, The National Archives)* **Police Athletic League Play Street** [opposite, bottom]. Street kids await eagerly the turning on of a fire hydrant in a street closed to traffic. The hydrant's spray was the slum kid's answer to the old swimming hole. *(WPA Photo No. 69-N-16192D, The National Archives)* **Dangerous Playground** [above]. An abandoned building makes a great jungle gym, as every generation of street kids discovers. *(Mary E. Callaghan. Museum of the City of New York)*

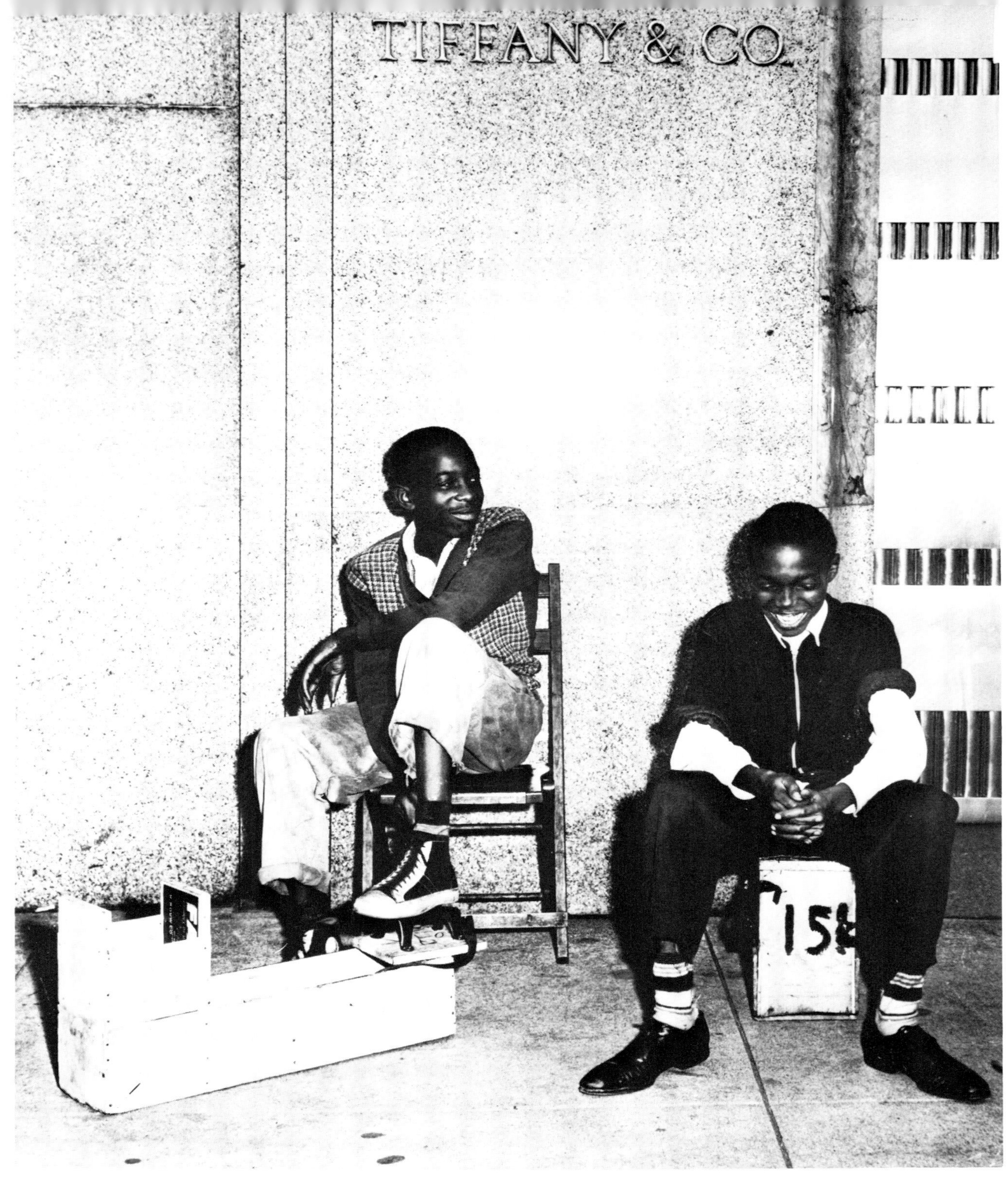

Shoeshine Boys [above]. *(Weegee)* **Shoeshine Boys** [opposite]. The 40s meant World War II, when fewer ablebodied young men were around and kids were able to dominate all sorts of job categories. A favorite continued to be shining shoes, which, at a dime a pair plus a tip, meant a fairly decent income. At the time candy bars were a nickel, comic books a dime and movies but 20 cents. The three shoeshine boys seen here bespeak the 40s with outfits that are vaguely militaristic—boots, pea jacket, wool watch cap and short haircuts which laid waste to the areas around the ears. *(Morris Huberland)*

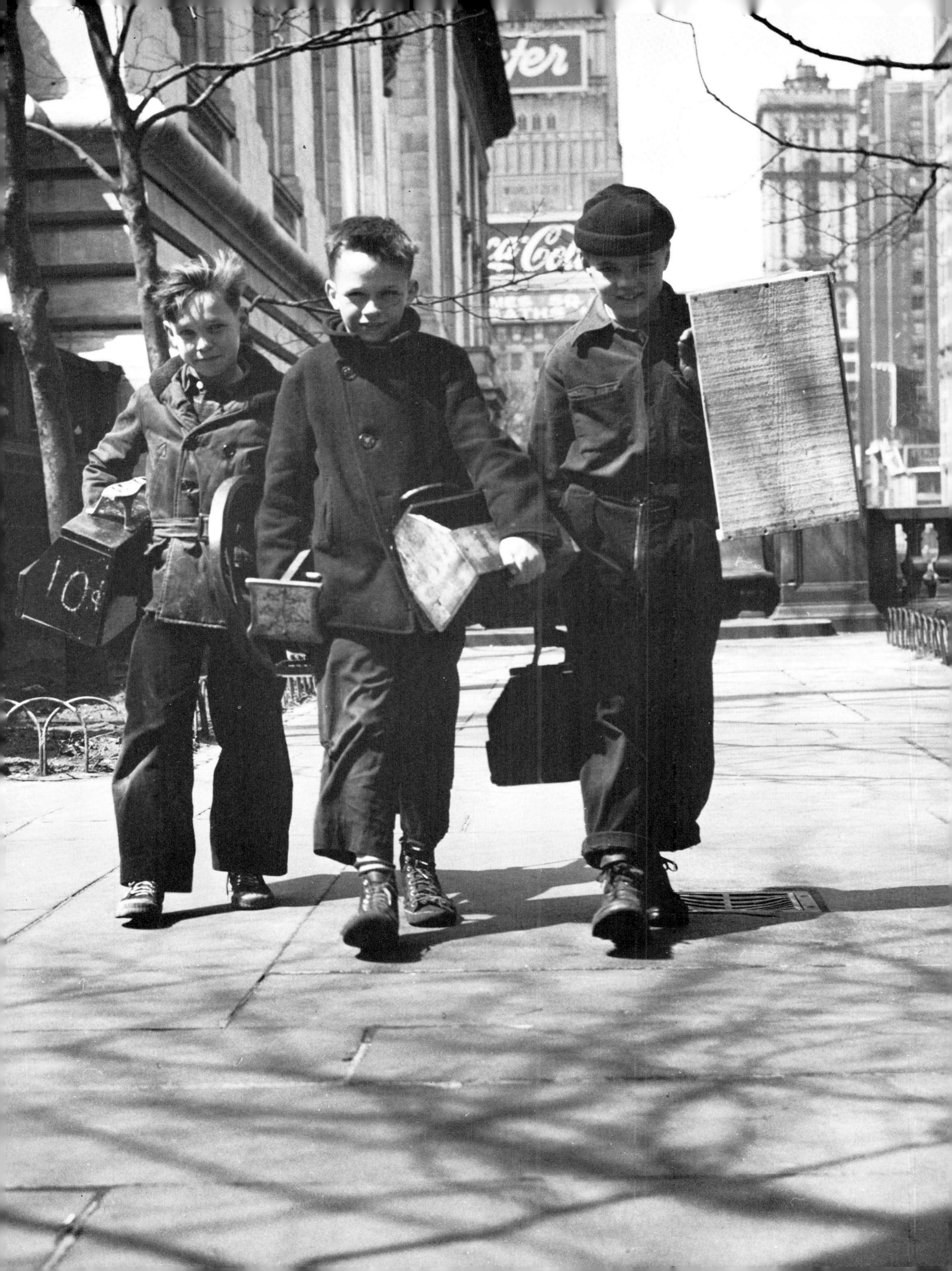
10¢

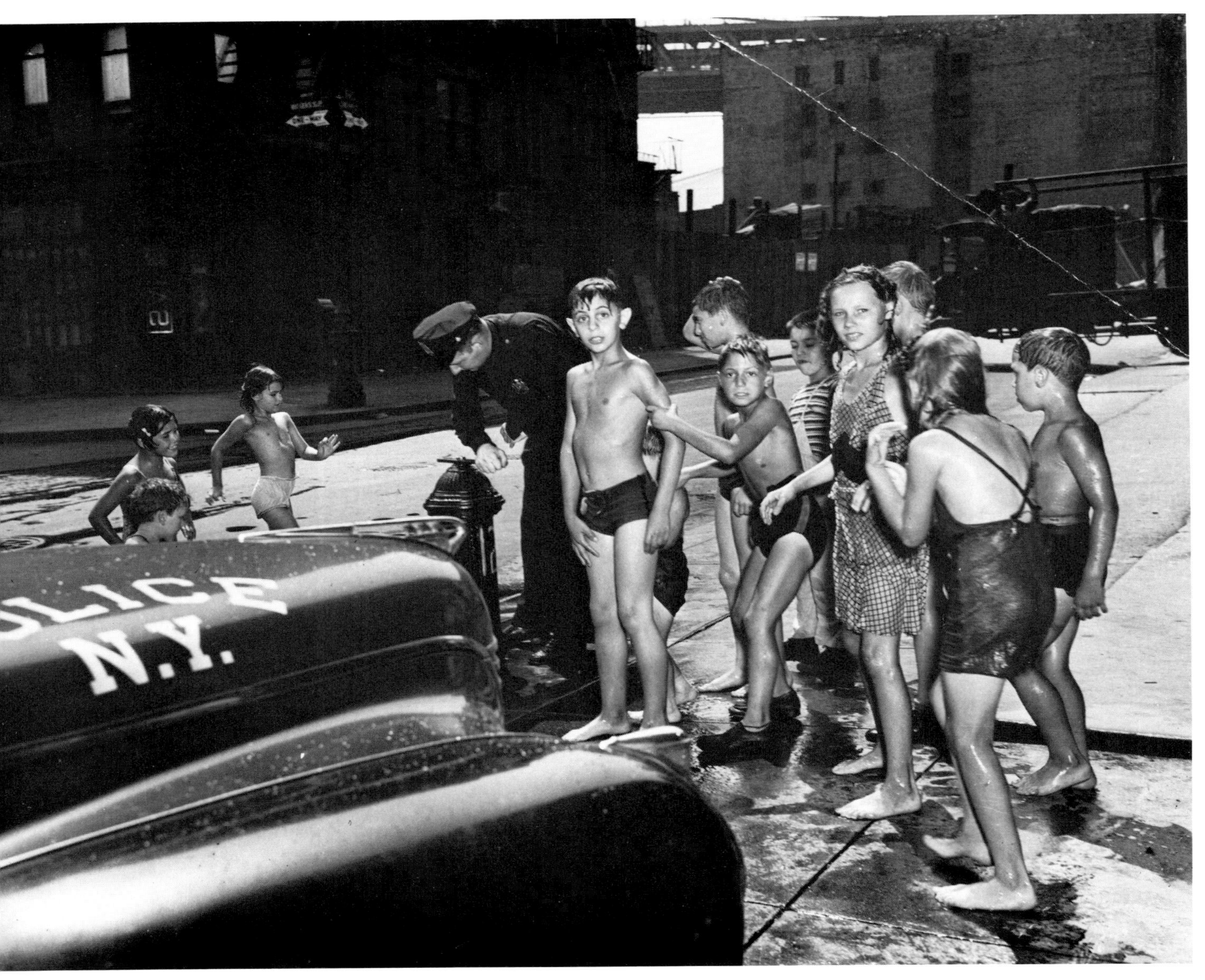

Policeman Turning Off Hydrant. Wet and disappointed neighborhood kids watch as a policeman turns off the hydrant that has been spraying them. No cop enjoys this job but open hydrants cause the water pressure to drop drastically, denying water to the upper floors of the tenement apartments and endangering the efforts of firemen at their job. *(Weegee)*

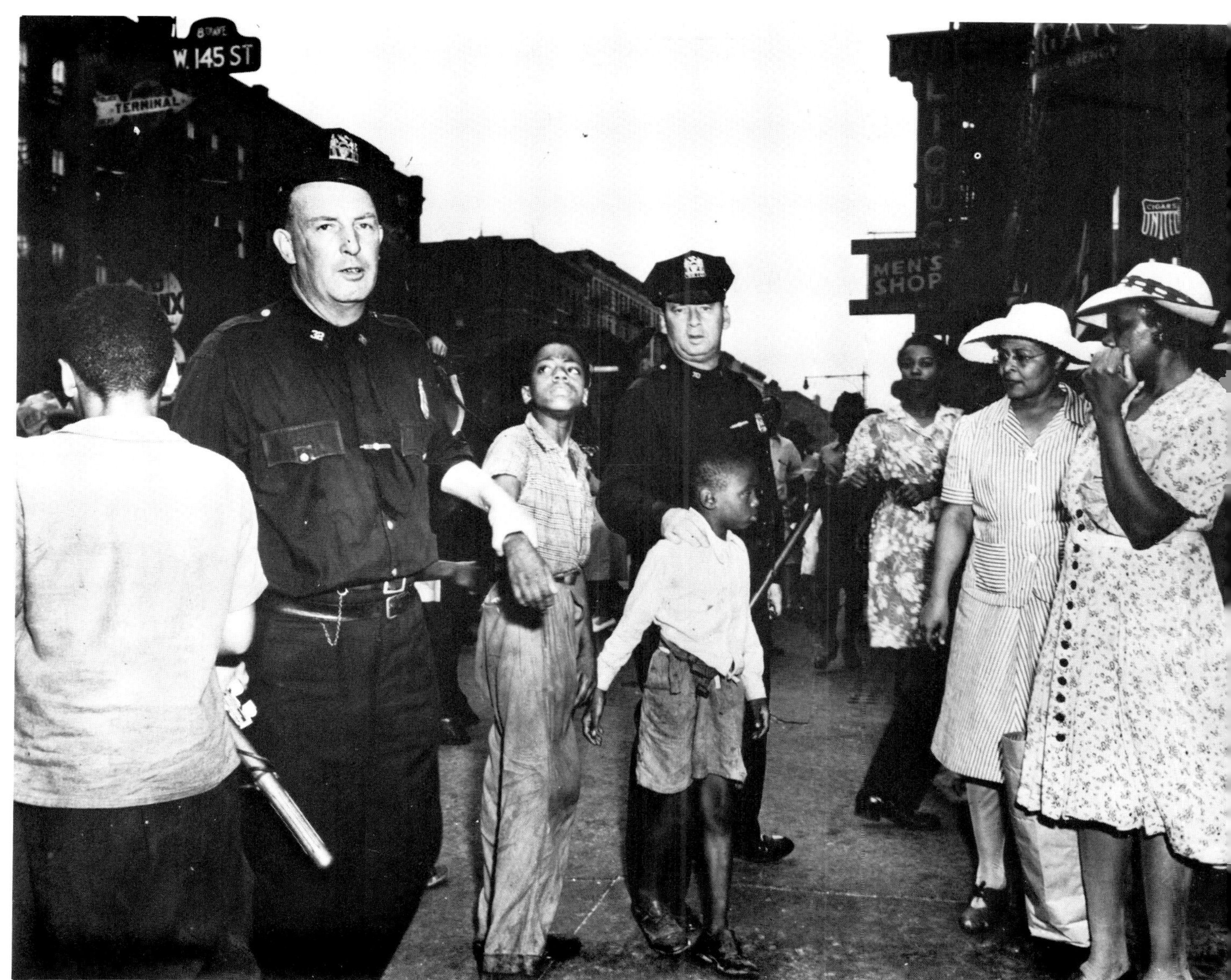

Two Black Boys, Mothers And Cops. [above]. As two White policemen hold two Black boys, their mothers look on in agony, trapped between love for their sons and respect for the law. The picture suggests the New York City policeman's ambivalent role in the neighborhood. Essential to maintain order, he still represents antagonistic forces. *(Weegee)*

Chalk Games [over]. More than crayons and paper, chalk and the sidewalk were the art media for city kids. A box of colored chalk could be bought for a few cents and no one objected if the entire neighborhood became a canvas because the scribblings defaced only until the next rain. Boats, submarines, flags and cowboys came alive on the city street. Chalk was also the essential marker for potsy, street checkers, puss-in-the-corner and countless other street games. *(Arthur Leipzig)*

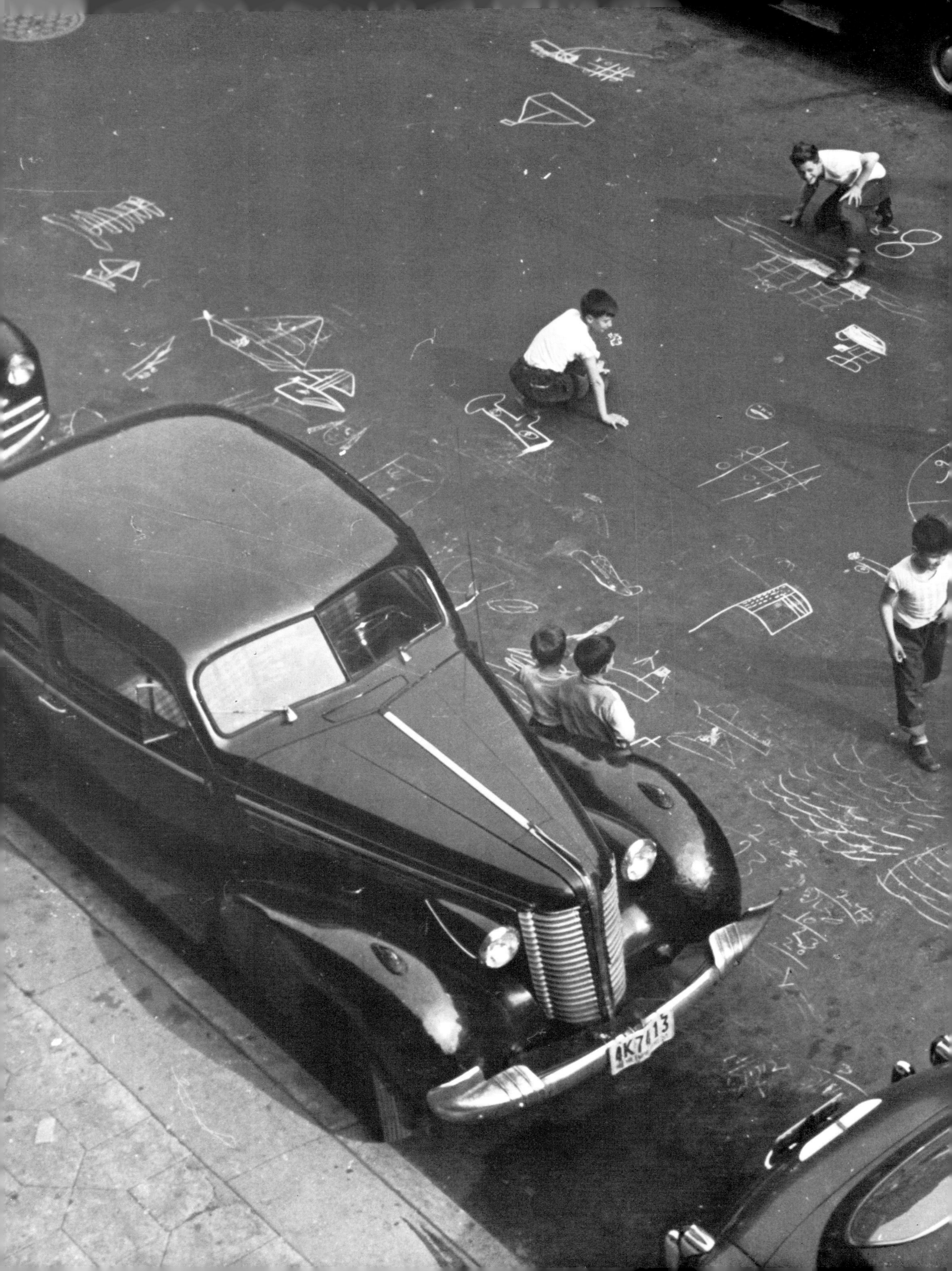
4K7413

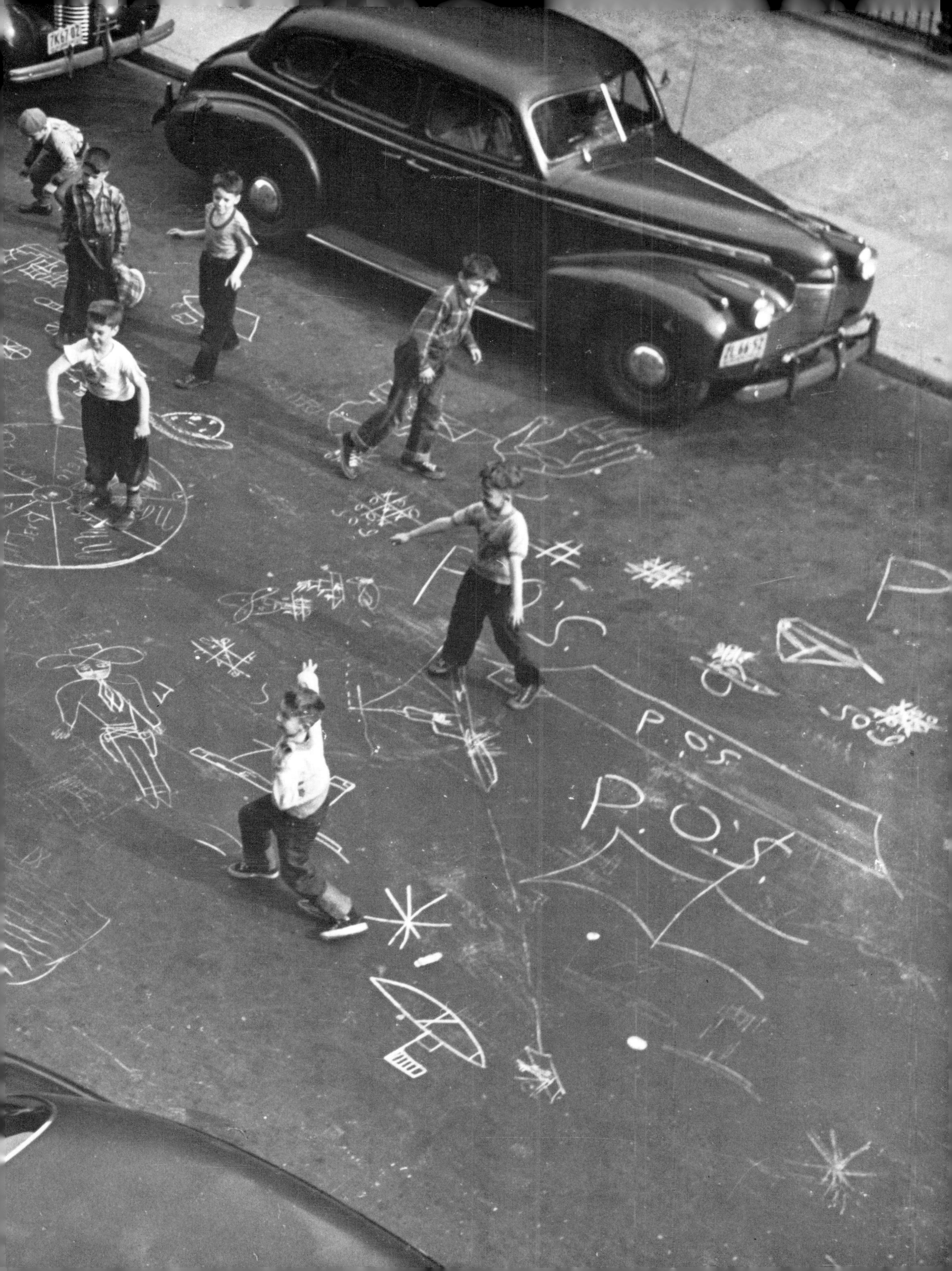
P.O.S.
P.O.S.

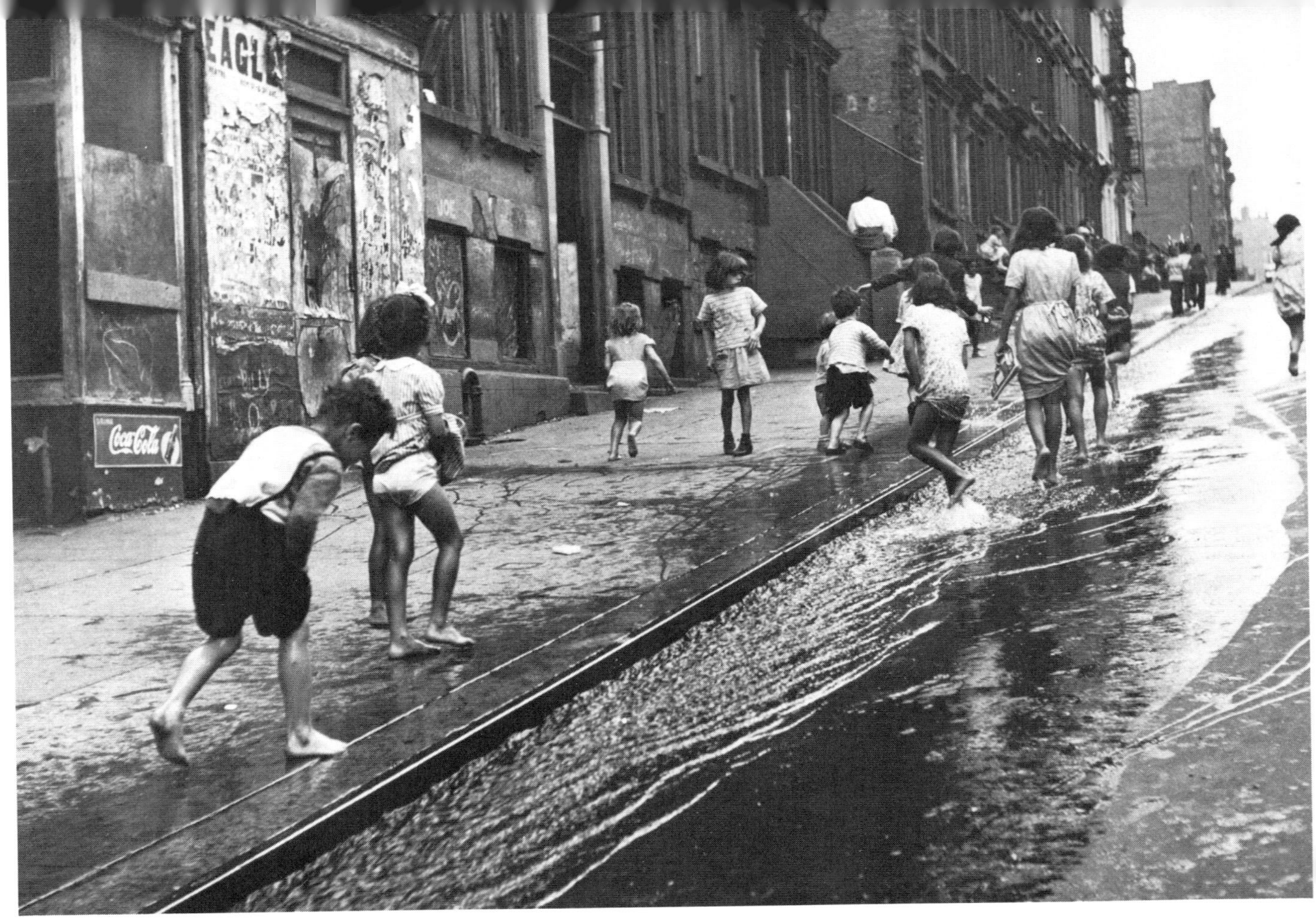

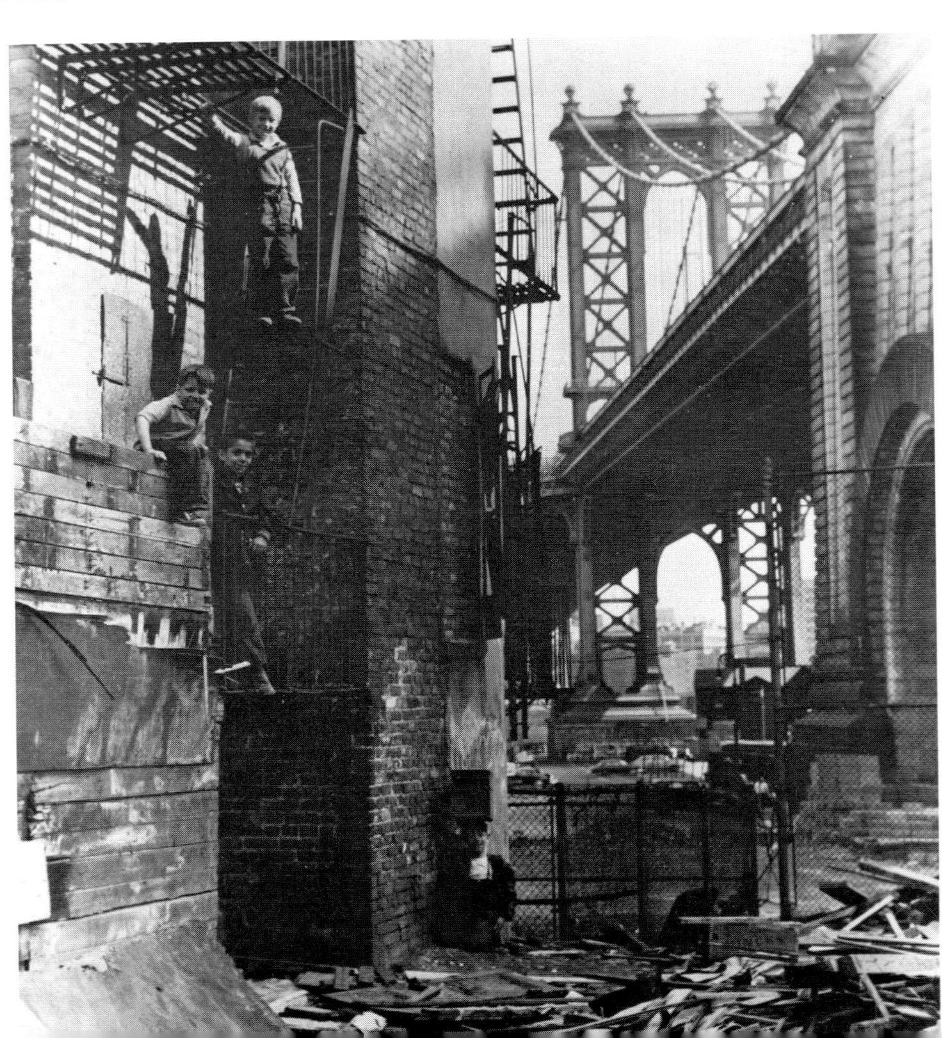

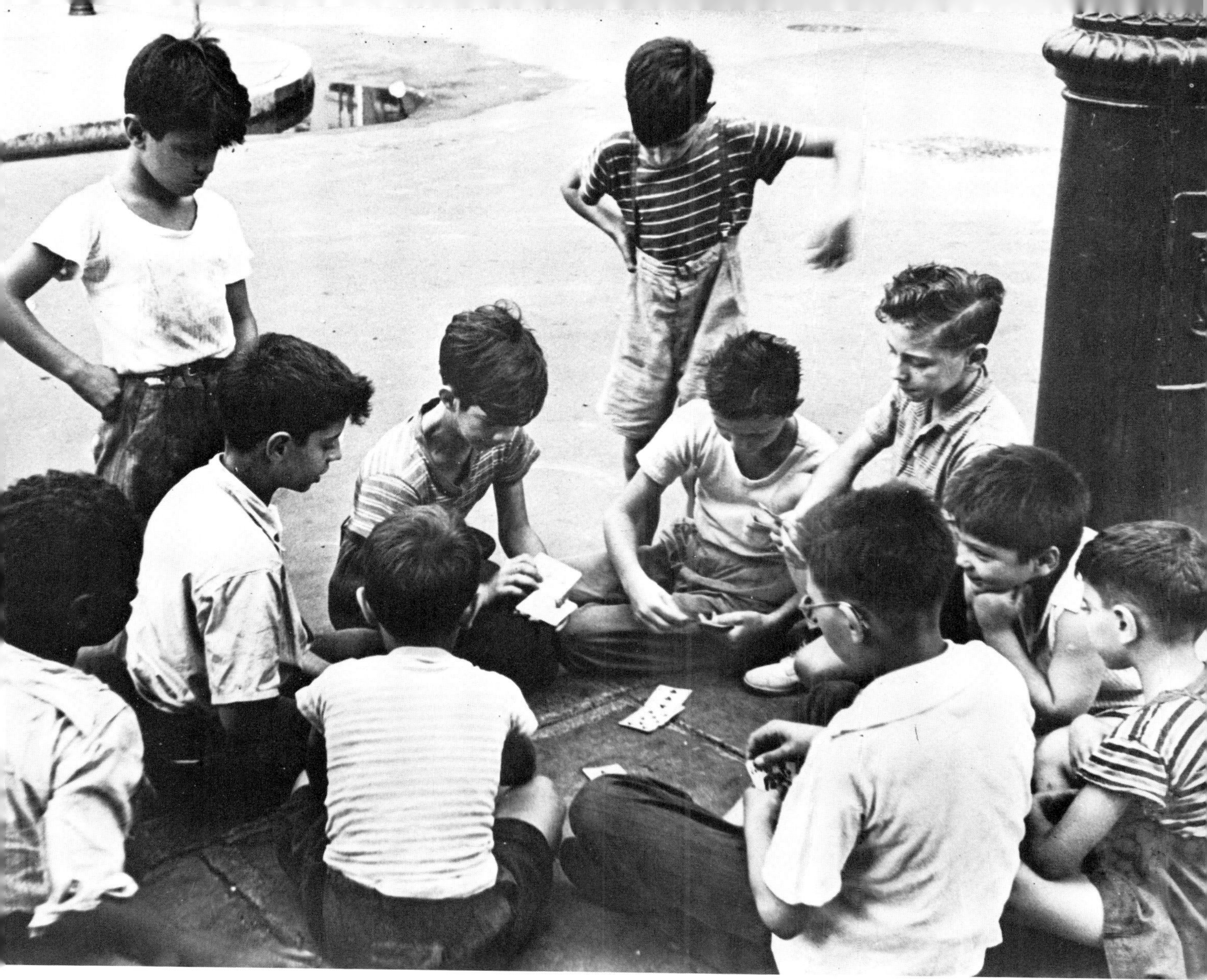

Kids Playing on Street [opposite, top]. Hitching up their skirts, girls wade in the stream flowing from an open hydrant on West 103rd Street, probably feeling the same excitement felt by kids a hundred years earlier, when Manhattan was crisscrossed with natural streams and ponds. *(Ralph Morse.* Life *Magazine © Time Inc.)* **Water Street Area, Lower East Side** [opposite, bottom]. The 40s saw the beginning of monumental renovation on the Lower East Side. Old tenements and factories were leveled and new apartment complexes rose in their place as streets were widened and parks added. Between the time when a building was vacated and the moment it fell before the wrecking crew, the city kids claimed the structure for themselves. *(Morris Huberland. The New-York Historical Society)* **Playing Cards in Brooklyn** [above]. Few street kids were above the temptations posed by a deck of playing cards. The street card game was a way to act grown-up. It had the added bonus of irritating the adult world with the brazenness of youth. Kids quickly learned the card games their parents played. Poker, pinochle and blackjack were widely and often skillfully played with tattered cards. The games were discouraged by elders only when money stakes were involved. *(Alfred Eisenstaedt.* Life *Magazine © Time Inc.)*

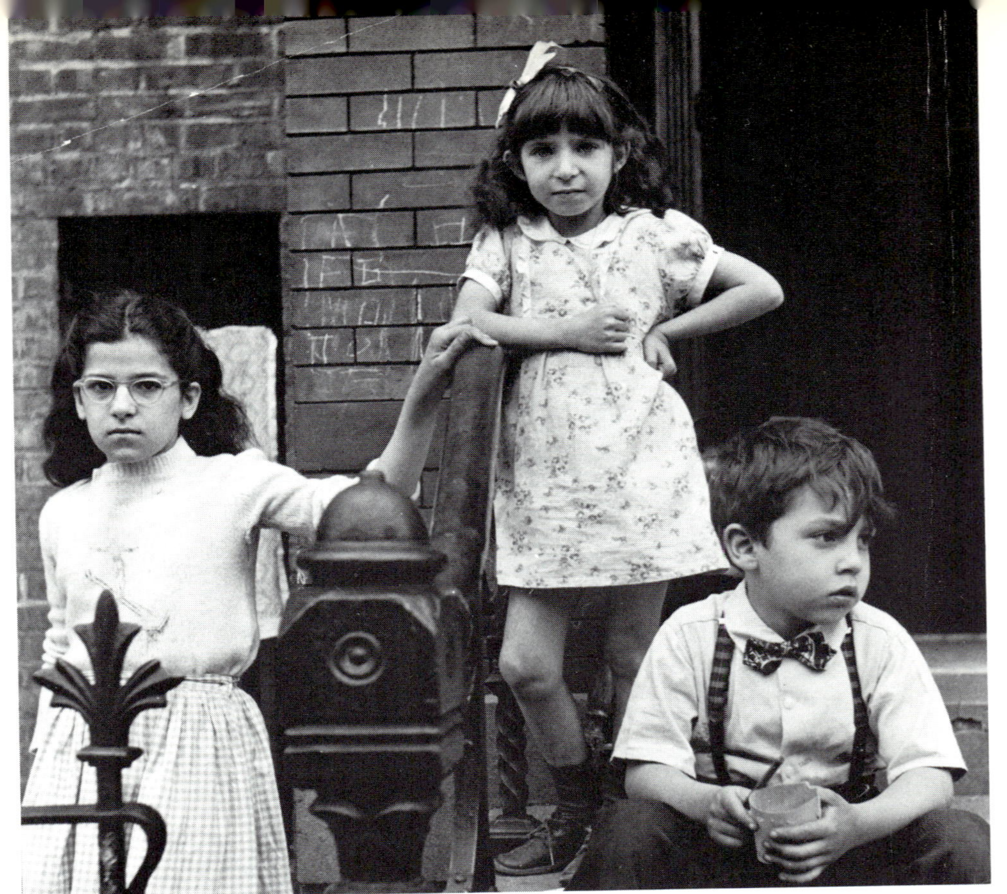

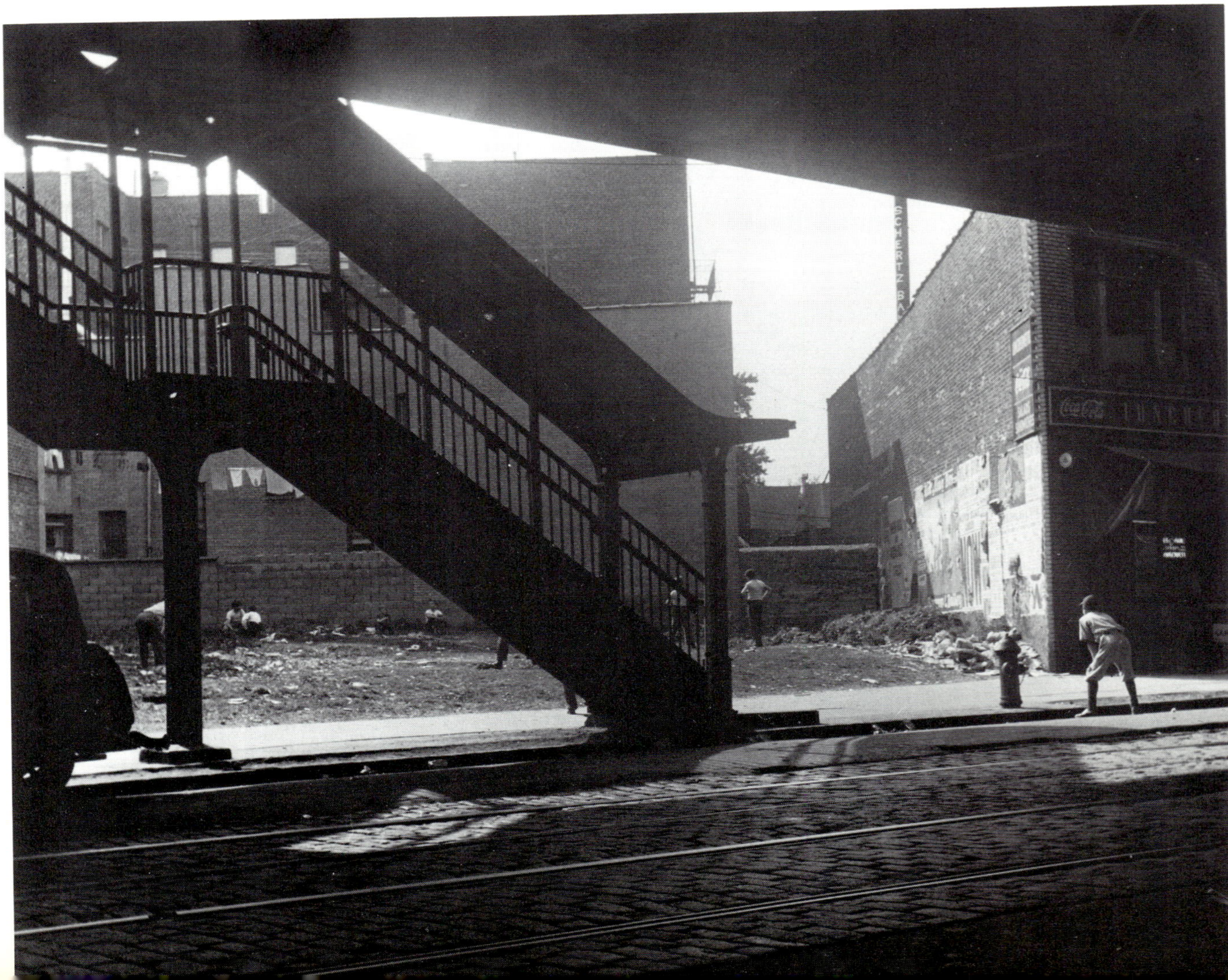

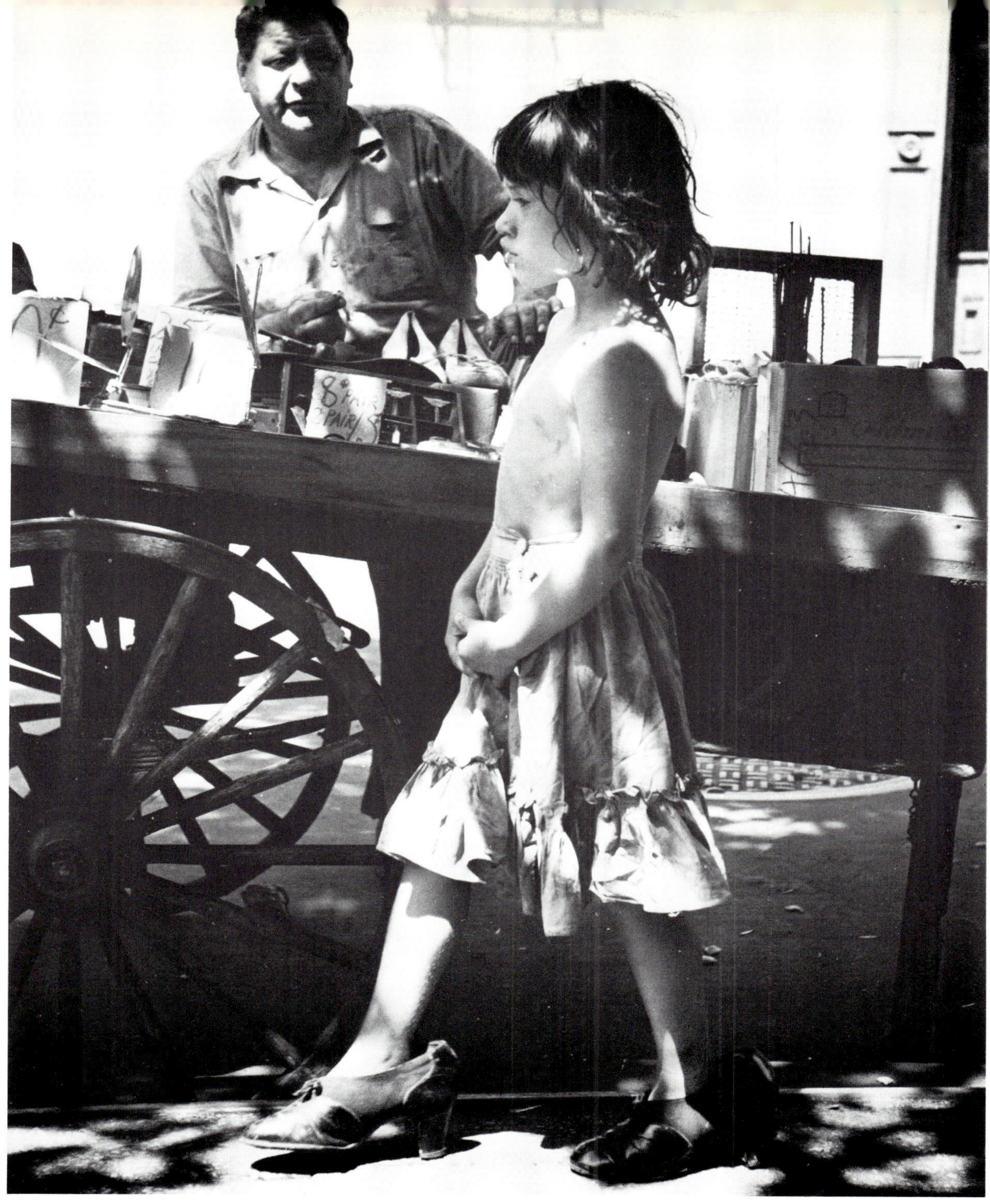

Kids on a Stoop [opposite, top]. The stoop is the front porch of the world to the city kid. Arrayed on this tiny grandstand, kids survey the passing scene or find someone sympathetic to sit with. So much information is imparted on a stoop that it serves as much a part of the educational process of urban kids as the classroom seat. *(Morris Huberland)* **Boys Playing Baseball** [opposite, bottom]. Baseball in one form or another can be played in almost any city space, as these boys demonstrate. With enough room to swing a bat at a thrown ball, field rules can accommodate the layout. A hit off the left-field wall is a single, over the left-field wall to a right-hand batter is a double, into the elevated tracks a double—but the batter must retrieve the ball. Although complicated to the outsider, the rules are strictly understood by the players. In fact, there was a better chance of seeing heated arguments at Ebbets Field or the Polo Grounds, where the rules were more clear-cut than in this trash-littered back lot where the kids play. *(Morris Huberland).* **A Girl Tries on Her First Pair of High-heeled Shoes** [above]. The young girl so intently contemplating her appearance is taking a giant step into womanhood. She is buying her maiden pair of grown-up shoes. Luckily, at eight cents a pair the financial gamble is not beyond her means. The shoes are used, but this young lady has seen few brand new clothes in her day. And they are slightly large, which gives her more to grow into. As any city kid knows, the important fact is to look and act grown-up. *(Jack Manning)*

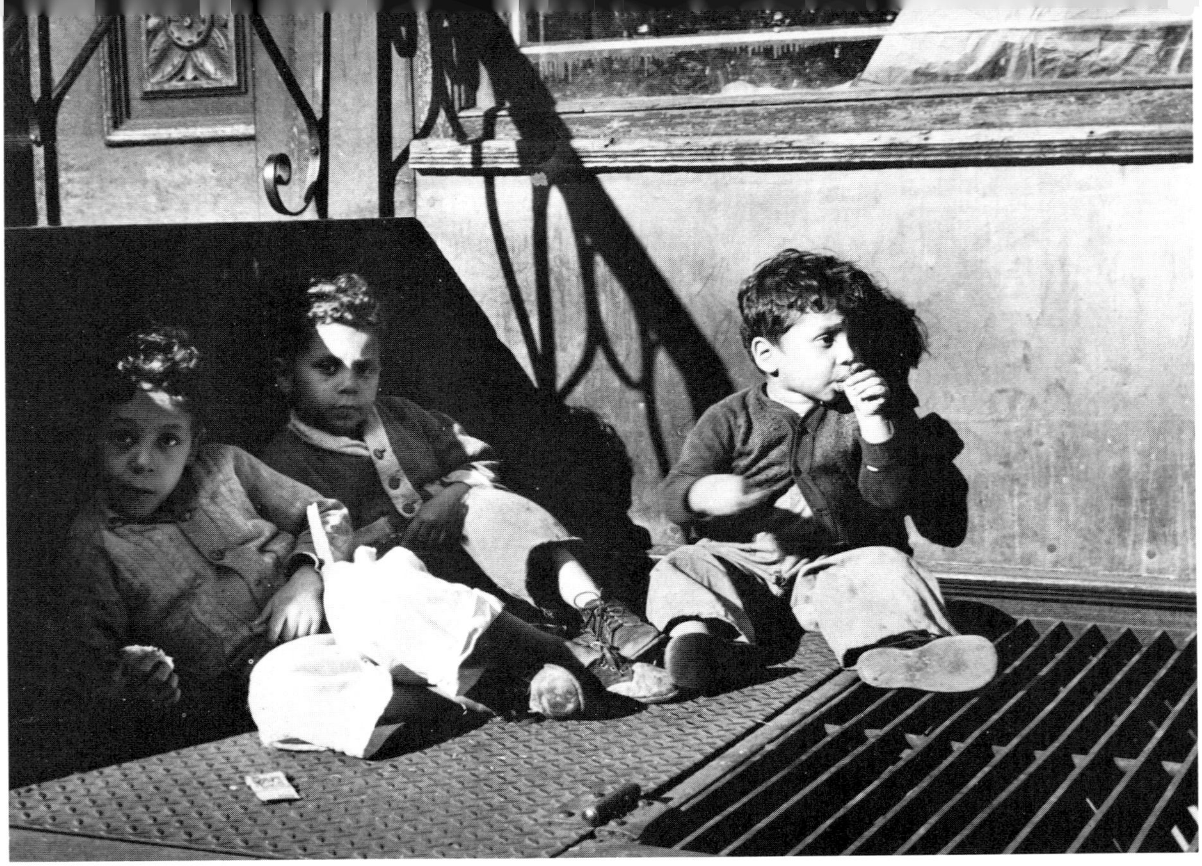

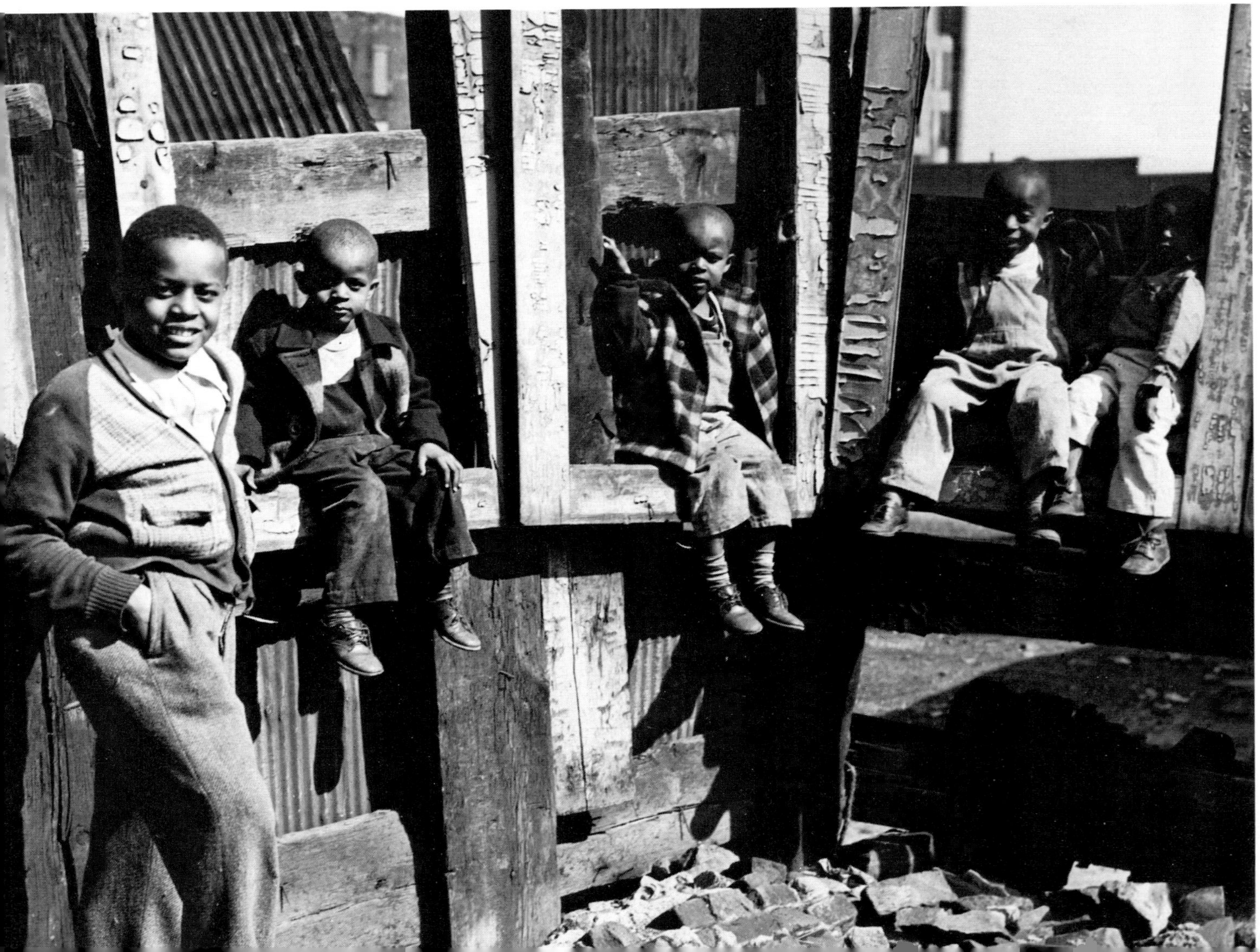

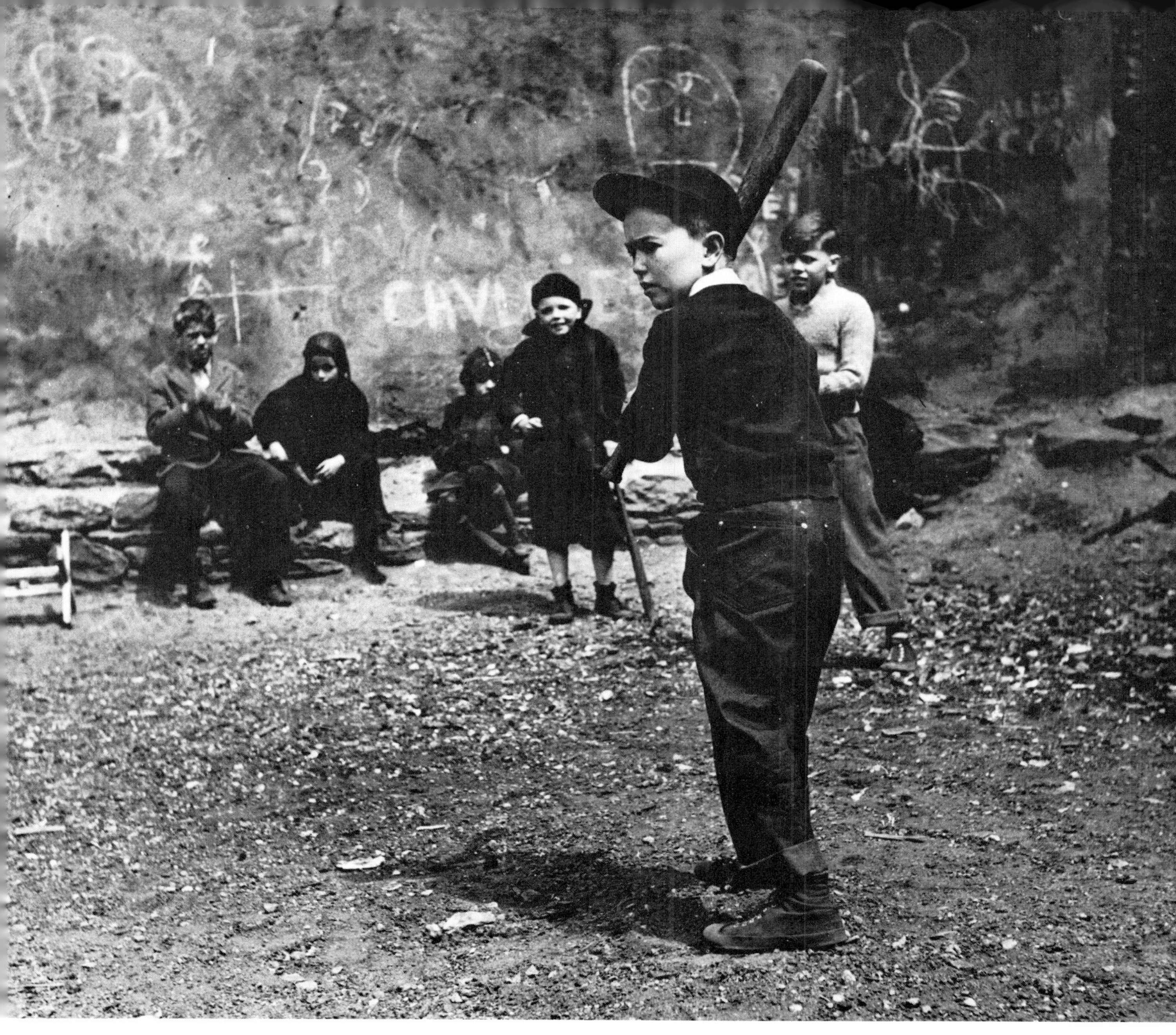

Kids at Rest [opposite, top]. The older boys grab the shade in a protected corner so favored by the urban kid. Meanwhile their younger colleague is left with the sun and the solace of his thumb. *(Morris Huberland)* **East Side Kids** [opposite, bottom]. There is no space so inimical to the human anatomy that a city kid can't occupy it. Kids can perch on a fence, as seen here, find repose on the tops of battered garbage cans, curl up in abandoned machinery or stretch out on the narrow platforms of a fire escape. The city's jumble of shapes, often so puzzling and nonutilitarian to adults, is nothing less than furniture to kids. *(Morris Huberland)* **Batter Up** [above]. *(Morris Huberland)*

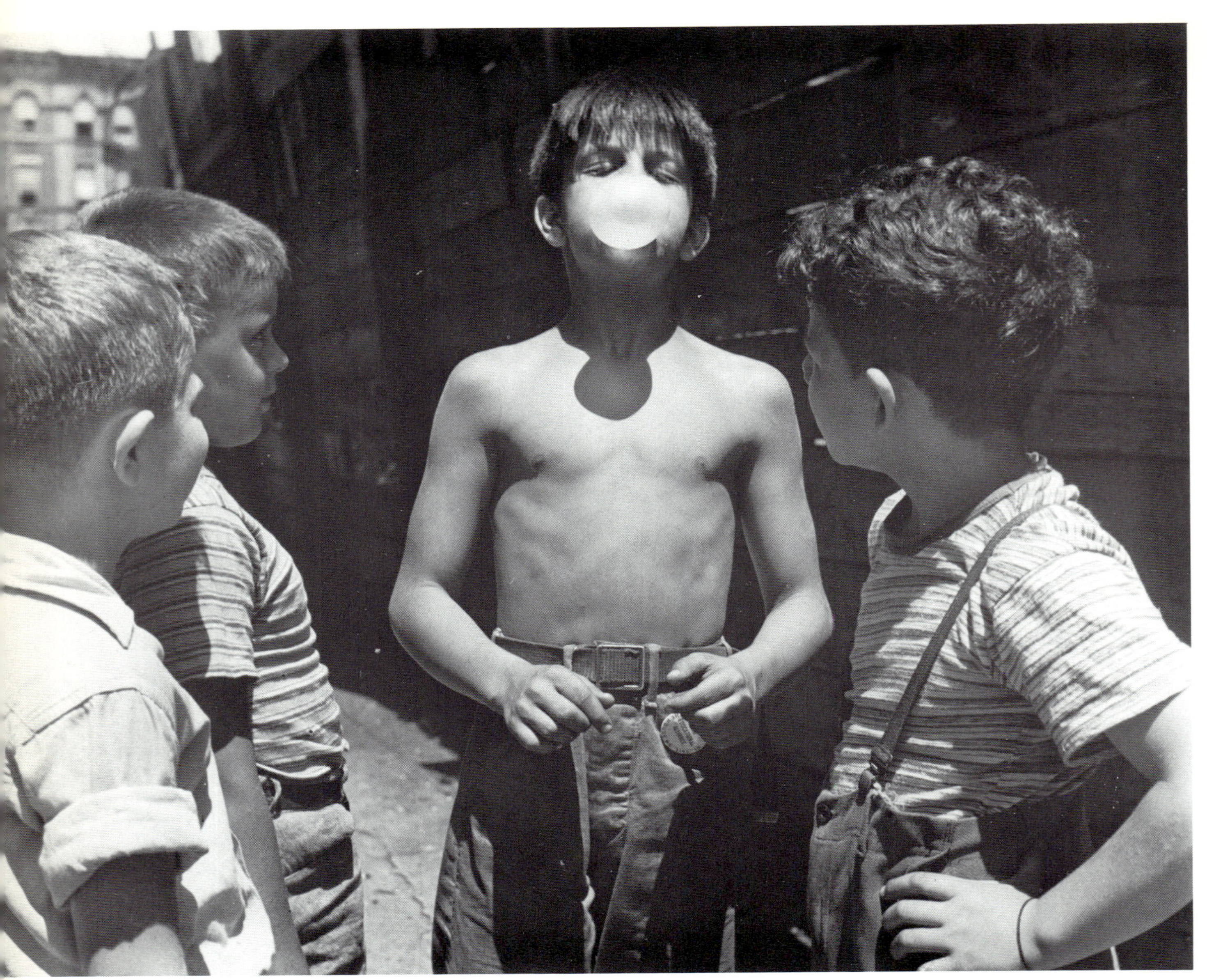

Bubble-gum Champ [above]. It takes a lot of training to be the best at anything and city kids need no goading to practice bubble-gum blowing. There are two steps in championship bubble-gum blowing: to blow as large a bubble as humanly possible; to deflate the bubble without having the gum burst, plastering the hair and face. Those who can master these two steps are given the satisfying ego-building respect of their peers that is so rarely received from their elders. *(Morris Huberland)* **Children, East Side, New York City** [opposite]. The ragamuffins that scale the fences of an abandoned East Side building once again demonstrate their dauntless spirit. *(Jerome Liebling)*

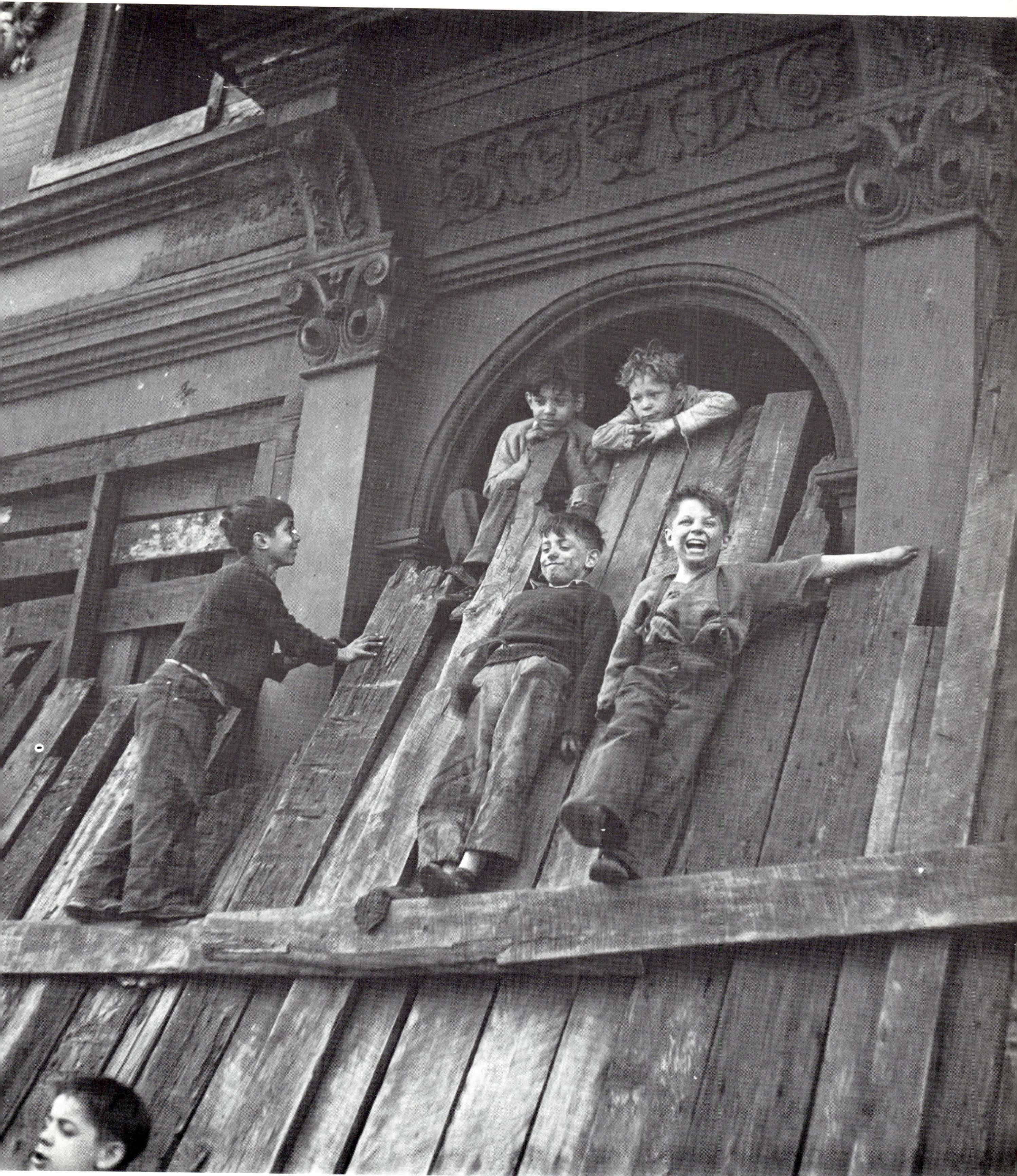

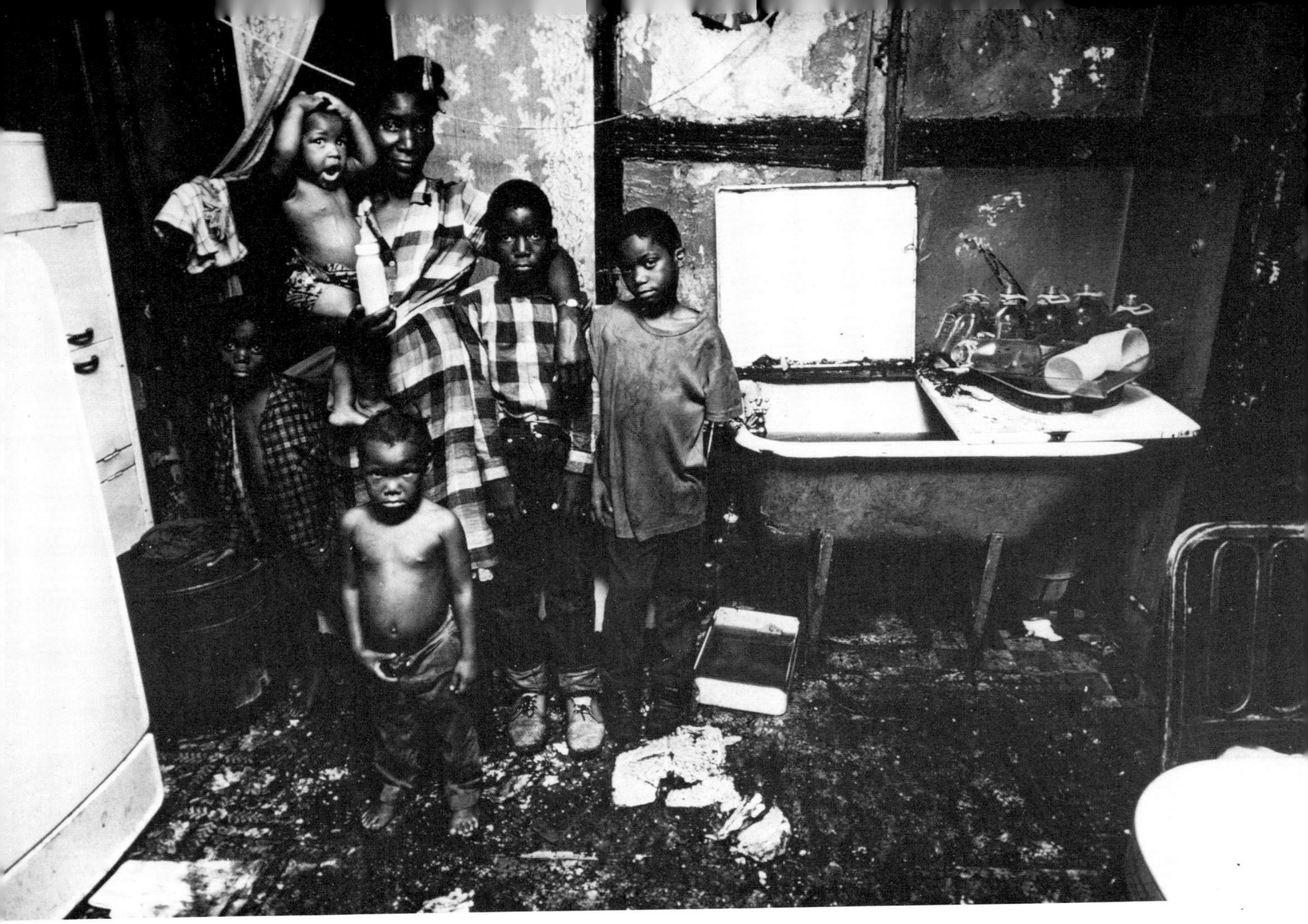

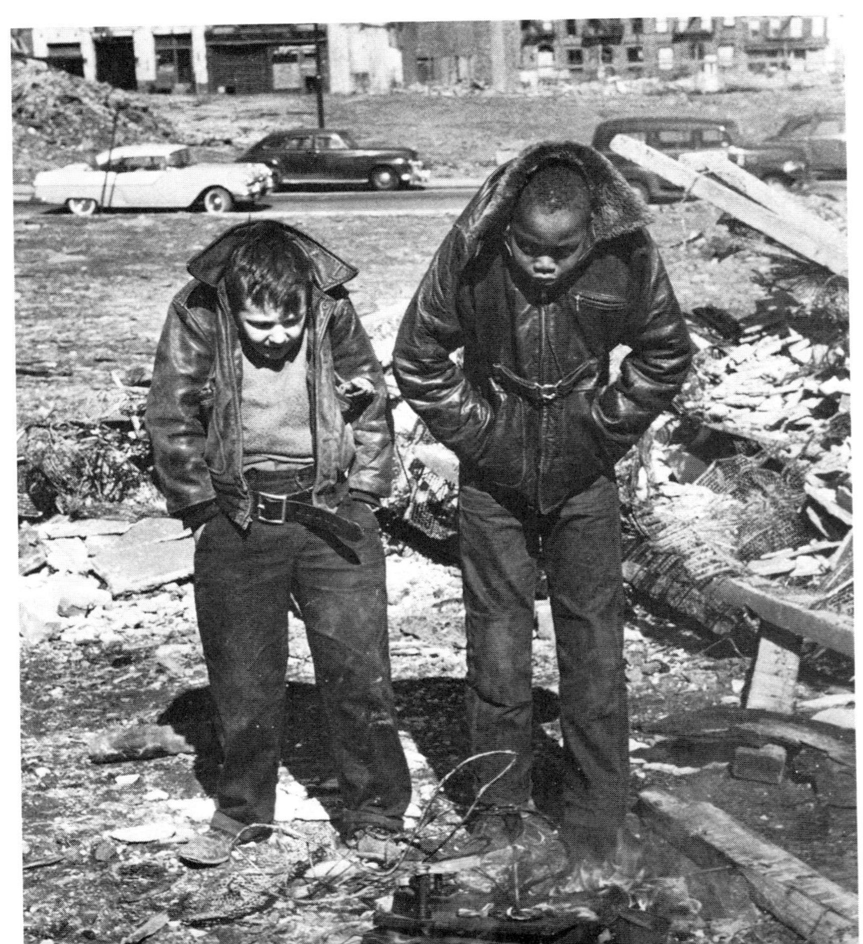

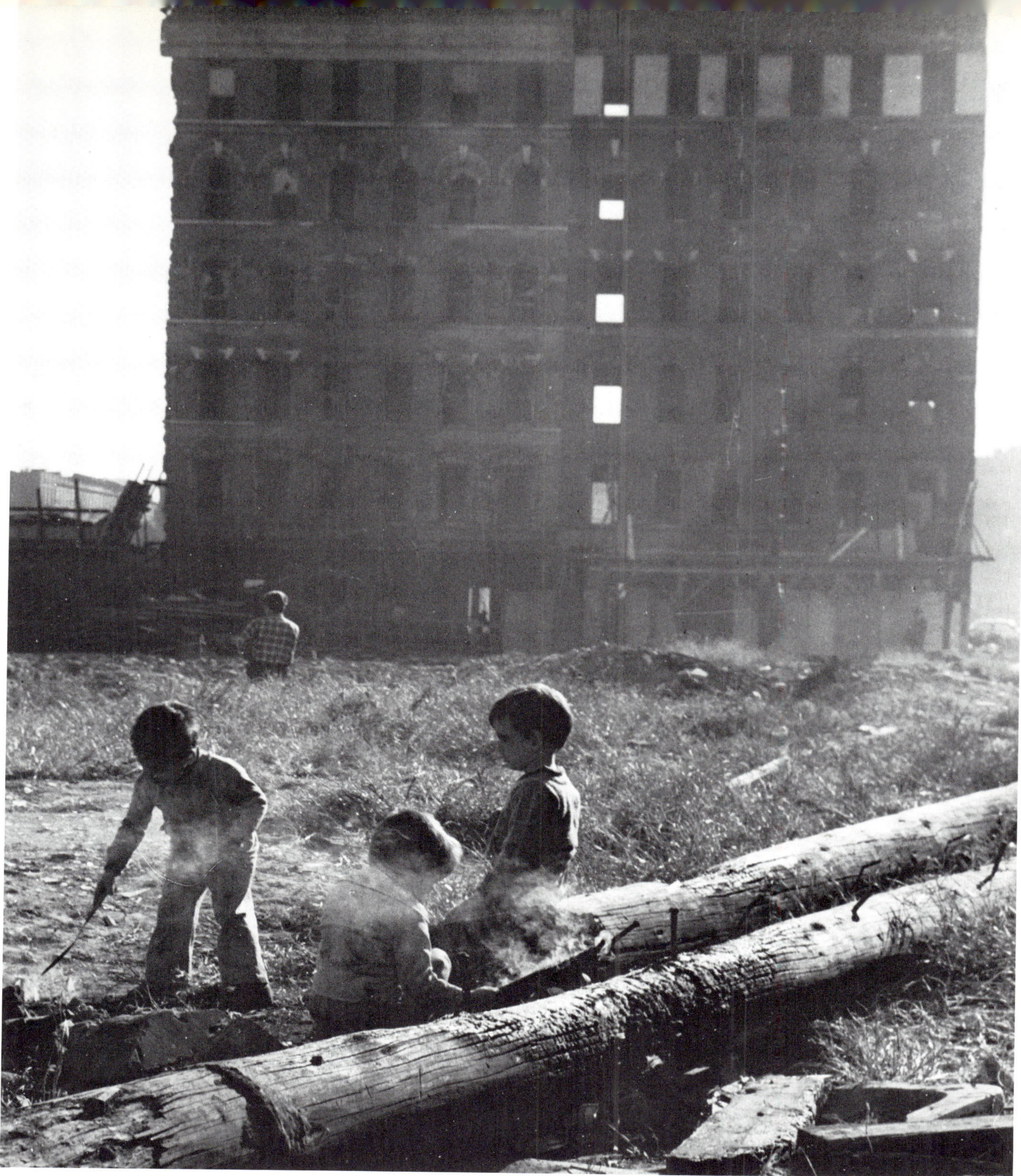

Harlem Family [opposite, top]. The poor kids of the 50s inherited the same ratty tenements that had housed immigrants since the 19th century. The new tenement dwellers, however, were Blacks from the rural South and Puerto Ricans fleeing their island in the hopes of economic improvement. This new rush to the city began during World War II and crested during the 50s and 60s. Some found the work and dignity they sought; most traded country shanties for crumbling tenements. *(John Launois. Black Star)* **Two Boys in Open Lot, Harlem** [opposite, bottom]. There was friction between the arriving Blacks and Latins and the remaining Whites who clung to their tenement neighborhoods. Similarly, there was antagonistic competition between the Blacks and Latins, but this tension was often lost on the kids. *(Morris Huberland)* **Boys in Vacant Lot** [above]. To these kids poking around a smoldering telephone pole, the vacant lot is an exciting playground. Actually, the lot and the shell of a building behind it are symbols of a problem during the 50s when whole neighborhoods were abandoned. *(Morris Huberland)*

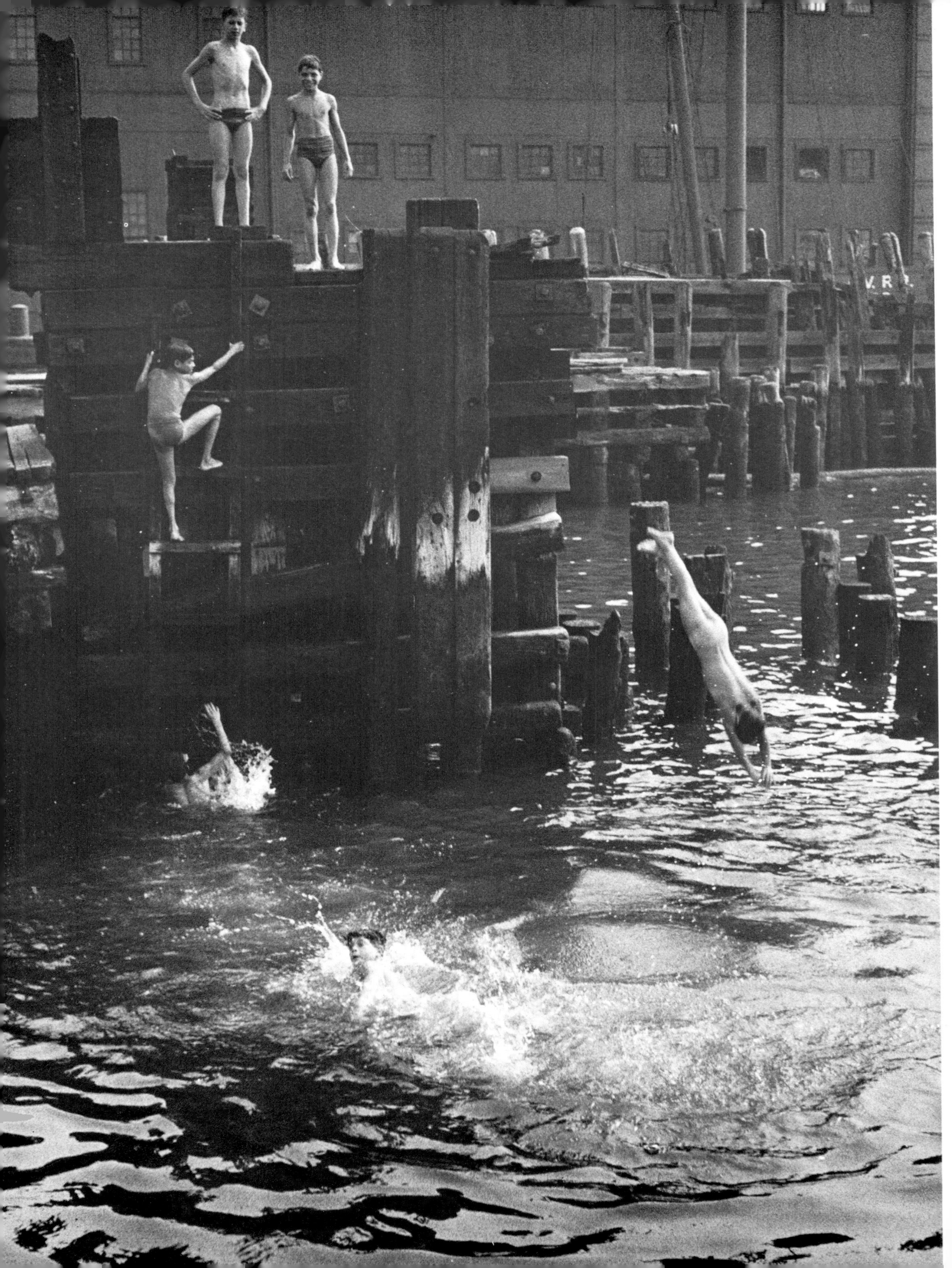

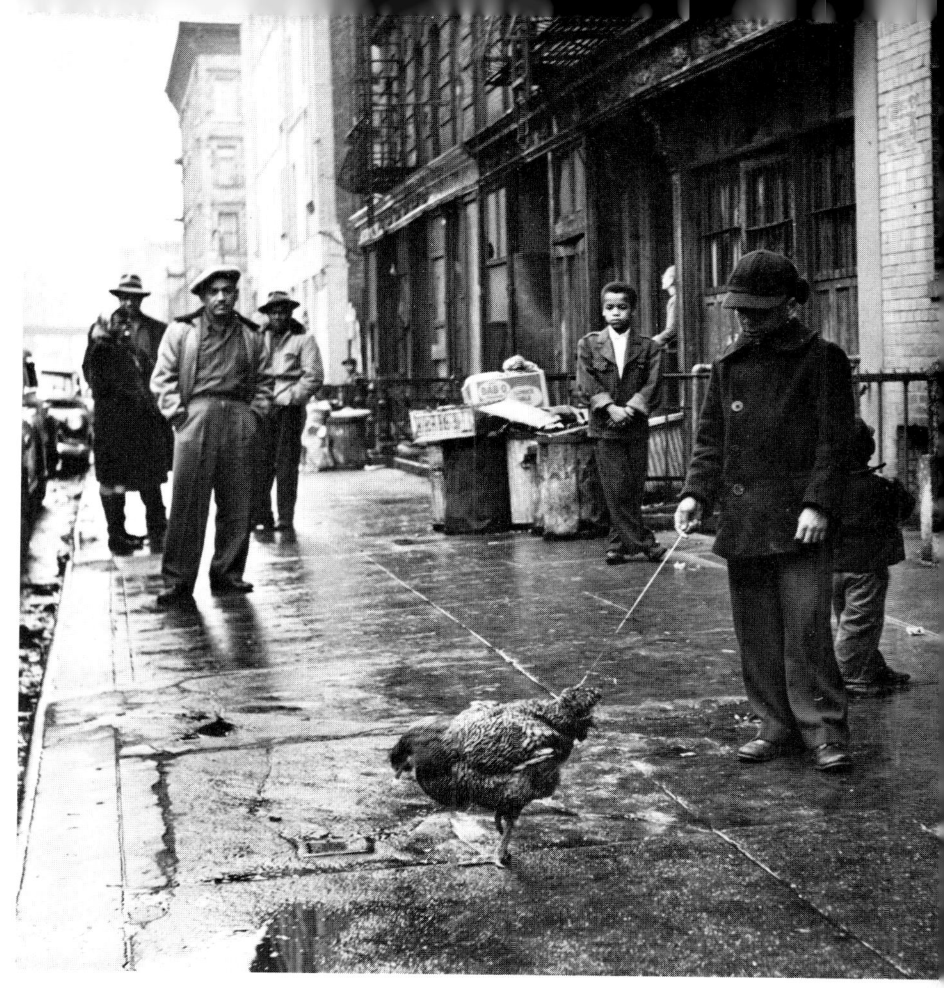

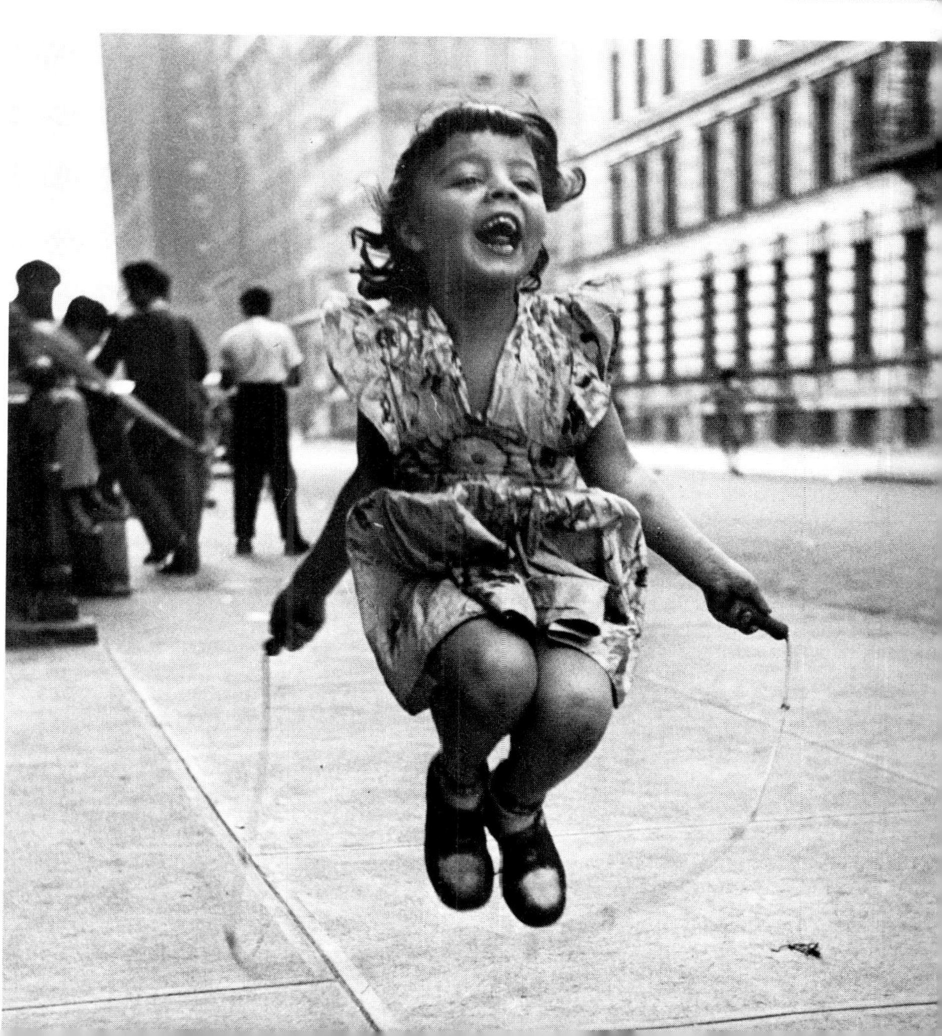

Hudson River [opposite]. The heat of the city's summer drives boys into the Hudson River, as it did 50 and 100 years earlier. *(Kaplan)* **Boy With Pet Chicken** [right, top]. Street kids, like all kids, are notorious for their odd pets —chickens, pigeons, mice, gerbils, hamsters, fish, snakes and other animals, as well as the more common dogs and cats. Almost anything that creeps, crawls, flies, swims, walks or demands constant attention could end up as the ward of the street kid. *(Morris Huberland)* **Skipping Rope** [right, bottom]. The bleak cityscape means nothing to this little girl as she exults in her skill at jumping rope. As it has through the decades, this ritual frees the mind and lifts the soul. A girl like this one is the recognized master of the art—even a professional prizefighter might have trouble keeping up with her skips. And as she burns up her prodigious energy and wears out the soles of her shoes, she is intoxicated with life and her place in it. *(Lester Talkington)*

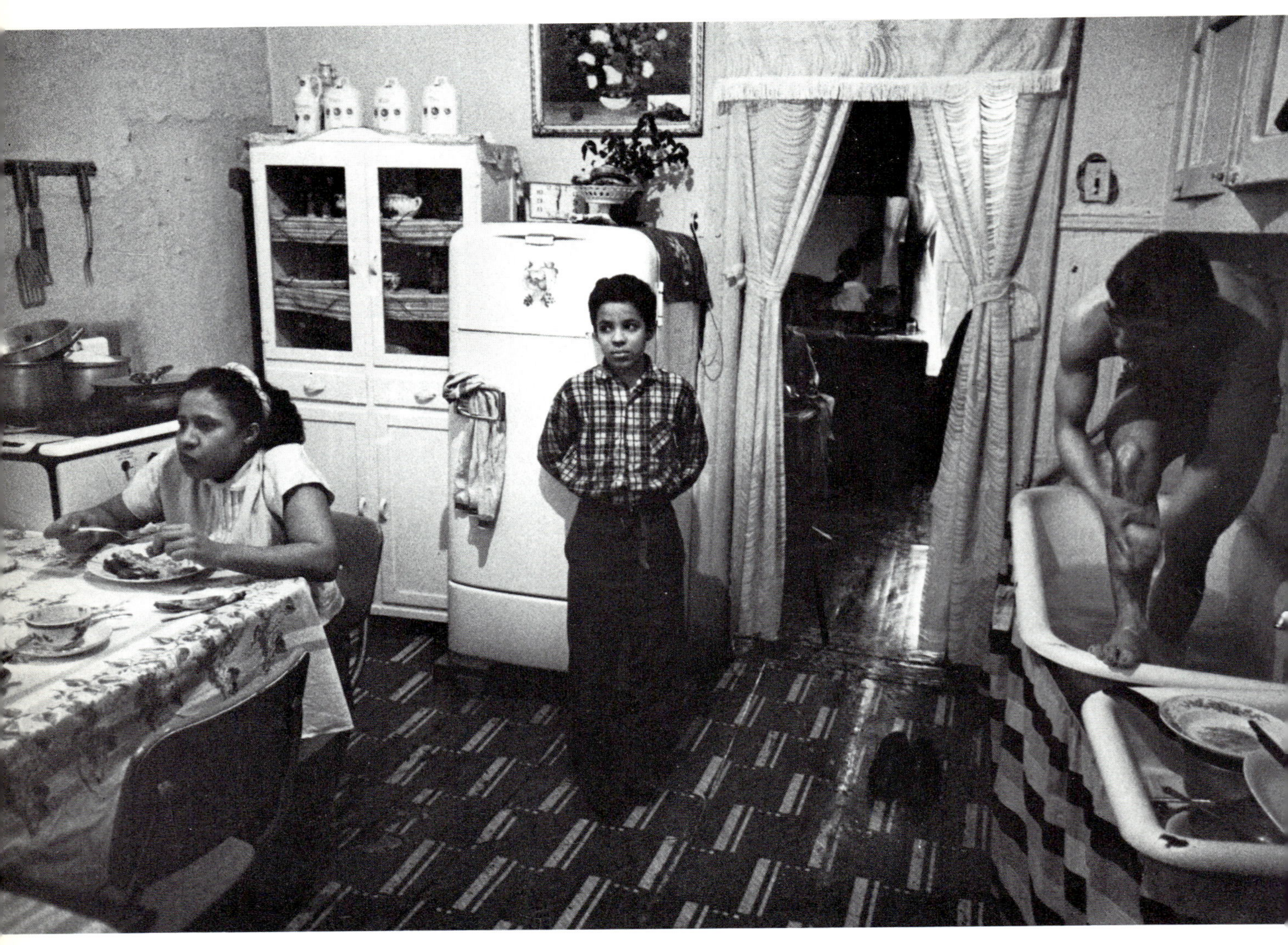

Kitchen Scene [above]. The tub-in-the-kitchen tenement apartment remained home for street kids growing up in the 60s, although many apartments, like this one, had been improved through modest renovation. From 1950 through 1964, 1.7 million White middle-class New Yorkers left the city for the suburbs to be replaced by Latins (mostly Puerto Ricans) and Blacks. The 60s saw the entrenchment of these immigrants in wide sections of the city as increasing numbers of Black and Spanish kids played in the streets and new languages were heard in the tenements. *(Charles Harbutt. Magnum Photos, Inc.)* **Boy Delivering Cleaning, Brownsville, Brooklyn** [opposite, top]. Kids could still earn some money as delivery boys—a job that is always available. Many other jobs that street kids had vied for in previous times no longer existed by the 60s—Western Union delivery boy, corner newsboy. Even the opportunities for shoeshine boys dwindled. Unskilled jobs in general were hard to find as manufacturing factories and lofts left the city for rural areas with cheaper labor, lower taxes and less congestion. *(Mike Levins)* **Friends—Lower East Side** [opposite, bottom]. Two buddies sit for a minute on an old cushion in a Lower East Side alley. Next to them is the residue of modern kids' culture, a broken and abandoned tricycle. *(Mike Levins)*

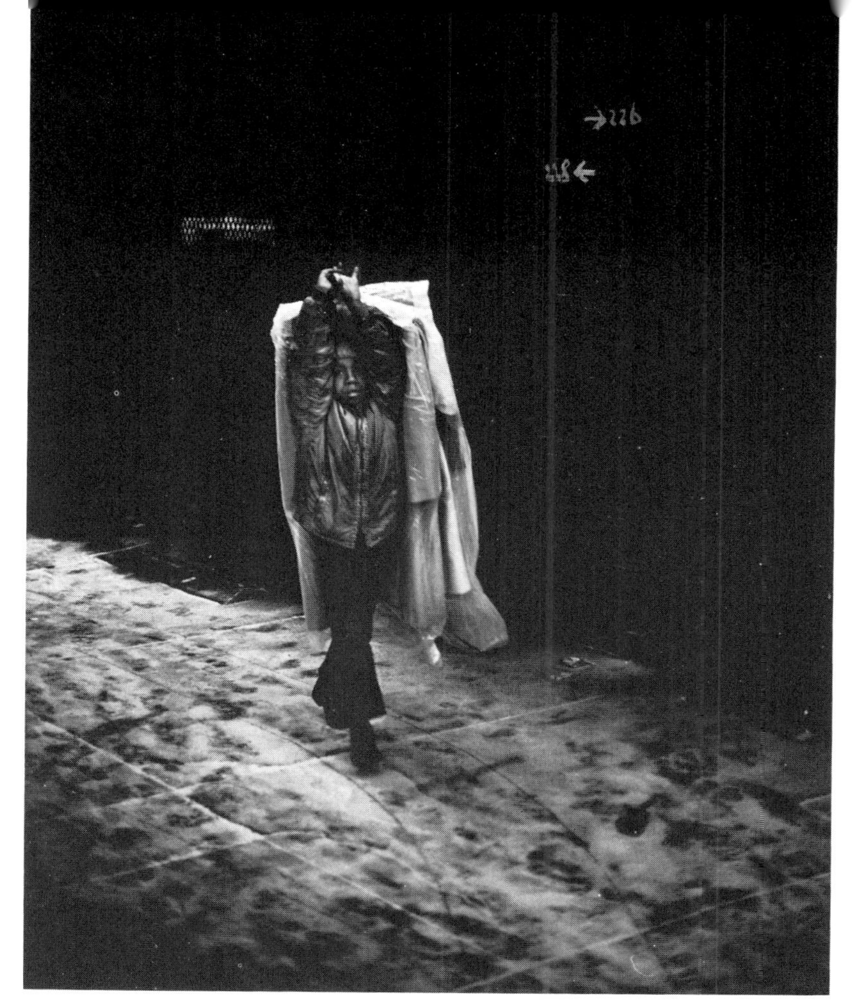

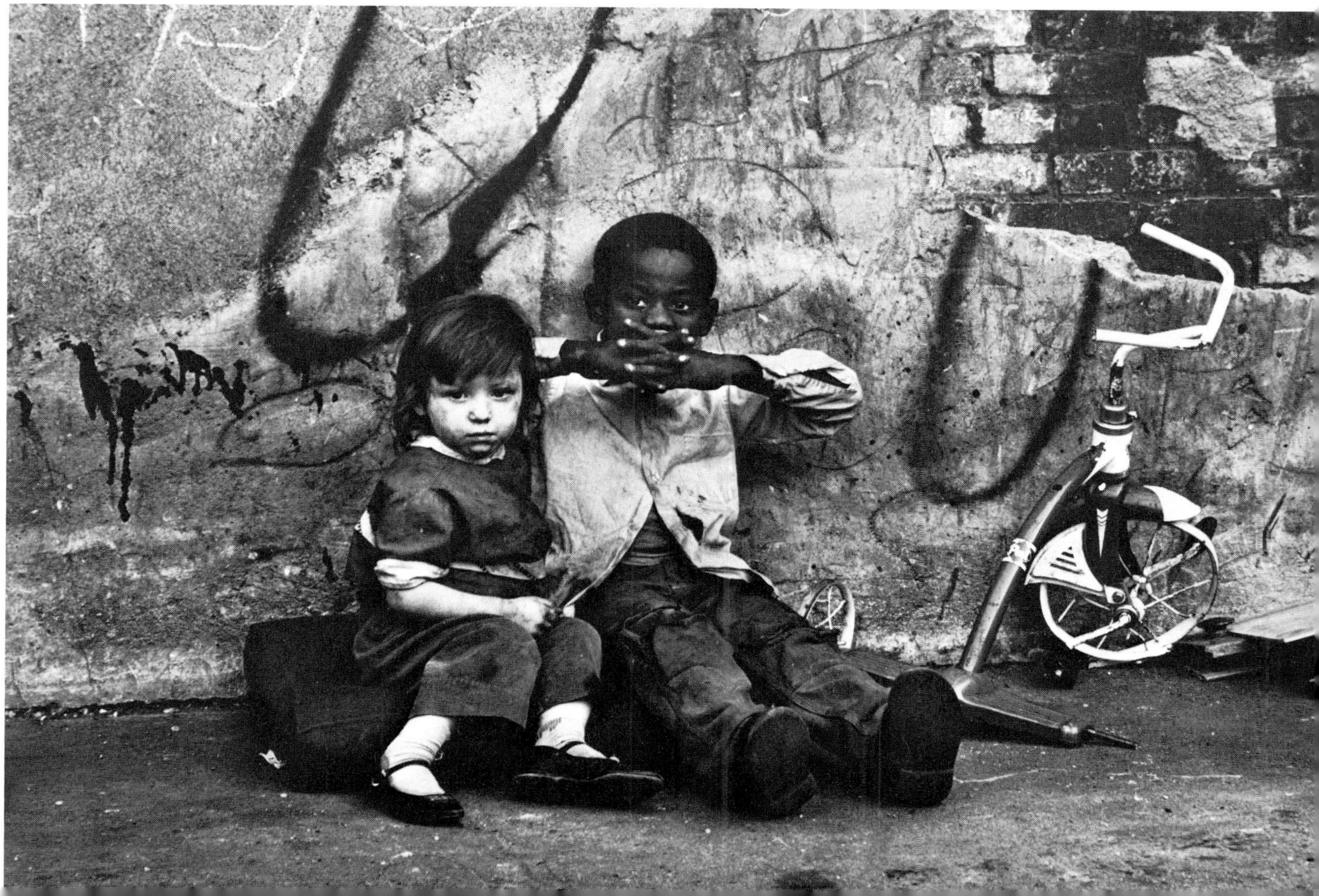

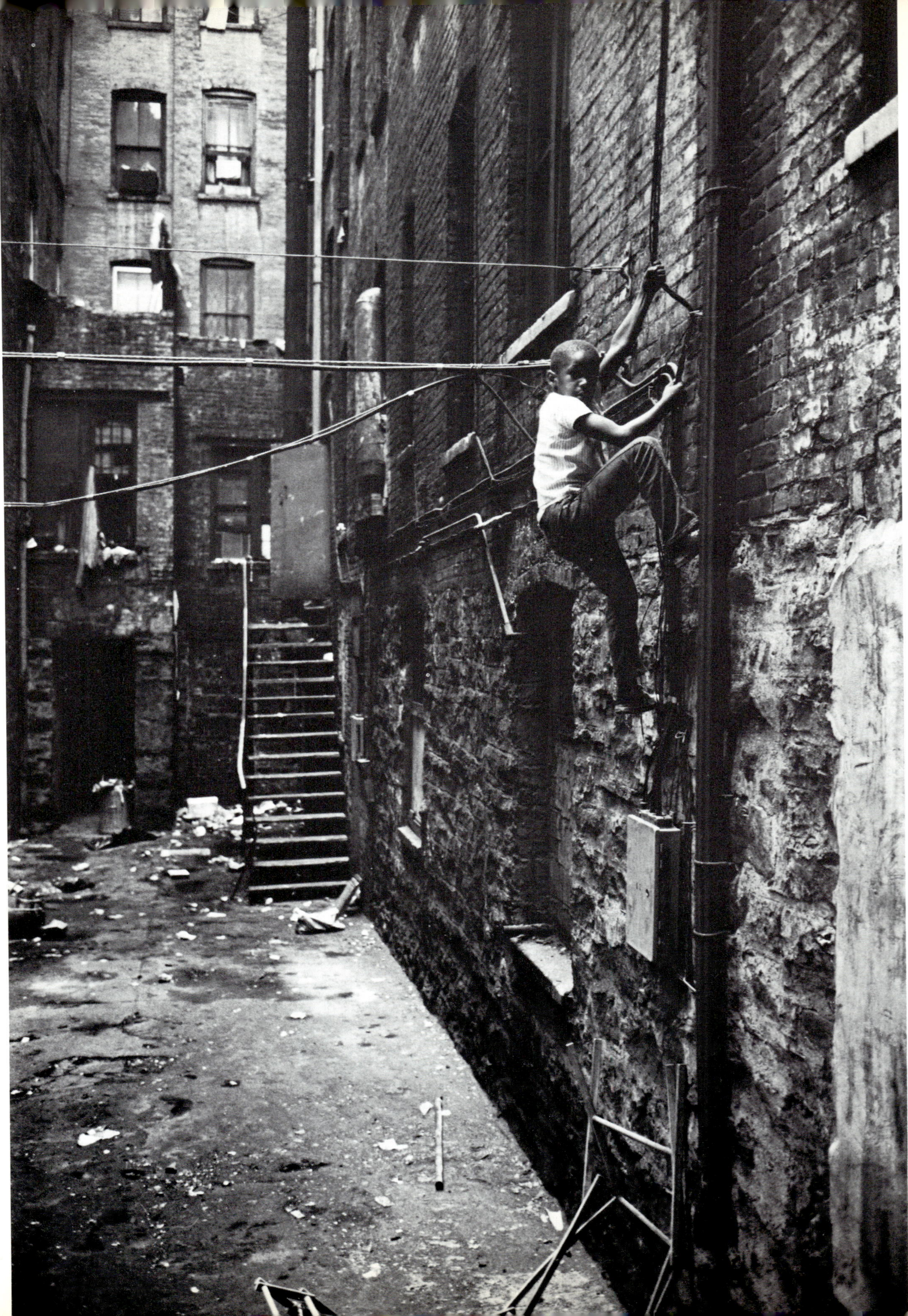

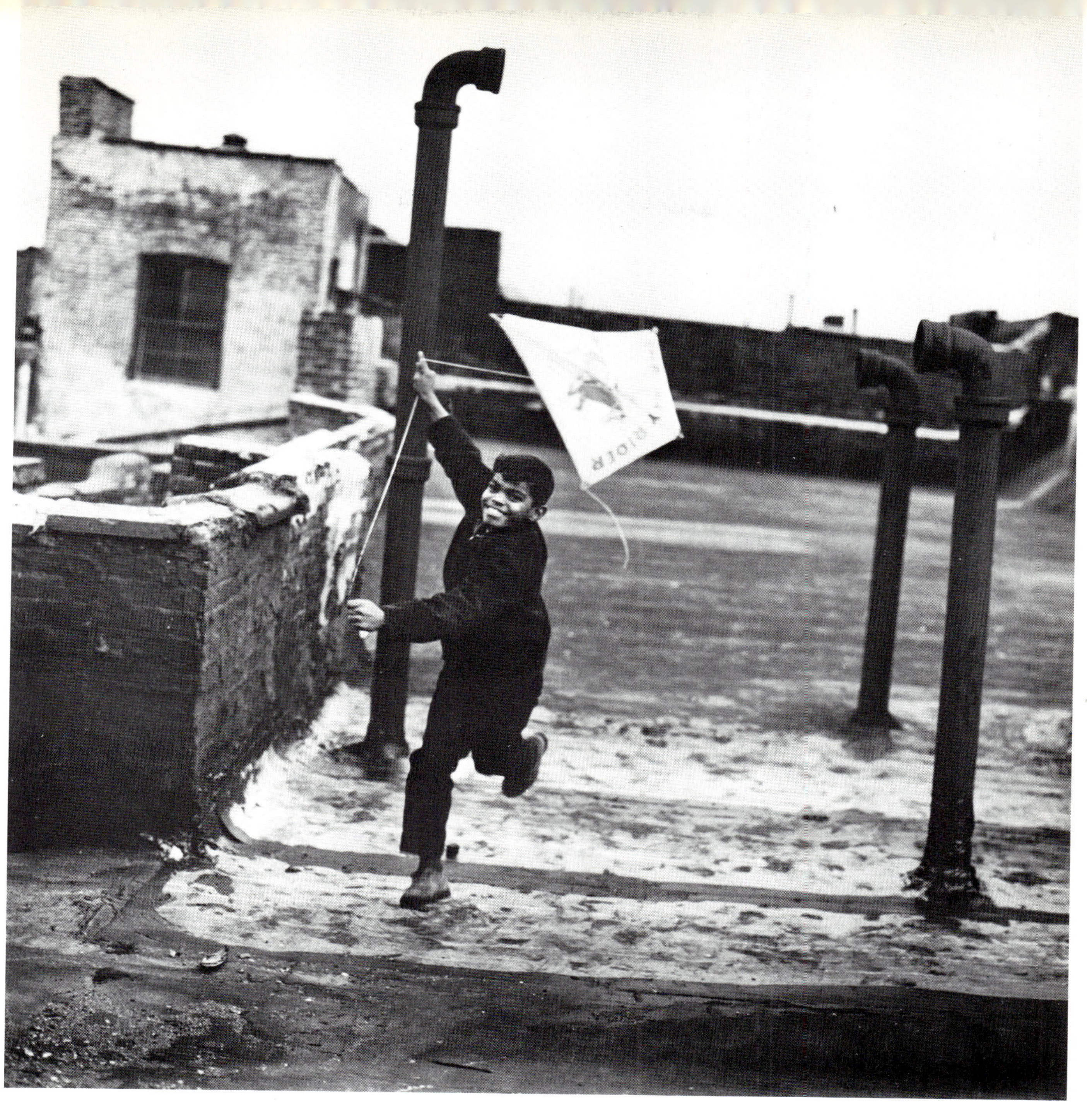

Boy Scaling Wall [opposite]. *(Bruce Davidson. Magnum Photos, Inc.)* **Boy with Kite, East 100th Street** [above]. Flying kites from city rooftops is an old tradition, although one that is not always looked upon kindly by landlords and the law. Kites were such a plague in the 19th century that they were outlawed south of 14th Street. *(Bruce Davidson. Magnum Photos, Inc.)*

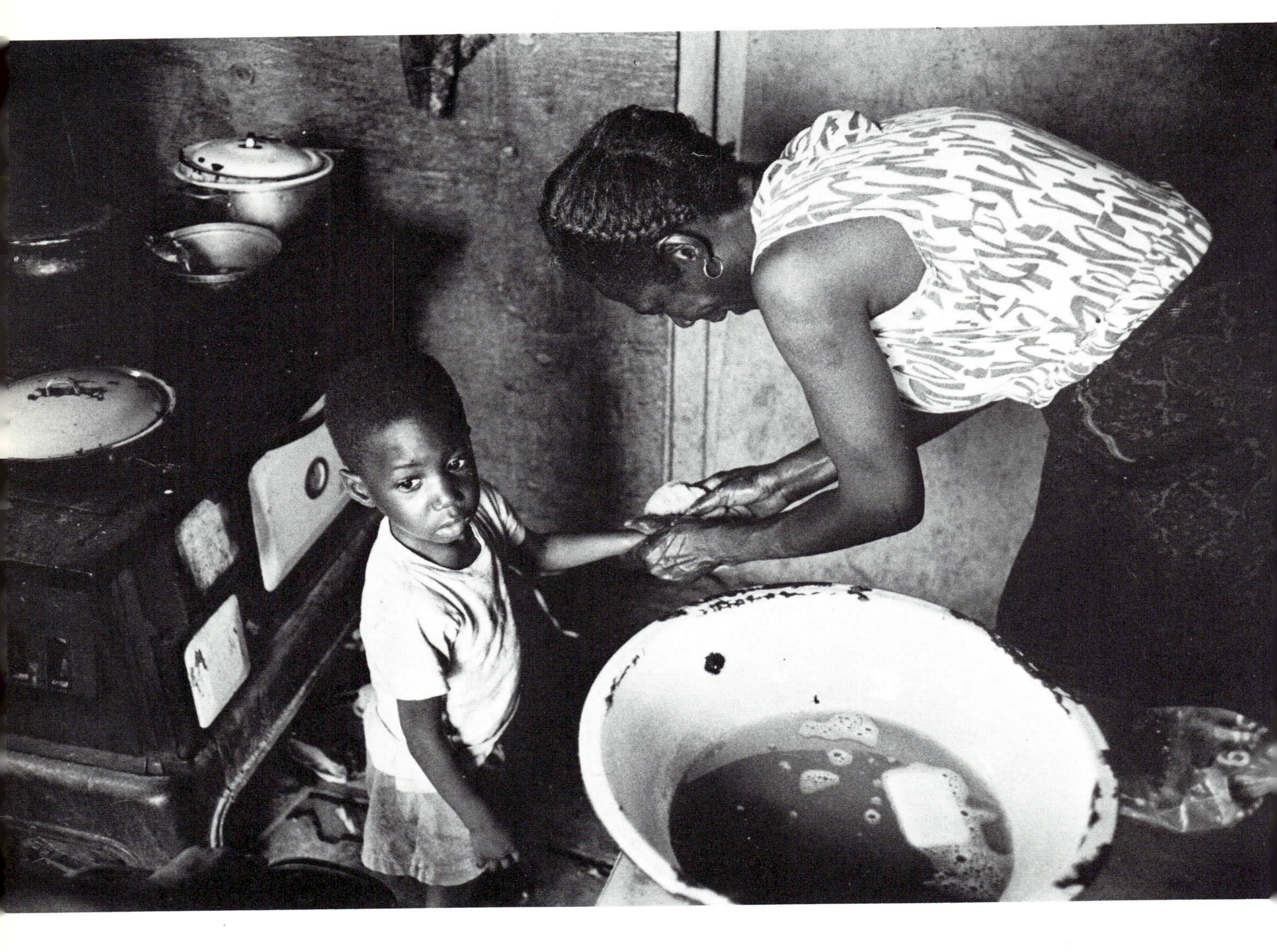

Black Mother and Child [above]. *(Shelly Rusten)* **I Have a Dream** [opposite]. *(Lucia Woods)*

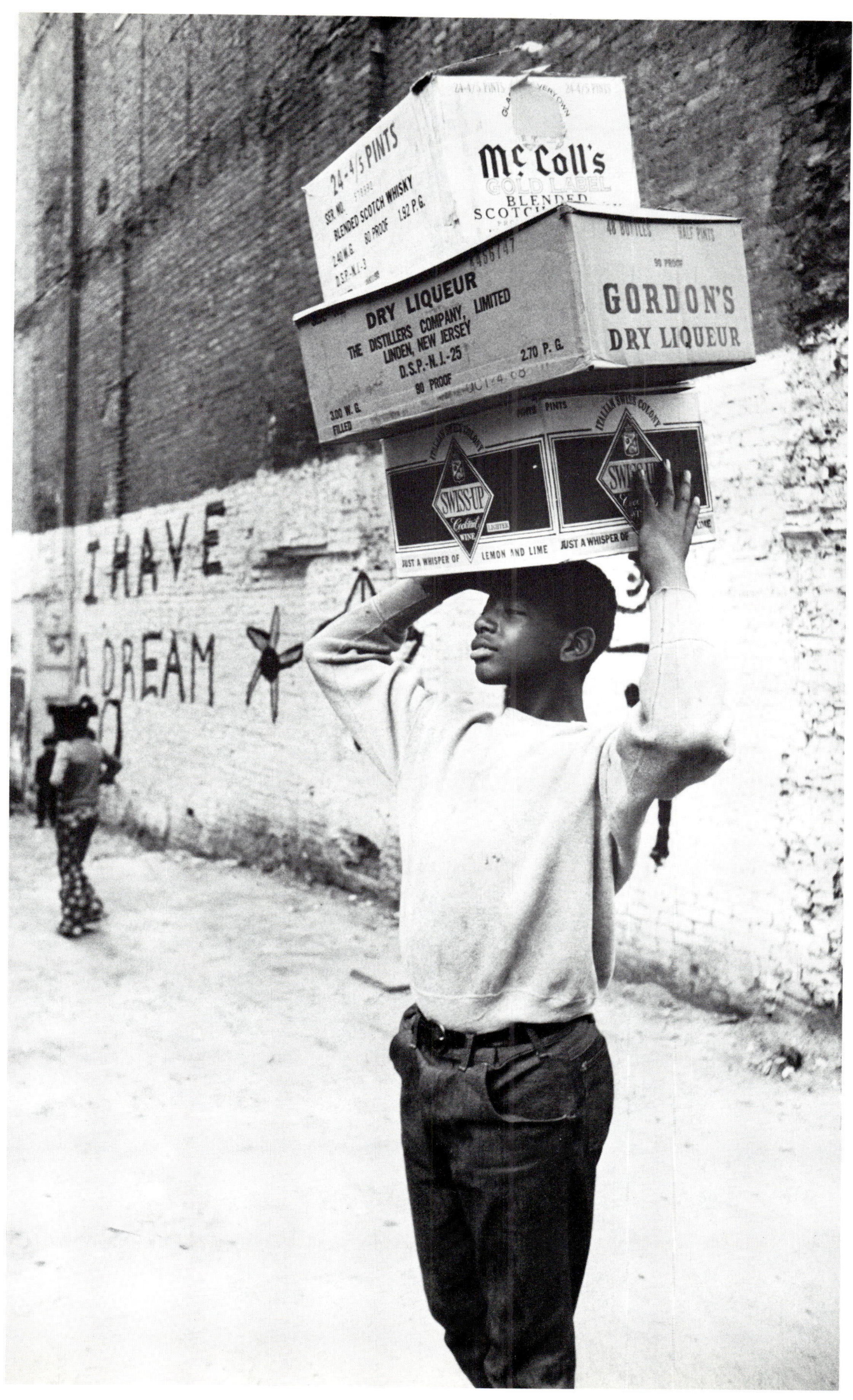
24-4/5 PINTS
McColl's
BLENDED SCOTCH WHISKY
2.40 W.G. 80 PROOF 1.92 P.G.
DRY LIQUEUR
THE DISTILLERS COMPANY, LIMITED
LINDEN, NEW JERSEY
D.S.P.-N.J.-25
2.70 P.G.
90 PROOF
GORDON'S
DRY LIQUEUR
SWISS-UP
JUST A WHISPER OF LEMON AND LIME
I HAVE
A DREAM

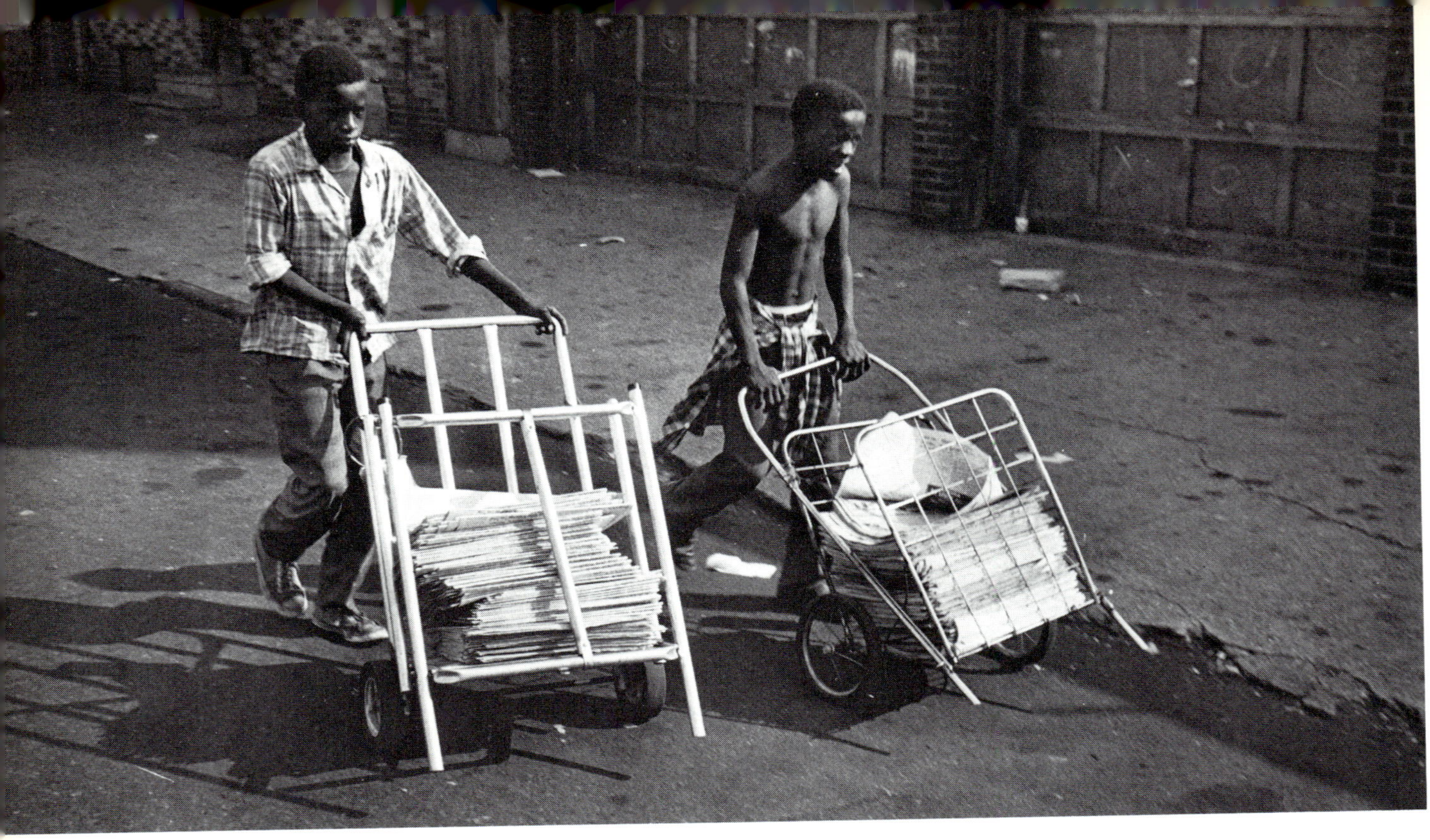

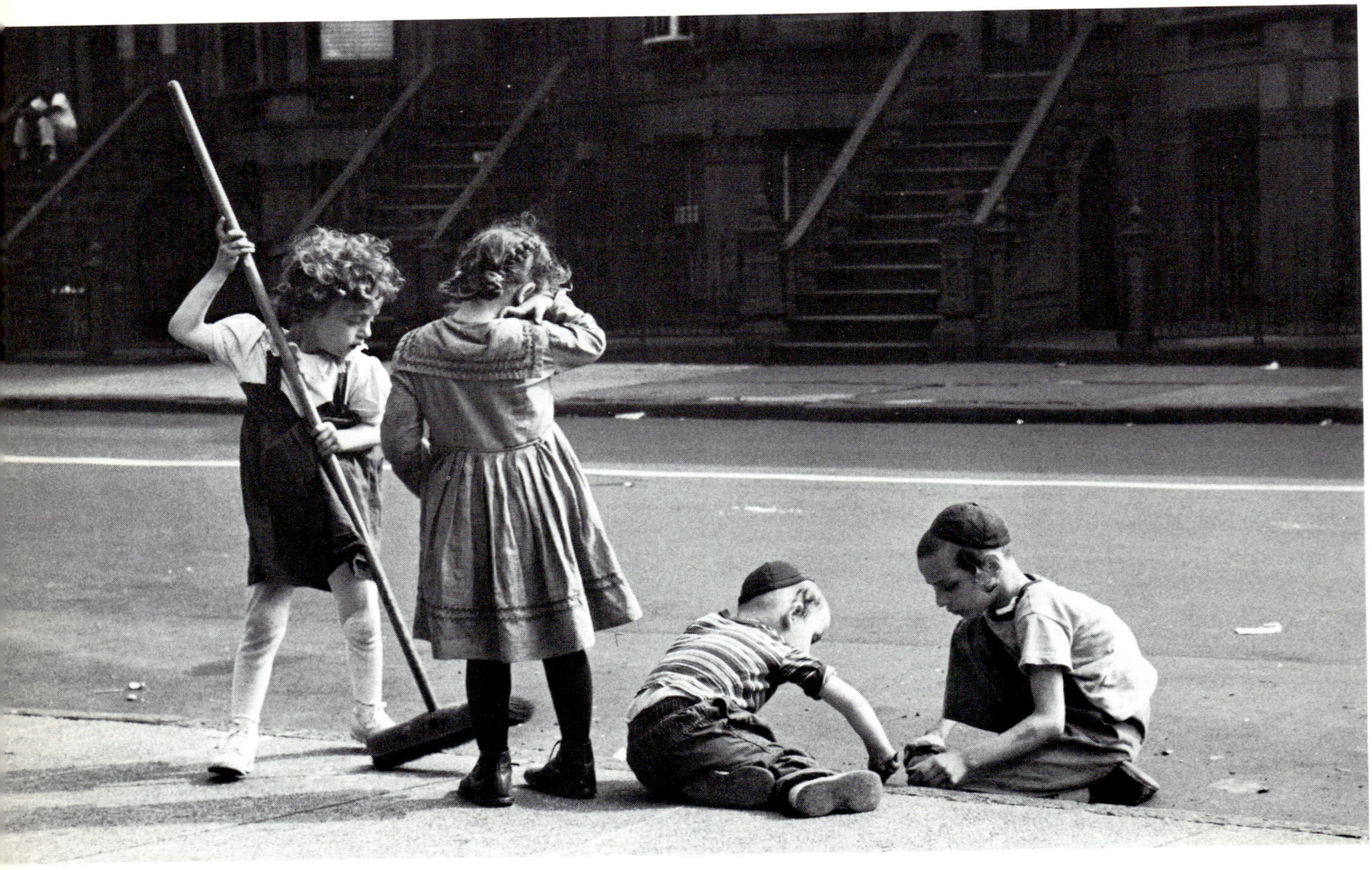

Carting Newspapers [top]. *(Mike Levins)* **Street Games** [bottom]. While two boys wearing yarmulkes play in the gutter, the girls sweep the sidewalk in a street scene in the Williamsburg section of Brooklyn, home to a thriving community of Hassidic Jews. *(Inger McCabe Elliott)* **Girl Reaching Out** [opposite]. *(Mike Levins)*

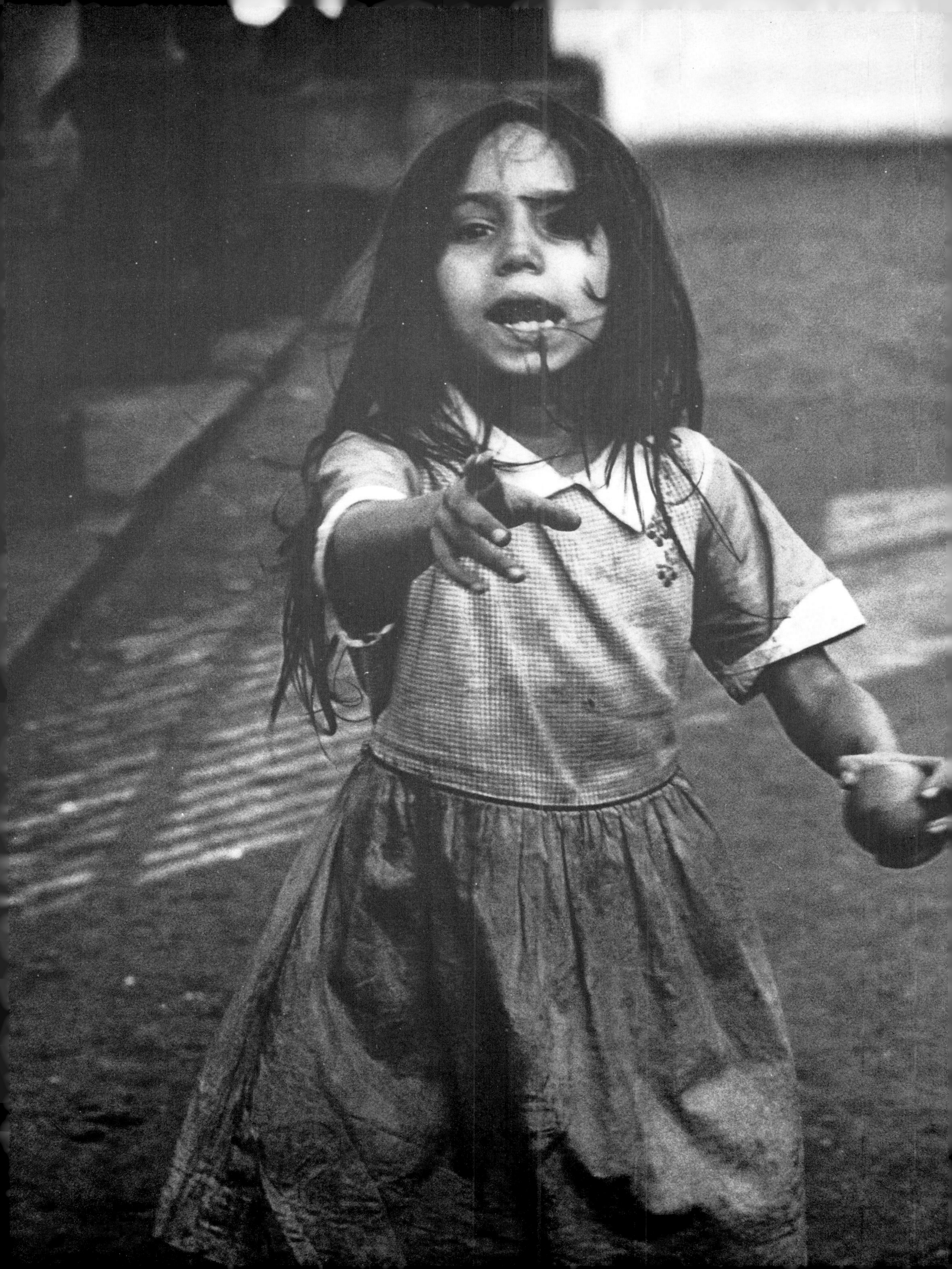

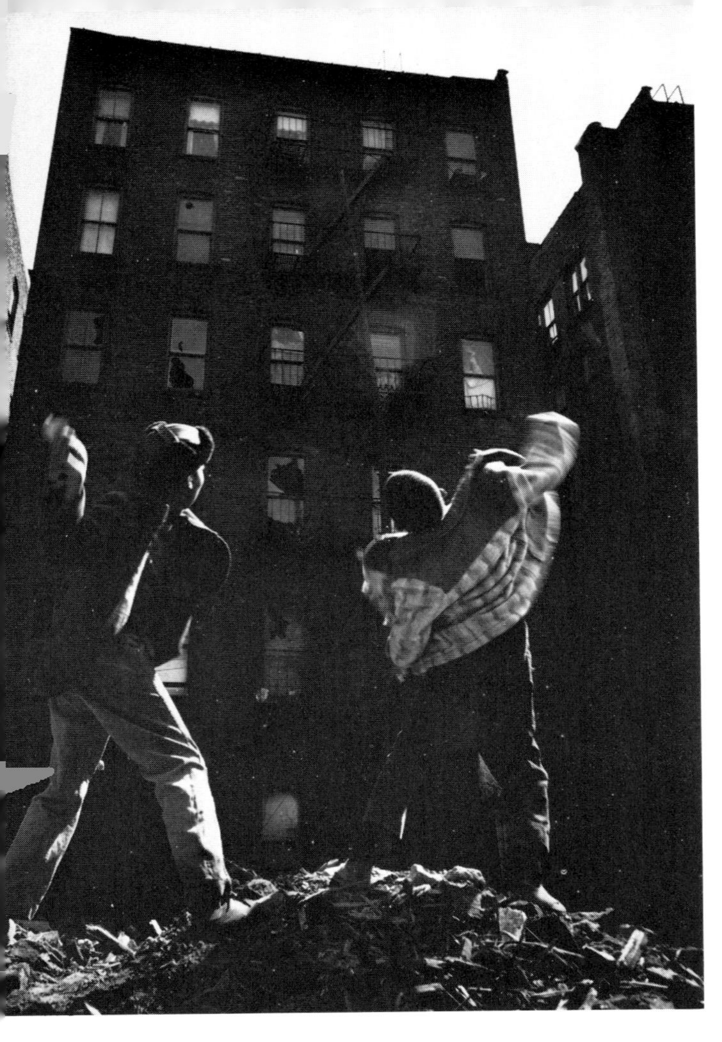

Throwing Stones, Lower East Side [left] The building has been deserted, some of the apartments left with the shades and curtains still in place. The windows now serve only as targets for boys with rocks. It's a pathetic sight, boys pelting a building that, with a little money and care, could be salvaged and restored. But the street kids of the 60s witnessed the logical extension of a society whose economic and legal forces operated to destroy housing when it was most needed. *(Mike Levins)* **Boys on Rooftop, Bronx** [below]. In the 70s, with the widespread destruction of housing, neighborhoods became open in a way they had not been in 100 years. Only kids, with their ability to live for the day, found delight in this sad condition. *(Mike Levins)* **Boys Playing on Car** [opposite, top]. Abandoned cars, like abandoned buildings, became instant playthings for street kids. Many of these cars have been stolen and stripped by thieves. The hulks are then left on the street where they become the property of the kids. Not only do the kids dance on the rooftops, as seen here, they smash the windows, swing on the doors and sometimes set the car on fire. *(Robert D'Alessandro)* **Youth with Bell** [opposite, bottom]. *(Larry Fink)*

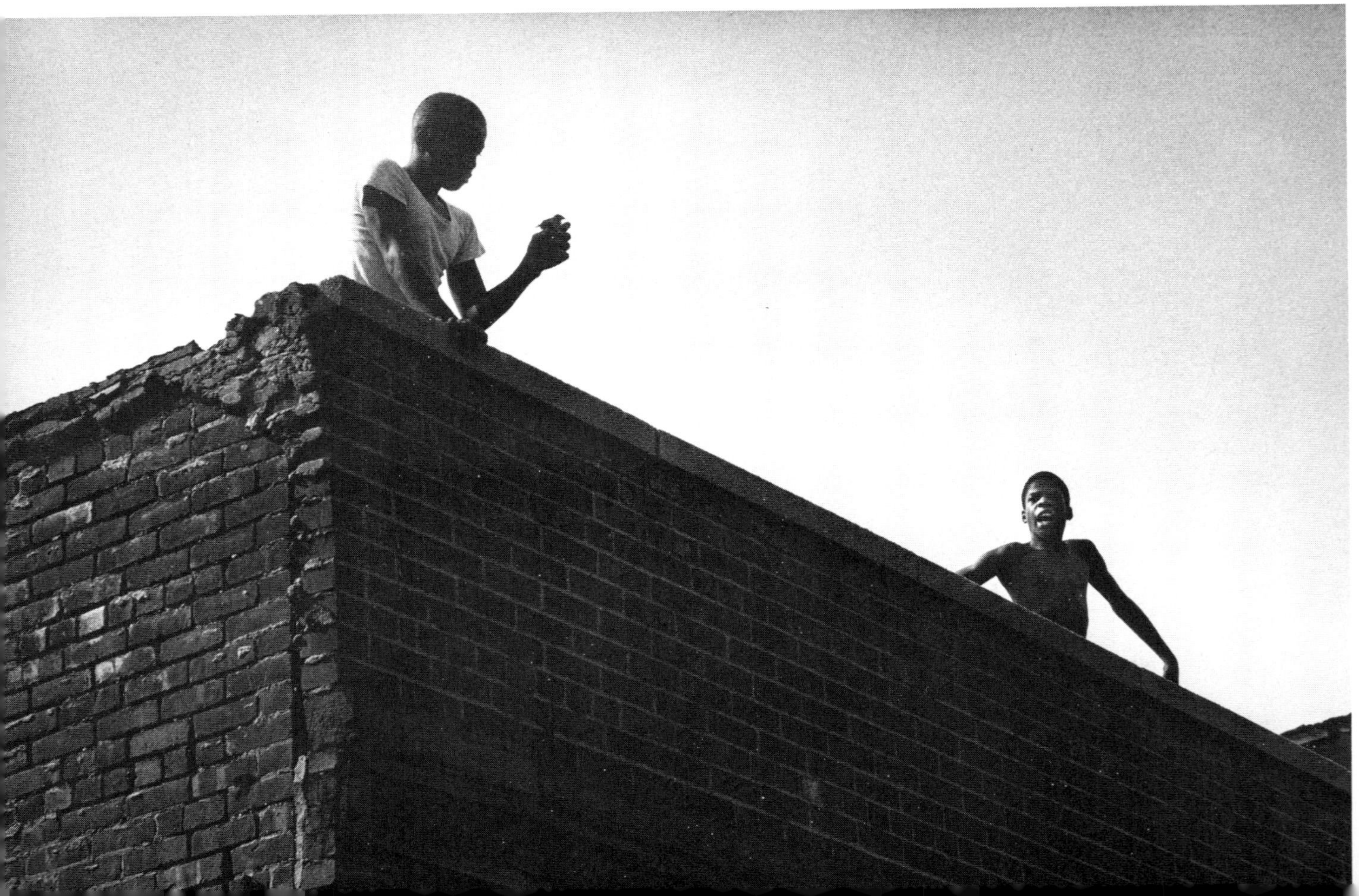

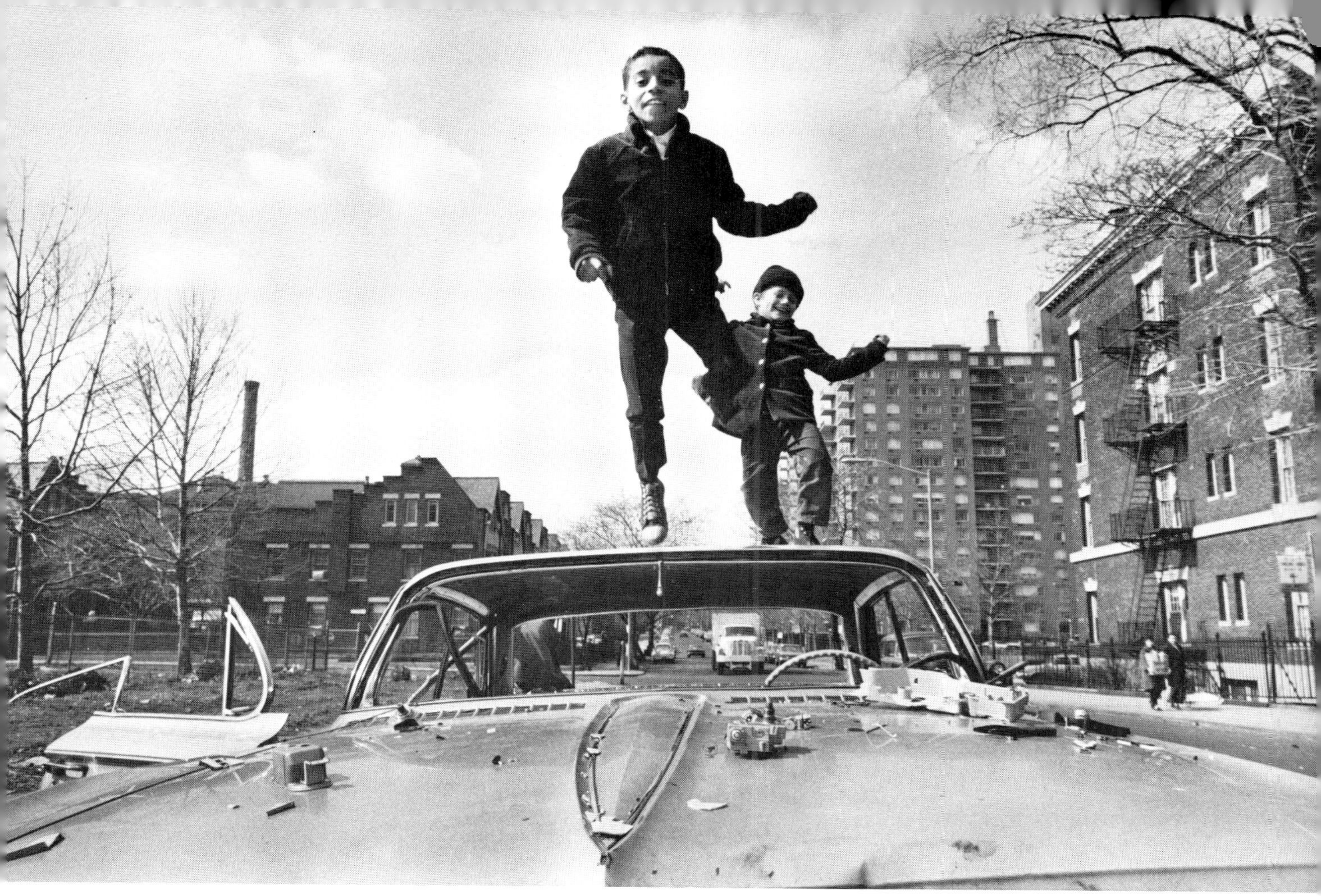

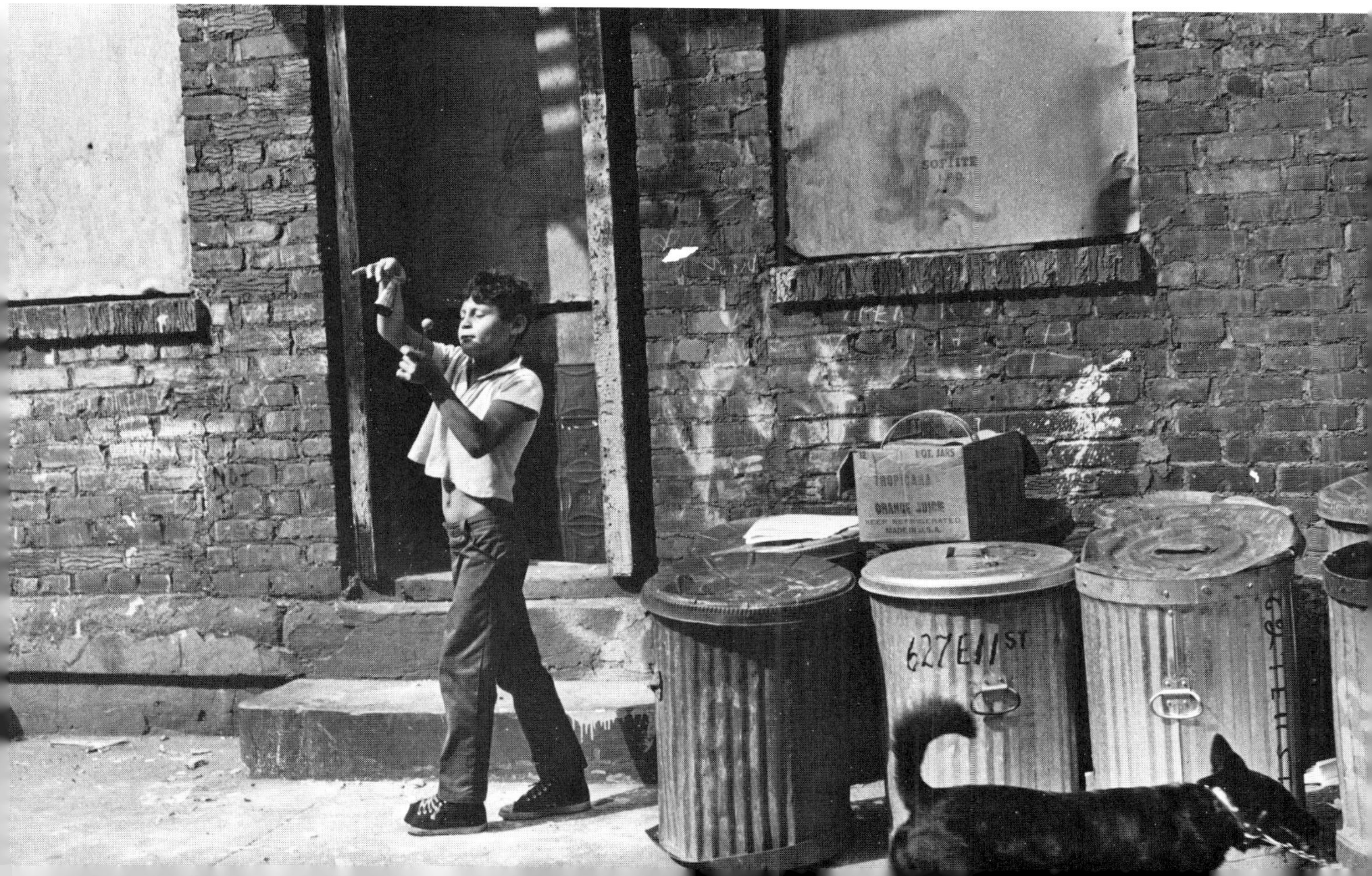

TROPICANA
ORANGE JUICE
KEEP REFRIGERATED
MADE IN U.S.A.
627 E 11 ST

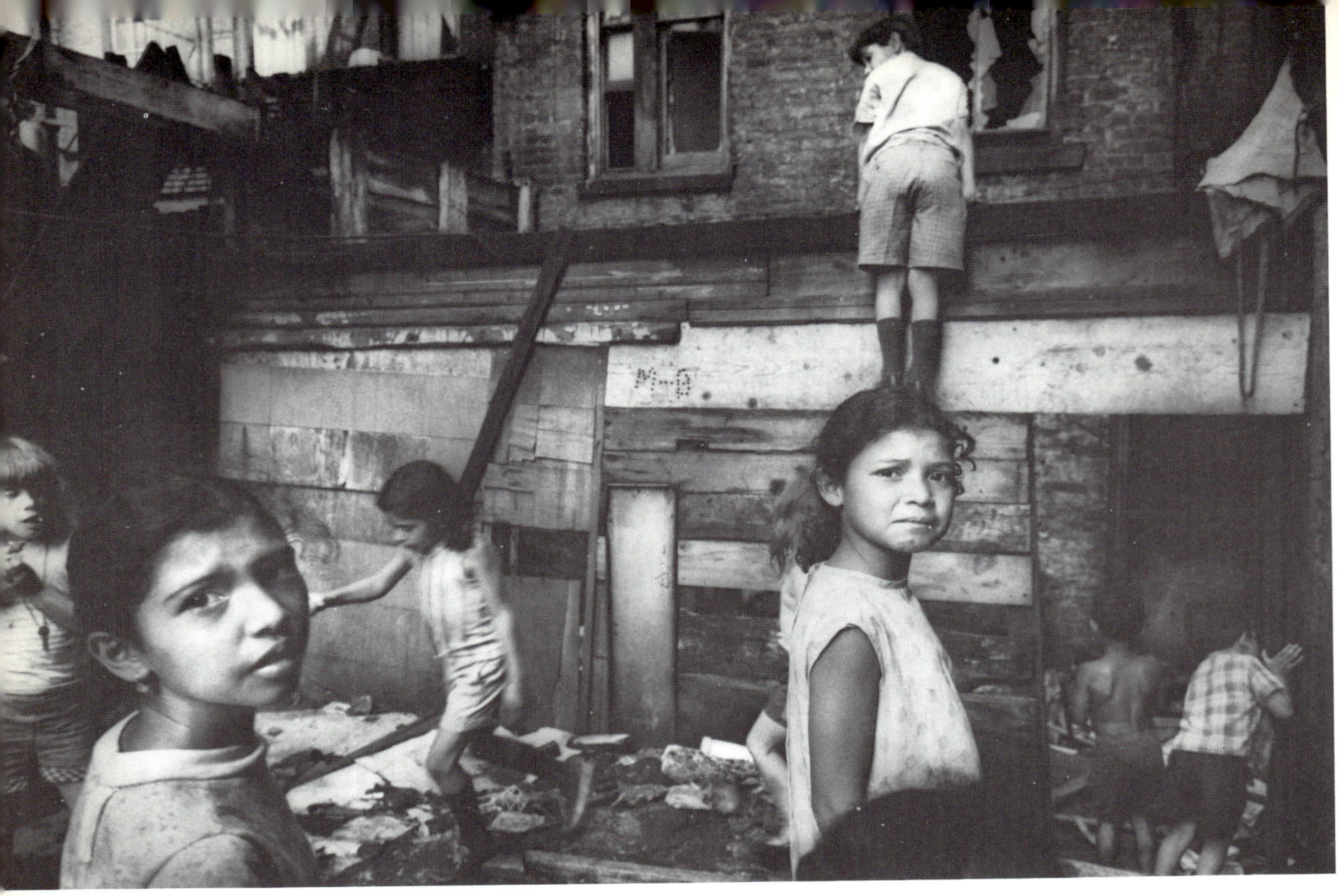

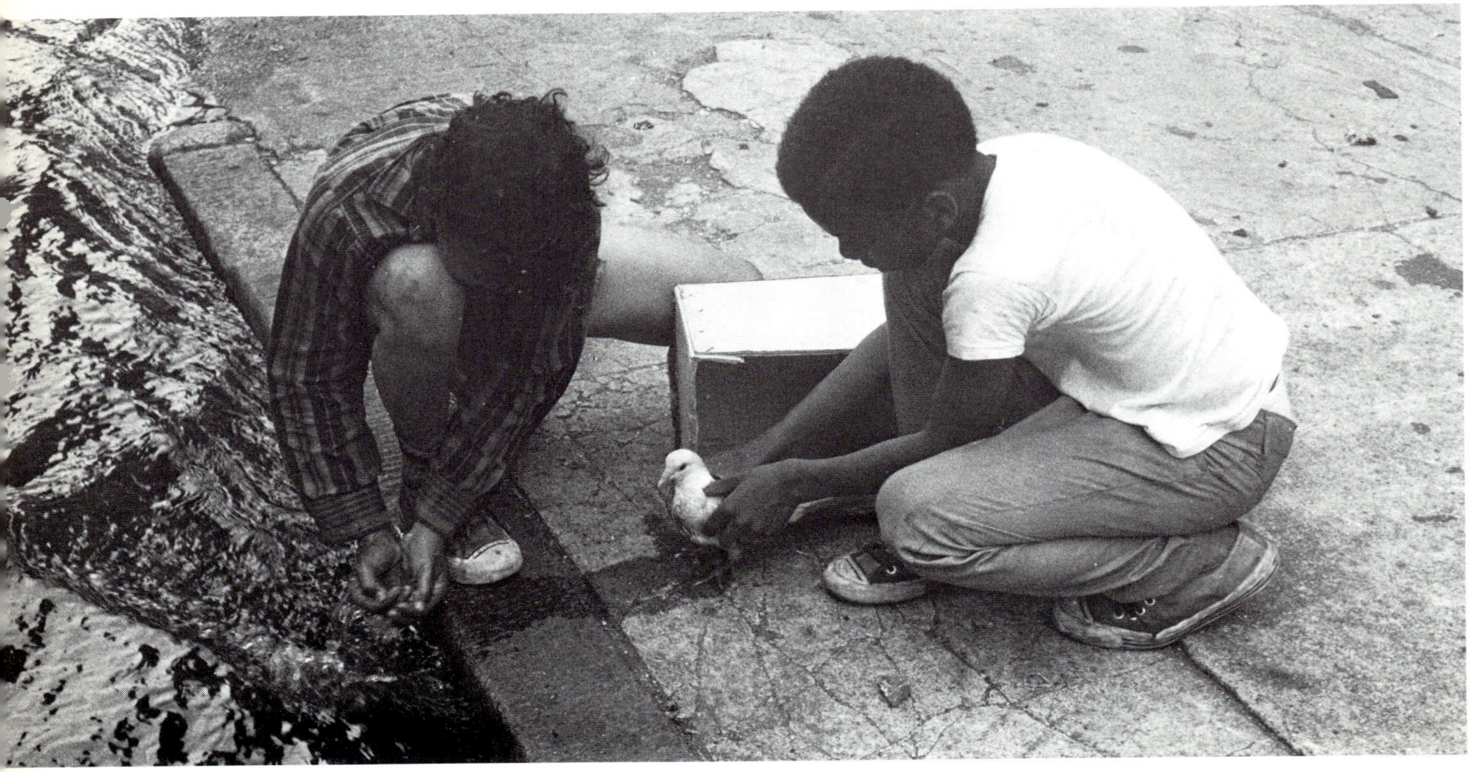

Children Playing in an Abandoned Building [top]. *(James H. Karales)* **Boys With Pigeon** [bottom]. *(Mike Levins)* **East 100th Street** [opposite]. *(Bruce Davidson. Magnum Photos, Inc.)*

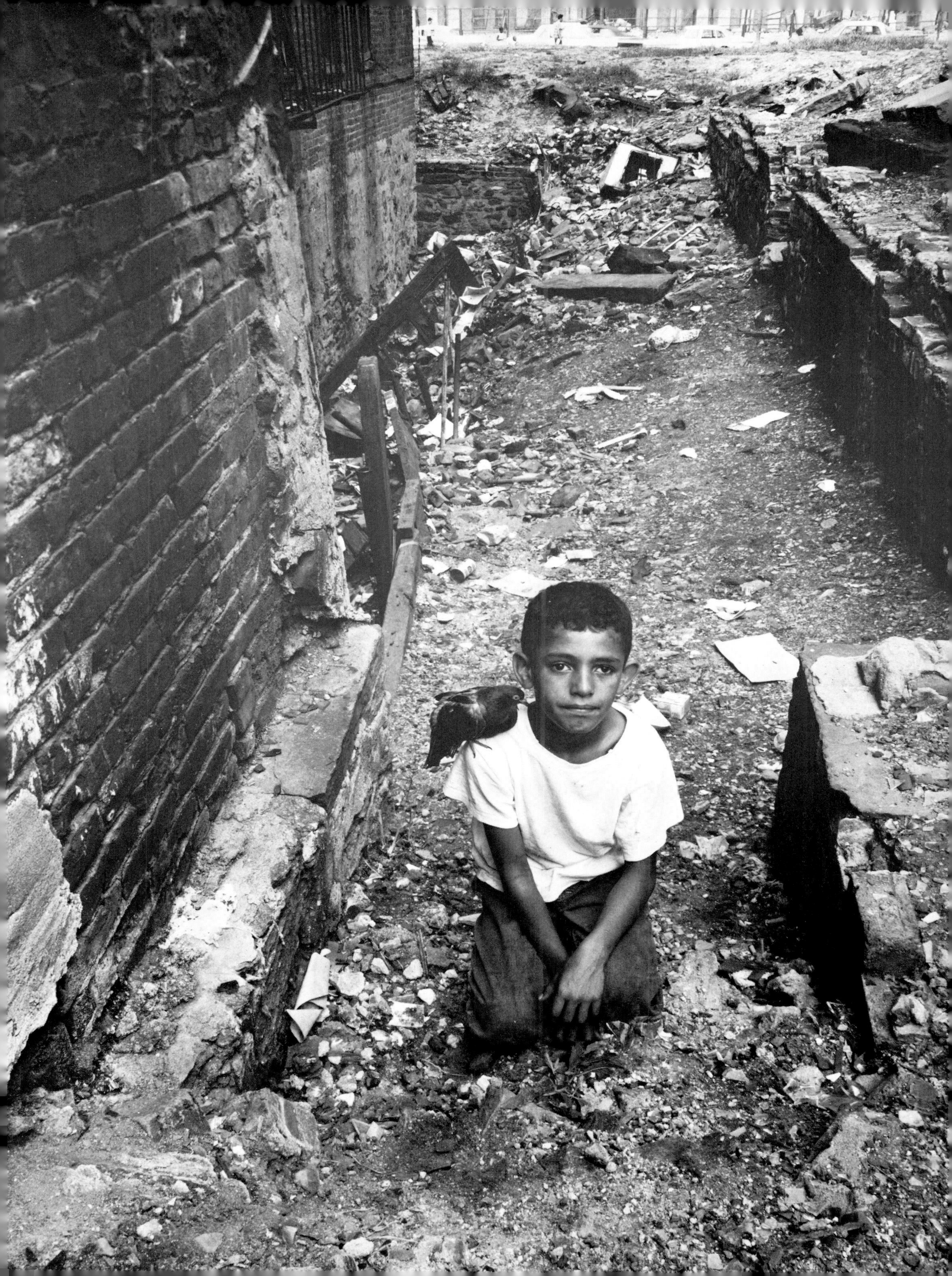

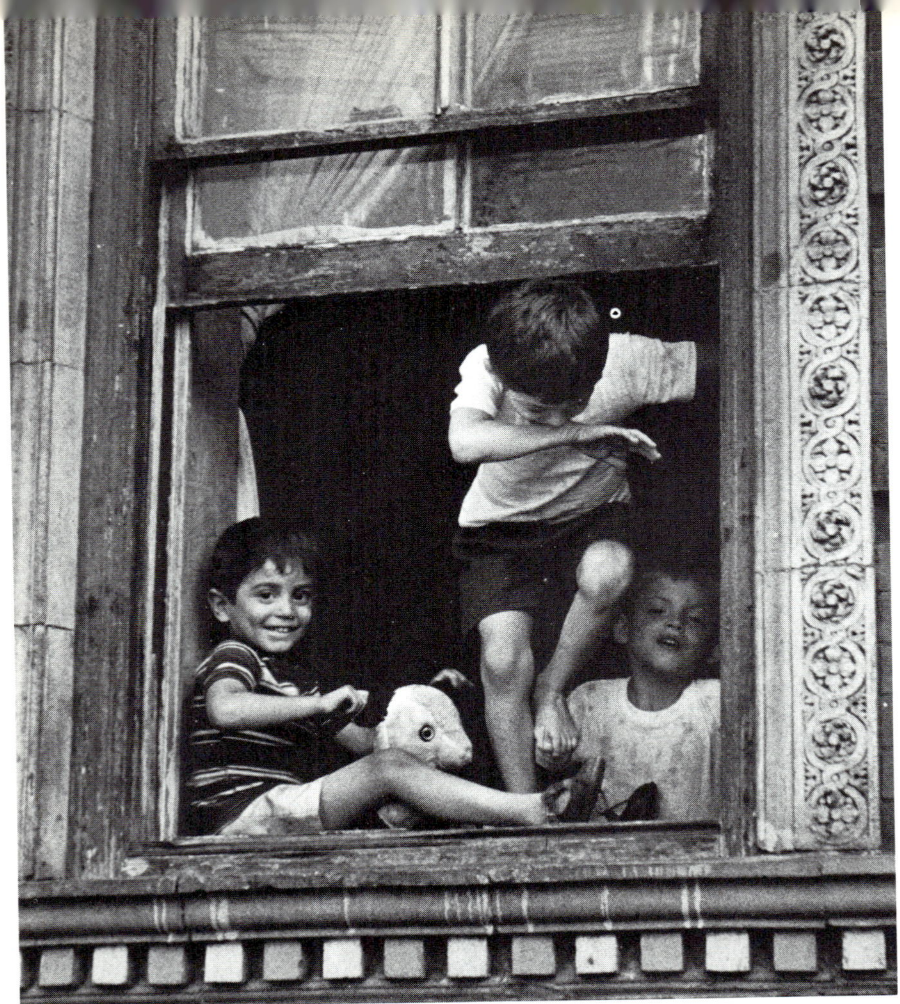

Window Kids [left and below]. These children of a Lower East Side family gaze out at the passing world from the ground-floor window of a tenement on East 6th Street between Avenues C and D. The intricate design around the window shows the surprising care and detail built into many tenements. These kids are but the latest of the generations of immigrants who have used the building relentlessly. *(Michael Weisbrot)* **Street Fight** [opposite]. *(James H. Karales)*

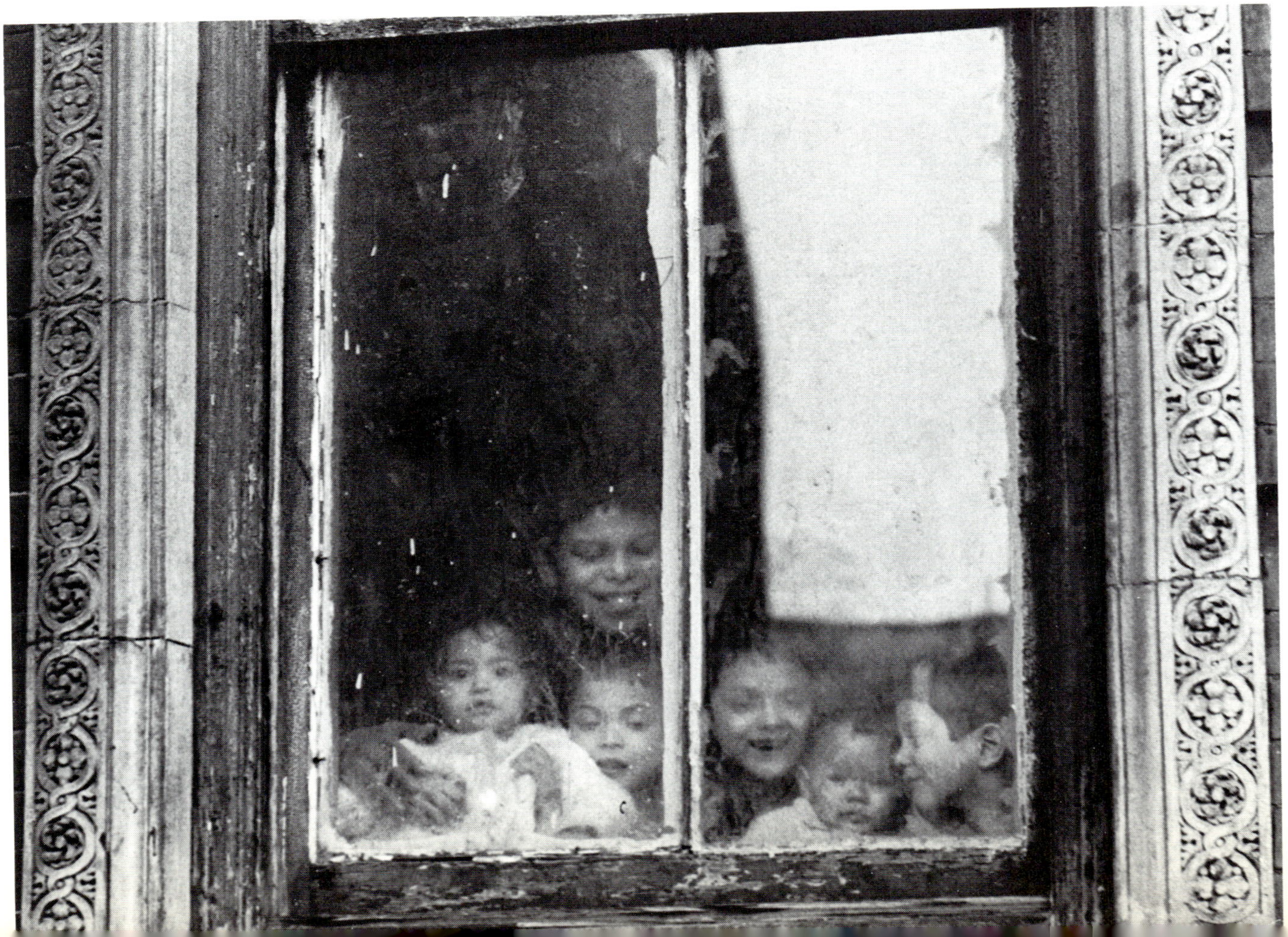

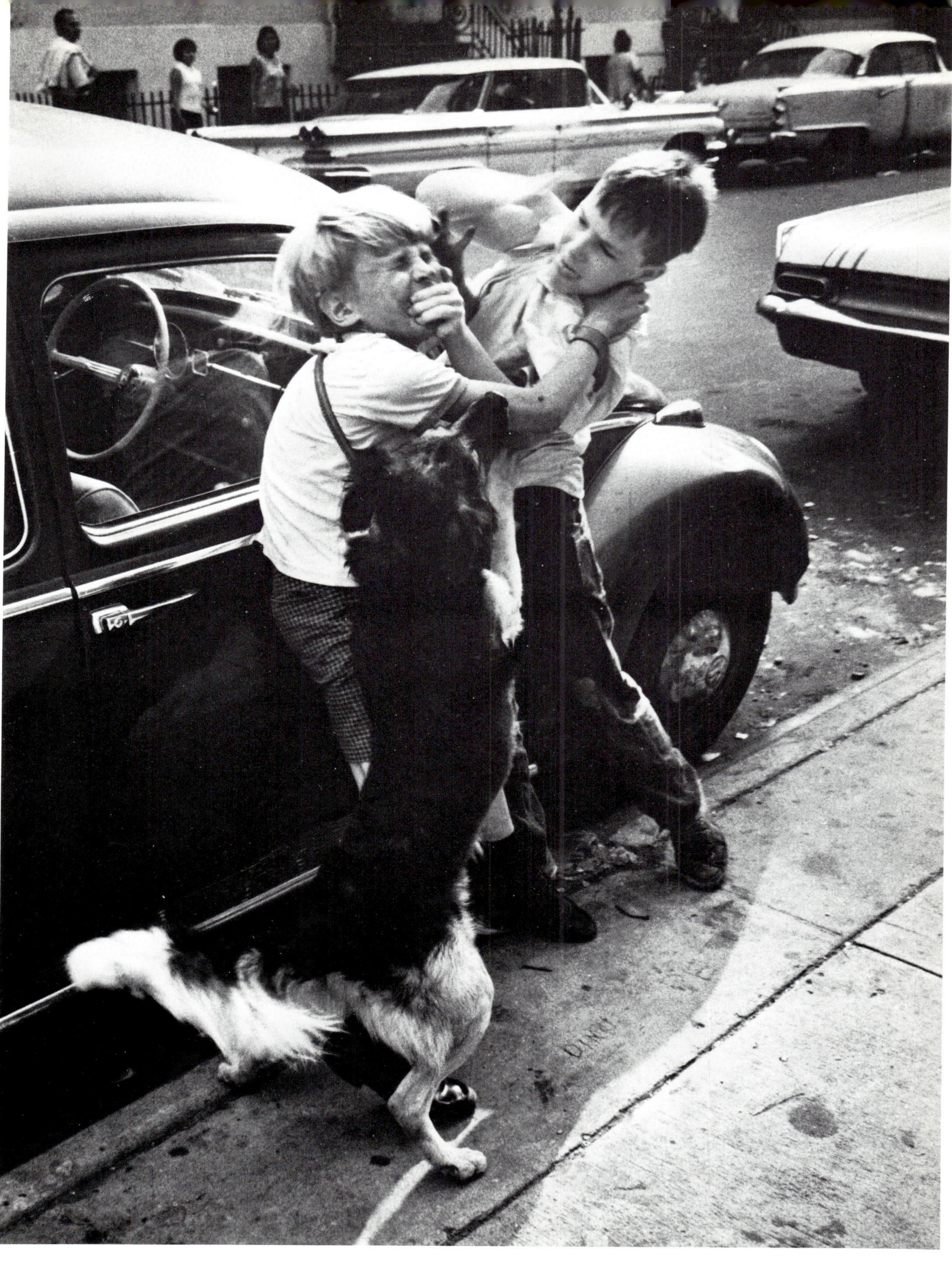

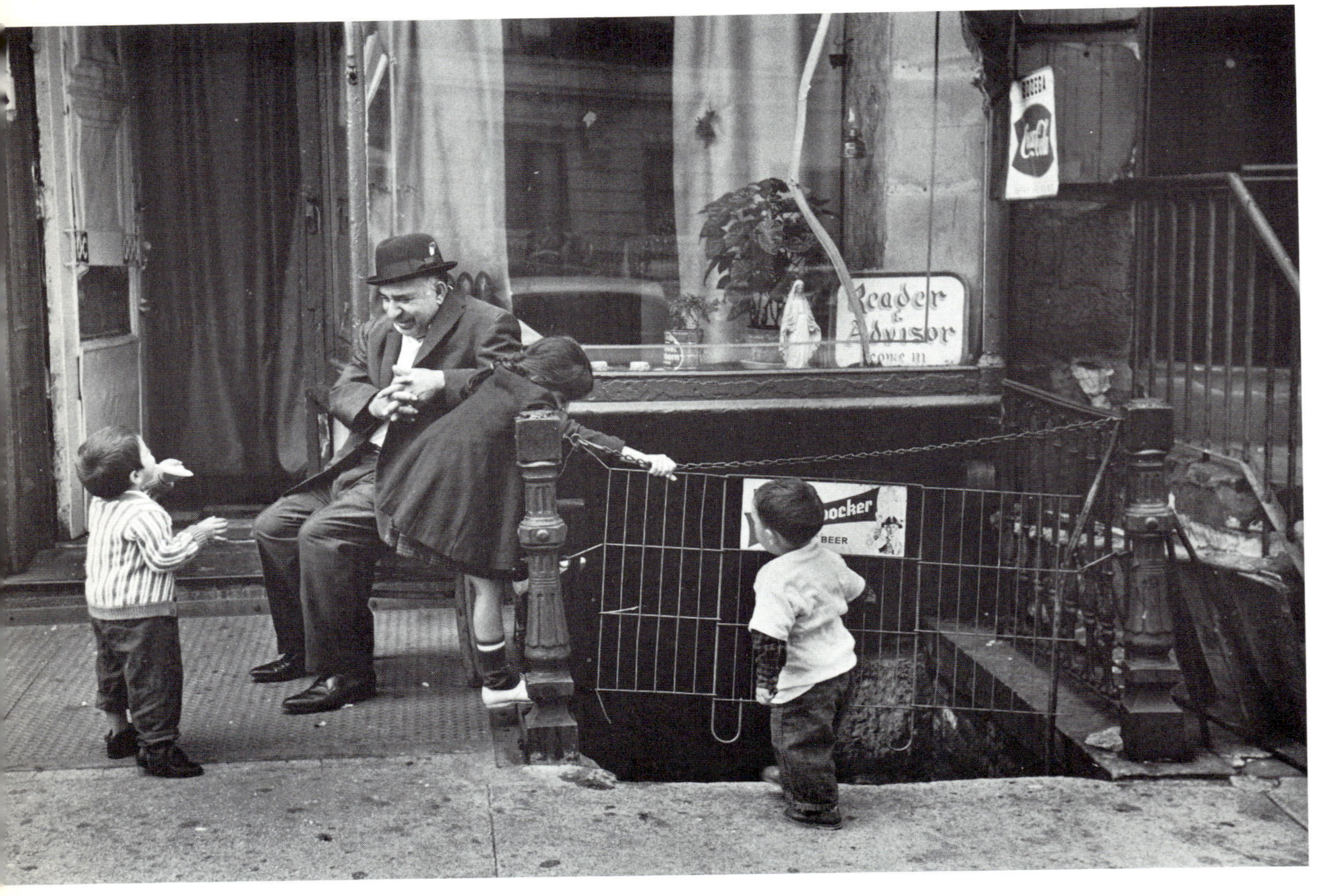

Gypsy Family, Lower East Side. With the growth of interest in astrology and the occult in the 70s, storefront readers and advisors became common in city neighborhoods. Most were family affairs with business and family life spilling from the store into the street. While many of these fortune-tellers were legitimate, others used the trade as a convenient front for backroom prostitution and vice. *(Larry Fink)*

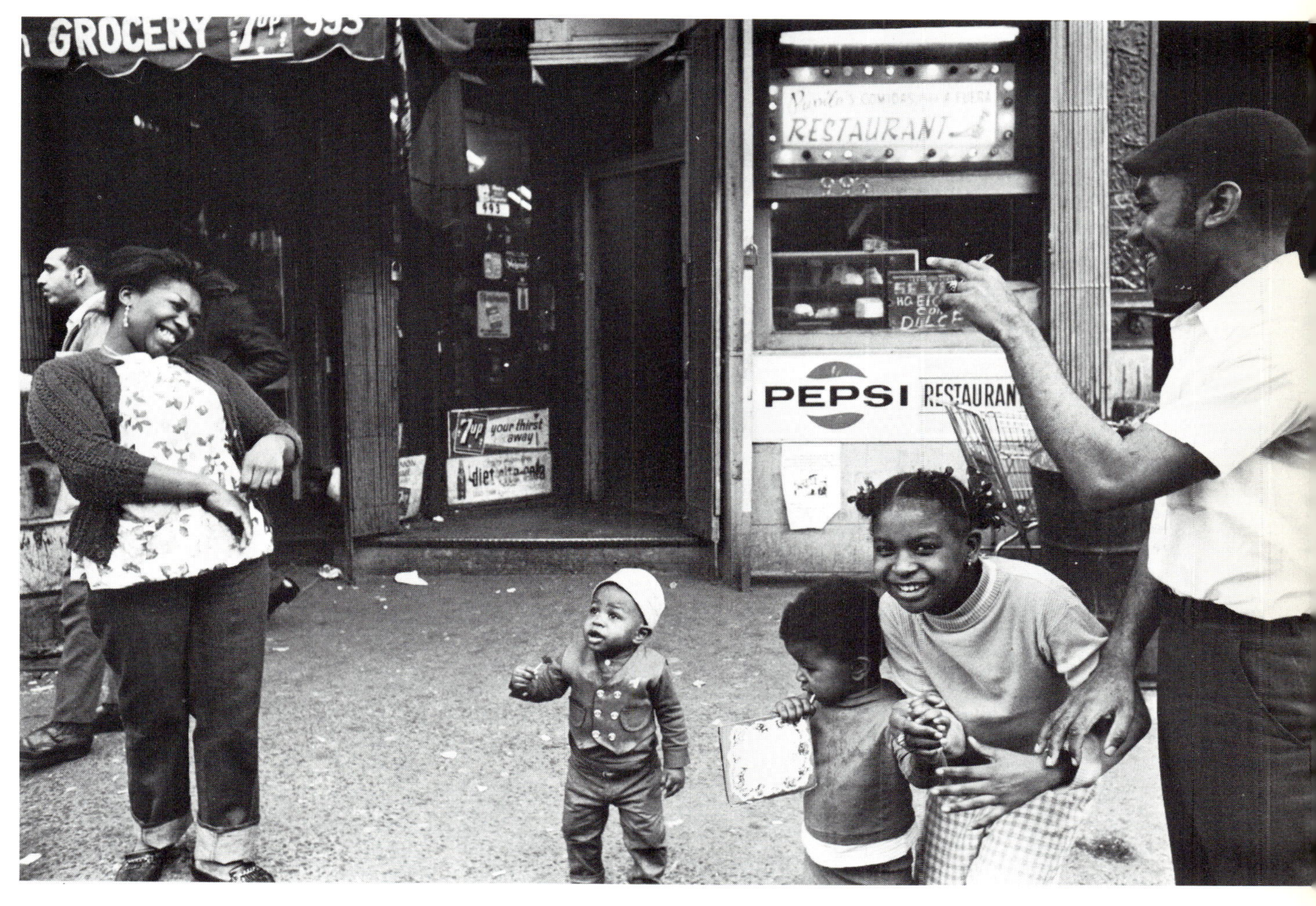

Amsterdam Avenue Scene. Life is tough in the slums but kids like these grow up with the wisecracking and joking of the street to lighten the load. *(Bonnie M. Freer)*

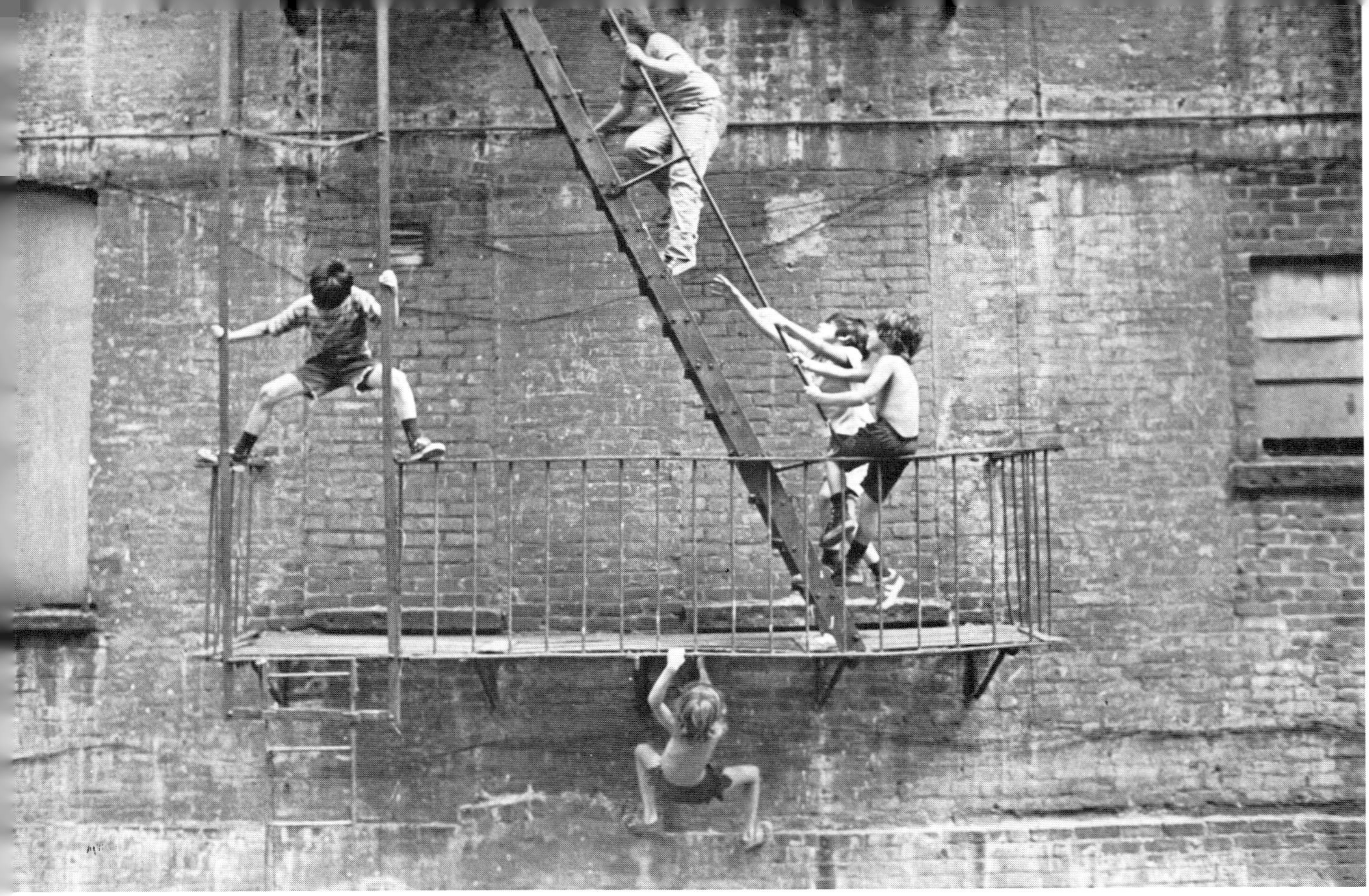

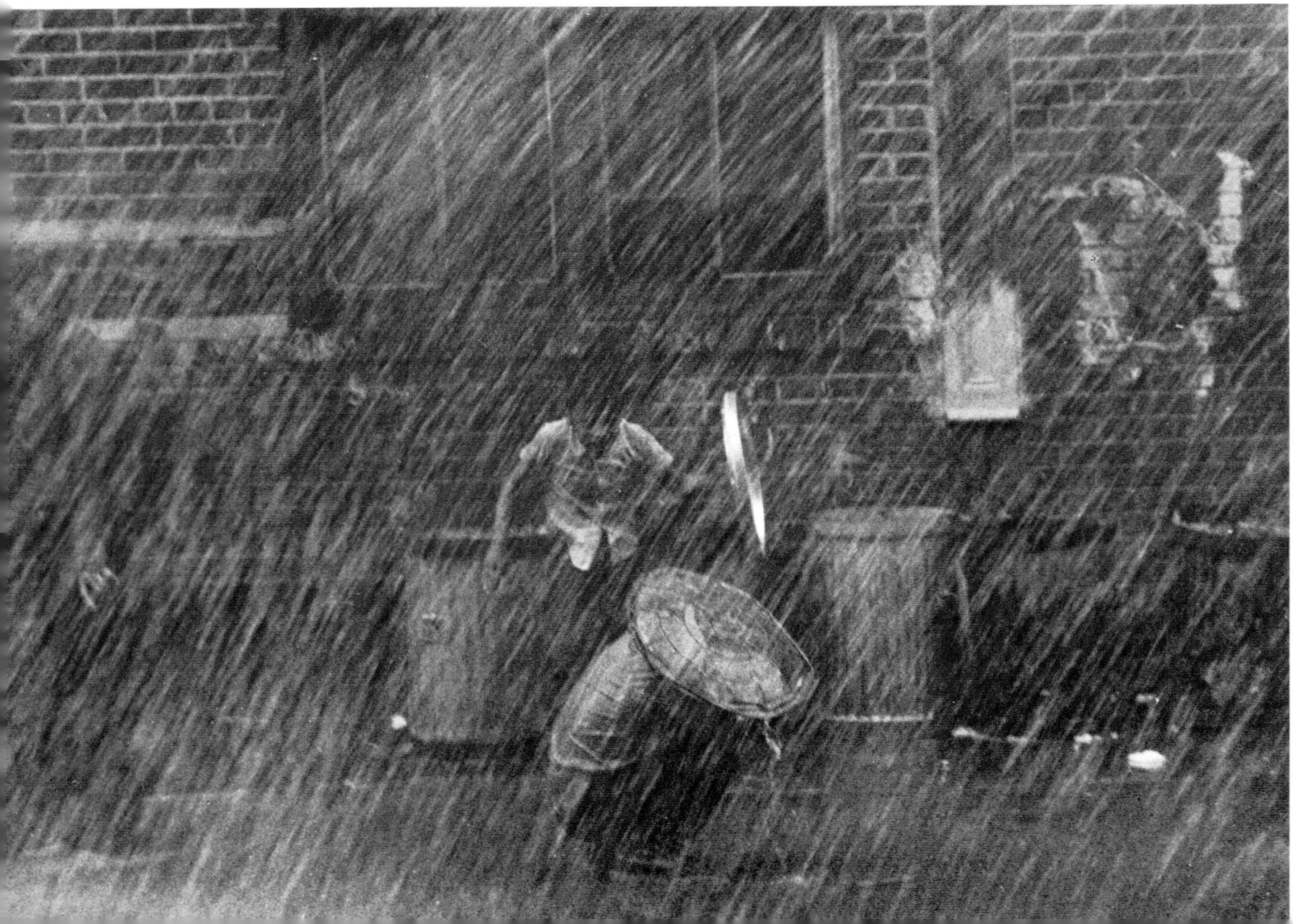

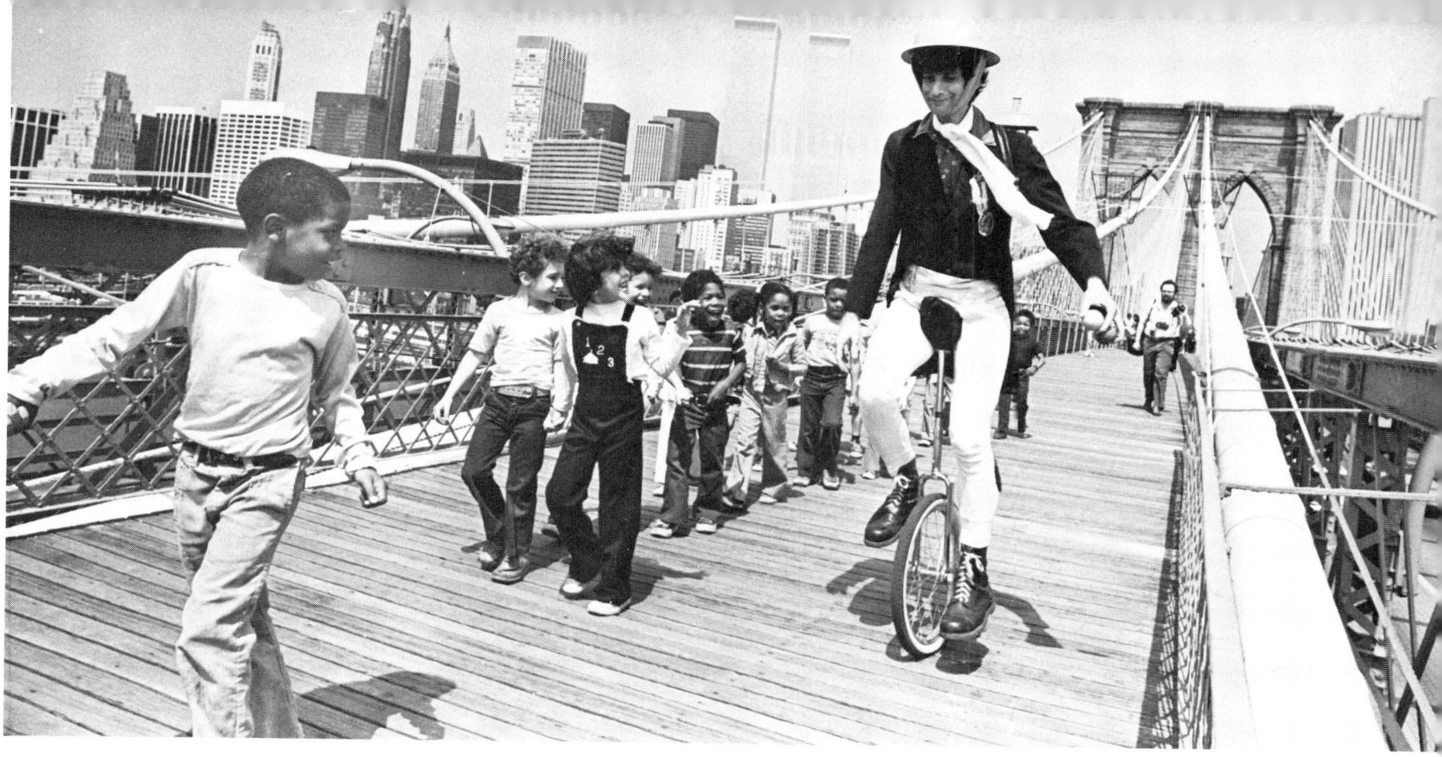

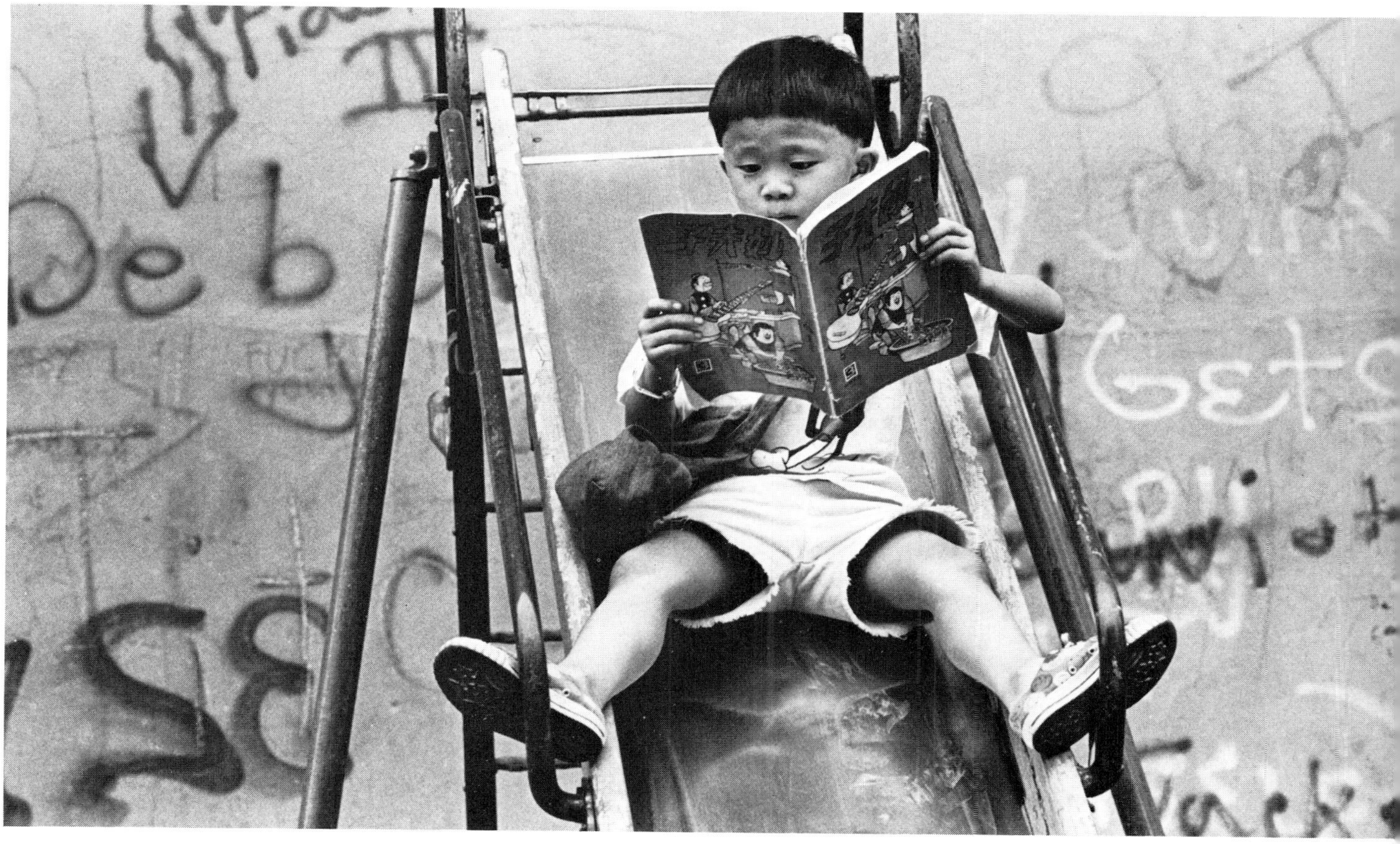

The Fire Escape [opposite, top]. *(Angel Franco, Jr. c.a.s.).* **Boys Playing in Water from a Fire Hydrant** [opposite, bottom]. These boys are using the tops of garbage cans as umbrellas as they crouch under the spray. *(Beuford Smith, Cesaire Photos)* **Pied Piper** [top]. *(Neal Boenzi. NYT Pictures)* **Boy on Sliding Board** [bottom]. It's not always easy to find a quiet reading niche away from the hectic street life on the Lower East Side. But this Oriental boy has found one, a place where he can absorb the latest exploits of his comic-book heroes. The Lower East Side, with its relatively inexpensive housing, continues to attract the latest immigrants. The 70s witnessed an influx of Orientals, Indians and Pakistanis, who, like the generations before them, add the color of their language, customs, cultures and restaurants to New York. *(Terry Bisbee)*

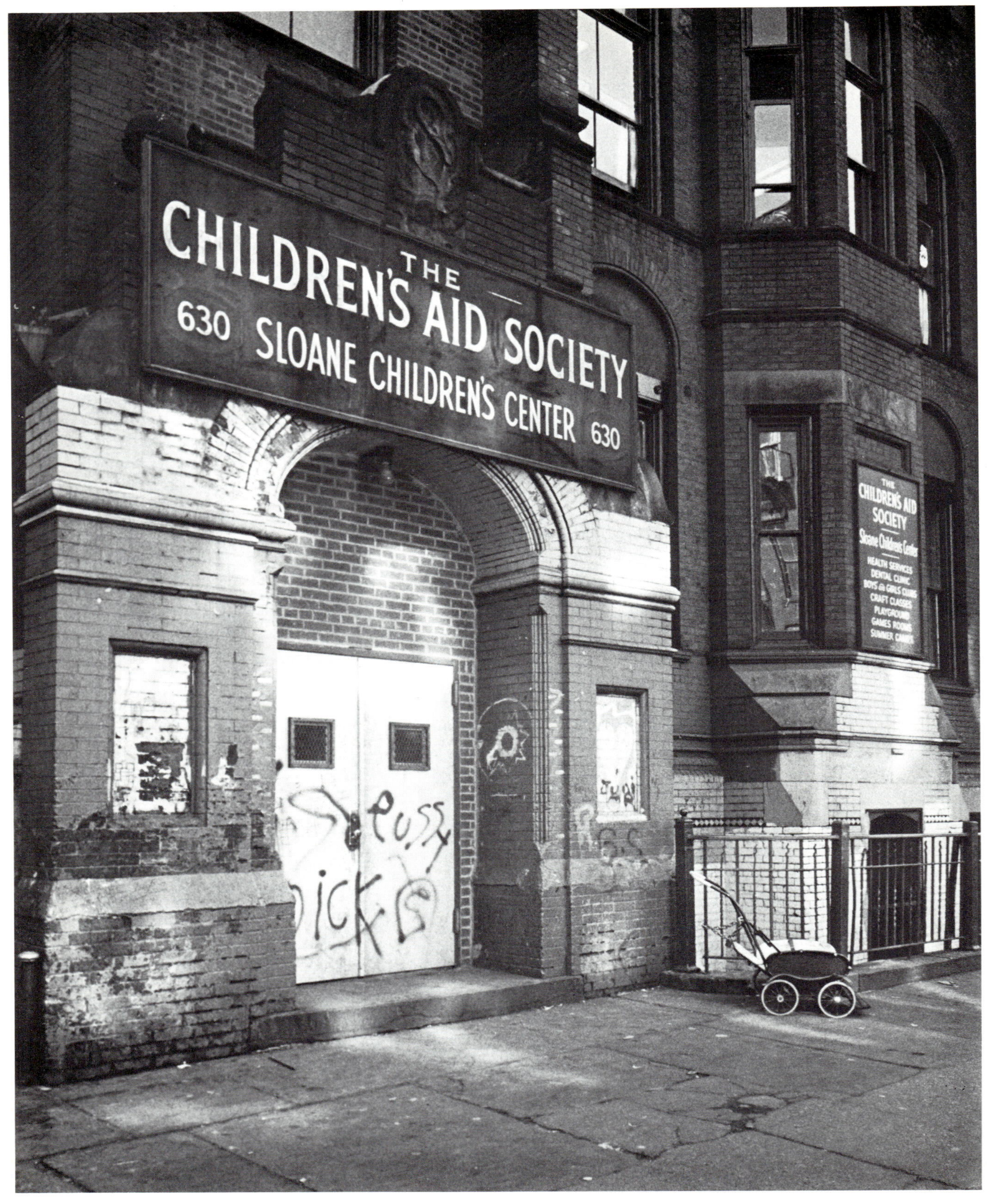

Sloane Center. The Sloane Center on East 6th Street was erected in 1890 as an industrial school, and was revitalized in 1946 as a special education and recreation center. Scarred by the graffiti of the slums, it symbolizes the enduring commitment of the CAS to its work in run-down neighborhoods. *(Michael Weisbrot)*

THE END